Magazine
Journalism

Journalism Studies: Key Texts

Journalism Studies: Key Texts is a new textbook series that systematically maps the crucial connections between theory and practice in journalism. It provides the solid grounding students need in the history, theory, 'real-life' practice and future directions of journalism, while further engaging them in key critical debates. Drawing directly from how journalism is studied and understood today, the series is a full-service resource for students and lecturers alike.

Series Editors: Martin Conboy, David Finkelstein, Bob Franklin

Published Titles
Radio Journalism Guy Starkey and Andrew Crissell
Alternative Journalism Chris Atton and James Hamilton
Newspaper Journalism Peter Cole and Tony Harcup
International Journalism Kevin Williams

Magazine Journalism

Tim Holmes and Liz Nice

Los Angeles | London | New Delhi
Singapore | Washington DC

SAGE Publications Ltd
1 Oliver's Yard
55 City Road
London EC1Y 1SP

SAGE Publications Inc.
2455 Teller Road
Thousand Oaks, California 91320

SAGE Publications India Pvt Ltd
B 1/I 1 Mohan Cooperative Industrial Area
Mathura Road
New Delhi 110 044

SAGE Publications Asia-Pacific Pte Ltd
33 Pekin Street #02-01
Far East Square
Singapore 048763

Library of Congress Control Number: 2010943034

British Library Cataloguing in Publication data

A catalogue record for this book is available from the British Library

ISBN 978–1–84787–029–2
ISBN 978–1–84787–030–8 (pbk)

Typeset by C&M Digitals (P) Ltd, Chennai, India
Printed and bound by CPI Group (UK) Ltd, Croydon, CR0 4YY
Printed on paper from sustainable resources

CONTENTS

ACKNOWLEDGEMENTS

The authors would like to thank the many magazine professionals who gave so generously of their time to share their experience and perceptions of the multifarious universe that is the periodicals industry, and to students, past and present, whose searching questions caused us to look very carefully at what we all too often take for granted.

1

MAGAZINES: A HISTORICAL SURVEY

Magazines are the most successful media format ever to have existed.

This is a big claim when the apparent dominance of television in the last 50 years or the printed book across the last 500 are considered, but magazines are so ubiquitous and their consumption so engrained in habit that their importance almost ceases to register and is thus overlooked. As Buckminster Fuller once noted in a broadcast lecture, people place importance on food and water as the sustainers of life but on a day-to-day basis it's actually air that we consume most. That is our biggest fuel. Like air, magazines play an often disregarded part in our quotidian existence: the pleasure they bring, and the ways in which they bring it, give them a social value; their ability to influence patterns of behaviour or consumption or aesthetics a cultural one; and their role as educators and informers an intellectual one. What is more, when the magazine is in printed form this is achieved at a readily-attainable cost – and in the age of the internet the cost of consumption is sometimes zero.

Yet compared with other cultural products such as television, newspapers, cinema and radio, magazines have generally not been taken seriously by either the (self-professedly) more high-minded 'fourth estate' branches of the journalism industries or the academy. 'Academic disciplines have almost routinely concentrated on the other legs of the print triad [i.e., newspapers and books]' notes American media scholar Dorothy Schmidt, '... but scant attention is given to the continuing role of magazines as reflectors and molders of public opinion and political and social attitudes' (Schmidt 1989: 648, in Abrahamson 1996b: 4). Laurel Brake argues that magazine journalism was not highly regarded in the nineteenth century, '... the low status of periodical literature is associated with many of the same factors which figure in the feeble welcome Victorian critics accorded the novel' (1994: 30), and in the twentieth century Liesbet van Zoonen observed that the 'traditional press' perceived magazine publishing as one of the 'low-status fields of journalism' (1998b: 39).

Academics studying journalism often use the word 'magazine' almost as an unthinking pejorative; Chambers et al. (2004) note that women are concentrated in 'sectors considered to be "soft" news ... and the delivery of a magazine-style of journalism' (p. 1) but later concede that 'In Britain, periodicals played a vital role during the women's suffrage movement ...' (p. 152).

The landmark study of *Journalists at Work* by Jeremy Tunstall revealed that consumer magazines were:

> ... believed by many other journalists to be an extension of the advertising world rather than of journalism. The trade and technical magazines are a separate world again, with each one oriented primarily to the interest or industry which provides not only its readers and its advertising but also its news sources. (1971: 11)

John Hartley captures this tension when he contrasts serious journalism ('the profession of violence') with the 'smiling professions' that include lifestyle and consumer journalism and states, 'They are routinely despised by serious journalists'. Yet when it comes to a likely future direction for journalism as a whole, 'the magazine sector has been leading the way for at least the past decade' (2000: 40, 45).

Encouragingly, the latter idea has been picked up by other media researchers. John Tulloch (2000) identifies magazines as 'the main source of the innovations in the publishing industry that created the modern popular press' (p. 139), while Martin Conboy (2004) flags up 'the ability of magazines to influence the mainstream of journalism' (p. 162) and acknowledges that they have been 'heralds of social and cultural change' (p. 163).

The very word 'magazine' calls forth a variety of responses. It might connote a thick, luxurious, women's glossy or a throwaway weekly gossip sheet. It could just as easily be connected with a favourite hobby as with a profession. Perhaps it may be associated with a supermarket or a satellite television provider. Magazines are all of these things and more – they cover an incalculable range of subject matter, styles and modes of delivery. They give pleasure to millions, information to millions more, and frequently manage to marry pleasure and information in a way that is unique to the form. This combination of a kaleidoscopic nature, the provision of pleasure and an ability to evolve, adapt and survive has led to the axiom that opened this chapter: magazines are the most successful media form ever to have existed.

And yet even this straightforward magazine history remains a surprisingly neglected area, considering the magazine has had a fundamental and intrinsic influence on publishing history. Conboy (2004: 163) notes the 'cross pollination' process by which newspapers have appropriated magazine formats and genres – the transmission of aesthetics – while Rooney (2000: 107) has enlivened current debates about tabloidisation and dumbing down by considering whether 'tabloidisation' might in fact amount to a 'magazinization', although that argument implies a certain view of what magazines are and what they do (Tulloch, 2000: 139). Historical parallels with current journalistic practises have been observed at least as early as the beginning of the nineteenth century – for example the concepts of 'targeting' the reader, relying on reader contributions, and involving the reader with 'competitions, special offers and inducements to buy' (Beetham and Boardman, 2001), while as far back as the seventeenth century women's periodicals have been seen to provide an early (if fleeting) forum for disenfranchised women 'of lower and middle rank' to participate in 'an alternative and competing public sphere' (Halasz, 1997, in Conboy, 2004: 129).

The histories of newspapers and magazines have been closely entwined down the years and although there are obvious similarities – until very recently both could accurately be described as material that was printed on paper and issued at regular intervals – there are also significant practical and cultural differences in their production. According to James Playsted Wood (1956), 'The English newspaper developed in the late seventeenth century out of the political pamphlet and the newsletter. The English magazine developed out of the newspaper within less than fifty years after the first newspaper was founded'. Wood credits Daniel (*Robinson Crusoe*) Defoe with founding 'what is usually ... described as the first magazine in English'. In 1704 Defoe was serving a sentence in Newgate prison for writing and circulating *The Shortest Way With Dissenters*, a religious tract, but these circumstances did not prevent him from starting the *Review* and publishing it weekly. This periodical printed not only news but also articles on 'domestic affairs and national policy' and it survived until 1712 (Wood, 1956: 3–4).

However, while the *Review* may have incorporated the miscellaneous content characteristics of the magazine form, an equally strong argument could be made for the *Ladies Mercury* of 1693. Not only did this publication contain a miscellany of material (ostensibly generated from questions sent in by readers) it also targeted a very specific readership – women. Amongst other topics, *Ladies* promised to help readers with 'all questions relating to Love etc' (Ballaster et al., 1991: 47).

Neither the *Review* nor the *Ladies Mercury* used the word 'magazine' in their titles, and this was not widely adopted to describe a particular form of print publication until 1741, when Edward Cave first published the *Gentleman's Magazine*. There had been magazine-like periodicals published in the UK before then, among them the *Athenian Mercury* (1690), a forerunner of the *Ladies Mercury*, and then the *Tatler* (1709) and *Spectator* (1711). Although the latter was a daily publication it was considered a literary journal rather than a newspaper, rather as the *Economist* currently describes itself as a newspaper rather than a magazine.

Media historians (Davis, 1988; Wharton, 1992; Reed, 1997) tend to name the *Journal des Scavans*, published in Paris in 1665, as the first 'magazine' on the grounds that it contained a miscellany of content that made it metaphorically like a storehouse (*magazin* means shop in French and the word derives from the Arabic work for storehouse – *makhazin*). The *Journal*, an adjunct to publishers' booklists, contained digests of books, writers' obituaries and bibliographies – a formula copied for the English *Weekly Memorials for the Ingenious* in 1682. However, like most historical 'firsts' it is a useful starting point rather than a definitive genesis: Morrish (2003: 5) argues that *Erbauliche Monaths-Unterredungen* (1663) has a claim to be the first magazine, while Tony Quinn of Magforum.com goes back to 1586 with *Gynasceum, sive Theatrum Mulierum* ... (*The Gynasceum or Theatre of Women, in which are reproduced by engraving the female costumes of all the nations of Europe*) published in Frankfurt.

As with 'What was the first?', the more general question 'What *is* a magazine?' has been asked many times in the past and, as we will see, continues to be asked today. The answers are many and varied, involve both logic and emotion, invoke both history and prediction, and leave us just as uncertain after we have heard them as we were before we raised this query. Until recently, common sense (that dangerous quality) had allowed us to believe we *knew* what the term 'magazine' meant; according to Frank Luther Mott, pre-eminent historian of the medium, the magazine is a 'bound pamphlet issued more or less regularly ... containing a variety of reading matter and ... a strong connotation of entertainment' (1930: 7). Furthermore Fred and Nancy Paine devote 690 pages to listing sources of information about magazines but still conclude, 'for all that magazines have been studied, analyzed, and written about, their number and purposes remain as elusive as their precise definition' (Paine and Paine, 1987: 15). The Periodical Publishers Association (PPA), trade body for the magazine industry in the UK, offers a definition on its website that takes us into all kinds of areas:

Magazine. (noun)

The word 'magazine' describes branded, edited content often supported by advertising or sponsorship and delivered in print or other forms. Traditionally, magazines have been printed periodicals which are most commonly published weekly, monthly or quarterly. These may be supported by printed one-off supplements and annual directories. Increasingly, magazines exist online where content is available through websites or in digital editions, or delivered by email as an electronic newsletter. Many magazine brands also deliver tailored information services to their audiences. Magazine brands also engage with their audiences face-to-face by organising exhibitions, conferences and other events. (www.ppa.co.uk/all-about-magazines/what-is-a-magazine/; accessed 21/5/10)

Barry McIlheney, chairman of the PPA, added his own opinion in an interview with *InPublishing Magazine* (July/August 2010). Having been recently appointed to the post, he was keen to explain his thoughts on the PPA's role, the essential nature of a magazine and its independence from any particular substrate:

> It's not just about saying magazines are great, but promoting high quality editorial content with a magazine heritage delivered across any platform. It sounds a mouthful, but I'm talking about the unique mix of words and pictures and the relationship with the consumer that 'magazine' means, and that's a mix that doesn't just have to be delivered via paper and ink. (www.inpublishing.co.uk/kb/articles/barry_mcilheney_interview.aspx)

Nevertheless, as far as print was concerned, for a long time it was possible to accept a working definition that stated a magazine 'should contain articles or stories by different authors, and that it should be published at regular intervals, which can be any period longer than a day' (Davis, 1988: 3). This was sufficiently flexible to allow for the examination of a wide range of publications while still acknowledging the etymology of the name, which could be understood to be 'descriptive of the publication's content rather than its format' (Paine and Paine, 1987 : 10).

However, using frequency as part of the definition (claiming that a magazine cannot be published daily or, rather, that anything published daily is *de facto* not a magazine) simply raises another set of questions following the emergence of newspaper supplements such as the *Guardian*'s G2, which calls itself a daily magazine, and newspapers that have adopted magazine-like, highly designed story treatments (Portugal's daily *i* is an excellent example of this – see http://timholmes.blogspot.com/2009/11/newspaper-news-magazine-aesthetic-i.html). We also face a problem that Davis and the Paines did not – the regularly updated digital manifestations of print titles – leading to the conclusion that frequency can no longer be considered a reliable or unproblematic indicator.

And neither can physical form or appearance. The magazine has moved on from paper and is now found on the internet as a website, on mobile phones as a WAP-site, on smartphones as an app, and in other evolving forms and formats that will change with advances in technology. Furthermore, it does not take much cultural exploration to encounter an ever-expanding range of postmodern artefacts that will push the boundaries of what anyone thought a magazine could be. For example:

- *Pop-Up* calls itself 'the world's first live magazine, created for a stage, a screen, and a live audience ... *Pop-Up* showcases the country's most interesting writers, documentary filmmakers, photographers, and radio producers, together, on stage, sharing short moments of unseen, unheard work. Books, films, journalism, photography, and radio documentaries in progress. Obsessions and digressions. Outtakes, arguments, and live interviews ... An issue exists for one night, in one place.' (www.popup-magazine.com/about_us.html; accessed 20/5/10)

- *Rotary Magazine* was a project that used 200 miscellaneous slides and a slide projector, all purchased from eBay. After organising the most interesting slides from the collection and creating typographic slides to complement them, the editors projected *Rotary Magazine* issue 1 to give 'an alternative browsing experience, allowing many people to view at the same time and at their own pace. As the magazine was projected this also meant no paper or printing was necessary for viewing, resulting in a more sustainable outcome.' (www.jackmaxwell.co.uk/index.php?/work/rotary/; accessed 20/5/10)

- *48 Hour* magazine was more conventional inasmuch as it resulted in a printed product, but the whole project was, as the name suggests, put together in a 48 hour period beginning on 7 May 2010. The editors revealed a theme and contributions were crowd-sourced (i.e. invited from all-comers). Not only did the idea work, after publication the magazine was granted a degree of legitimacy when it received a cease-and-desist letter from the American broadcasting company CBS claiming to own the rights to the name '48 Hours' for its television magazine programme. (48hrmag.com; accessed 20/5/10)

Are these artefacts magazines? Professor Samir Husni (a leading scholar of magazines also known as 'Mr Magazine'), of the University of Mississippi, would certainly argue they are not. Husni, director of the Magazine Innovation Center, starts from the position that print magazine publishers in the USA have been their own worst enemies by training readers to expect magazines to be cheap as a result of offering deeply discounted subscriptions (see Chapter 2 for more on this). In a blog post entitled *So, What Is A Magazine, Really?*, he states unequivocally:

> Magazines are much more than content. Magazines are much more than information, words, pictures and colors all combined in a platform that serves nothing but as a delivery vehicle. Magazines, each and every one and each and every issue of every one, are a total experience that engages the customer's five senses. Nothing is left to chance. It is a total package. Without the ink, the paper, the touch, the smell, the look, the taste, it will not be called a magazine. (mrmagazine.wordpress.com/2010/06/11/so-what-is-a-magazine-really-read-on/; accessed 1/7/10)

(See also www.stateofthemedia.org/2010/magazines_summary_essay.php)

On the other hand, Dr Susan Currie Sivek of the Mass Communication and Journalism Department at California State University, Fresno, believes that 'it's time for traditional magazines to learn from these projects that are on the boundary of our current understanding of a magazine. It's time to consider all the new ways the essential qualities of "a magazine" can be expressed' (sivekmedia.com/2010/04/29/definition-of-magazine/).

However, if we examine academic and commercial research into the form it is possible to perceive some underlying principles of the *ur-magazine* in a set of findings that are repeated across the literature. Click and Baird (1990: 5) struggle with the 'difficulty of arriving at an acceptable definition', before abandoning the attempt in favour of describing how magazines work by forming 'personal relationships that are built among the writers and editors of the magazines and their readers'. The specific role that magazines fulfil within the ecology of media forms is explained by David Abrahamson thus:

> ... it has long been the unique function of magazines, rather than newspapers or the broadcast media, to bring high-value interpretative information to specifically defined yet national audiences. (1996a: 1)

Johnson and Prijatel (1999: 5, 7) state that 'magazines are highly specialized in content and in audience', going on to note that 'audience and content work in tandem ... Magazine editors see their readers as part of a community; readers of a successful publication have a sense of ownership of *their* magazine'. When considering the reasons for success or failure, they identify three major factors:

1 a highly focused editorial philosophy;
2 a clearly defined formula;
3 a thorough understanding of and connection with the audience (1999: 109).

(There is, of course, one more very important factor for a *successful* magazine that we will come to in Chapter 2.)

This general pattern of focus and engagement can also be found in studies of specific magazines, such as Valerie Korinek's thorough examination of *Chatelaine*, the Canadian women's magazine, which focuses on how readers connected with this in the 1950s and 1960s:

> These readers were not passive consumers whose interaction with the magazine was limited to writing their yearly subscription cheque to Maclean Hunter, but an engaged, and engaging, group. (2000: 8)

Extrapolating from this material, the essential characteristics of the magazine form, a General Theory of Magazines as it were, might include the following:

1 magazines always target a precisely defined group of readers;
2 magazines base their content on the expressed and perceived needs, desires, hopes and fears of that defined group;
3 magazines develop a bond of trust with their readerships;
4 magazines foster community-like interactions between themselves and their readers, and among readers;
5 magazines can respond quickly and flexibly to changes in the readership and changes in the wider society.

Newspapers may fulfil one or more of those requirements – and there is evidence that some newspapers today are trying to fulfil more of them[1] – but not all of them simultaneously. Because of the newspaper's history/legacy as a vehicle of the Fourth Estate, it has been unusual (until relatively recently) for it to base its content on a consideration of the readers' *actual* needs or wishes, as opposed to a paternalistic provision of what the editor or proprietor determined that readers *ought* to need or want. Thus throughout the nineteenth and most of the twentieth centuries, although a newspaper may have been held in respect, it would rarely foster community-like interactions between readers and even less rarely be regarded as a 'friend' in the way that both academic and commercial research confirms magazines are able to do (see for example Hermes, 1995; Beetham, 1996; Korinek, 2000; Consterdine, 2002).

For the moment, although it is important not to allow the definition of the word to become fossilised, as far as print goes we can still claim to 'know' what is meant by 'a magazine' because we have had the best part of 300 years to become familiar with the term. As noted above, the first British publication to use it as part of the title was *The Gentleman's Magazine*, founded by Edward Cave, a printer, in 1731. Cave perceived 'there was a public among the middle classes for miscellaneous information of a kind not obtainable from the daily or weekly news-sheets' (Clair, 1965: 163) and used the name 'to mean a periodical drawing material from many sources, his 48-page monthly initially being mainly a digest from other publications, though gradually original contributions were introduced' (Davis, 1988: 5). Harold Herd (1952: 55) gives us an example of the contents from an edition of 1736:

I   Proceedings and Debates in Parliament.
II   Essays, Controversial, Humorous and Satyrical; Religious, Moral and Political: Collected Chiefly from the Publick Papers.
III   Dissertations and Letters from Correspondents.
IV   Select Pieces of Poetry.
V   A Succinct Account of the most remarkable Transactions Foreign and Domestick.
VI   Births, Marriages, Deaths, Promotions and Bankrupt.
VII   The Prices of Goods and Stocks, Bills of Mortality, and Register of Books.

As Katherine Shevelow puts it, Cave's publication 'evolved from a digest of summaries of other publications into an independent periodical issuing its own, distinct content' (1989: 174). This combination brought it a good audience, as Cave's contemporary Samuel Johnson remarked:

> Cave used to sell ten thousand of *The Gentleman's Magazine*; yet such was then his minute attention and anxiety that the sale should not suffer the smallest decrease, that he would name a particular person who he heard had talked of leaving off the Magazine,

---

[1]For example, the *Daily Telegraph*'s adoption of 'reader clubs'; see www.guardian. co.uk/media/pda/2010/feb/03/telegraph-website-stop-chasing-hits

and would say, 'Let us have something good next month'. (Quoted from Boswell's *Life of Johnson* in Clair, 1965: 164)

It is worth noting that Johnson contributed some of the illicit parliamentary reports at a time when such reporting was strictly controlled and licensed. This may have been one reason for the magazine's popularity – Marjorie Plant (1939: 57) cites a circulation for Cave's magazine of 15,000 after ten years.[2]

However, Cave himself was following in the footsteps of Peter Motteux who published *The Gentleman's Journal or the Monthly Miscellany* from 1692 to 1694. Shevelow describes this as 'an influential example of the "miscellany" periodical that later became the "magazine"' (1989: 26). *The Gentleman's Journal* contained not only articles of news, history, philosophy and poetry, but also music (Henry Purcell regularly contributed compositions), fiction in the form of short stories, and illustrations from woodcuts.[3]

---

[2]Ballaster et al. (1991: 50-54) have an excellent section on the emergence of the magazine, including more about Cave.

[3]There may be a connection between this flowering of periodicals for the 'gentleman' and the emergence of the category 'gentleman' which Habermas (1989: 9) outlines briefly in *The Structural Transformation of the Public Sphere*. If a social category has been defined in certain terms and is accorded certain attributes it seems likely that there will then be a demand for didactic material to assist existing members of that category to ensure that they meet the necessary requirements of general informedness, etiquette, social awareness (by which we could also mean gossip), and so on. Furthermore, given a degree of social mobility, or even the aspiration to social mobility, new members of that class or members of other classes who aspired to become members might well require sources of information to bring them up to the required standards. Such material published in book or periodical form would allow such novices to study in private either to supplement, or to obviate, the potentially embarrassing need for, or to overcome the lack of access to, personal tuition.

And since the new knowledge was based on humanistic learning, which required only the ability to read or to listen as someone else read, rather than ability at jousting or feats of arms, which required lances, swords, horses and large open areas, it became considerably easier to acquire as much knowledge as was needed from books and periodicals. Naturally the ability to read was itself a marker of class, although not necessarily of nobility or aristocracy. The ability to afford or obtain access to reading material was yet another marker of class and status, affluence and influence. In this need for knowledge as a means of making oneself socially acceptable we might be able to see the roots of specialist periodical publishing, especially after the capitalist commercial economy gave rise to the development of commodity fetishism, branding, and market segmentation.

If Machiavelli's *The Prince* could do this for a higher stratum of society, periodicals such as the *Gentleman's Journal* and *Gentleman's Magazine* and books such as the *Conversations* by Mademoiselle de Scudéry (Habermas, 1989: 10) could do the same for the emerging bourgeoisie. There may also be a connection between such material being published and the concept of 'the publicity of representation' which Habermas also describes.

All of the above titles share the 'miscellany' element that seems to be an important part of the early definition of a magazine. Another attribute of magazine-ness was discovered in 1691, when John Dunton and Samuel Wesley launched the *Athenian Gazette,* a publication predicated on the idea of supplying answers to questions sent in by readers. (This concept would be adopted by Alfred Harmsworth – later Lord Northcliffe – in the nineteenth century for his *Answers to Correspondents,* the magazine on which his fortune was based.) Dunton and Wesley renamed their magazine the *Athenian Mercury,* a title that Dunton adapted when he launched the *Ladies Mercury* in 1693. This was the 'publication that may fairly be called the very first periodical for women' according to Cynthia White (1970: 23), whose study of women's magazines was one of the pioneering works in this field. The *Ladies Mercury* targeted a well-defined group of readers (women who had intellectual capital, monetary capital, and the need for social capital), the material it published provided for its readers' information needs: by soliciting enquiries from them it encouraged a community-like two-way interaction, and readers trusted it to answer these enquiries honestly and accurately. As it first appeared in 1693 it can be seen to pre-date Defoe's *Review* by some 11 years. If White and others see this as the first women's magazine, an alternative label might also be the first specialist magazine — that is to say, the first one aimed at a specific niche in the market.

This is not to say that it was the first publication of any kind to be focused on a particular group, as Dr Louise Craven has noted, even though she appears to overlook the *Ladies Mercury*:

> Was there any conception of reader preference and buying habit in seventeenth-century England? Evidently, the audience for newspapers was larger than previously thought: in 1678 Henry Care pleaded for improved typography and layout in news books as 'they may fall into vulgar hands' where 'they have most need of good presentation'. The audience was also quite sophisticated, as diversification of newspapers in the later seventeenth-century reflects: specific geographical and social groups, as well as more familiar religious and political partisans were being catered for. Perhaps surprisingly, the female audience seems to have been ignored as yet. (The early newspaper press in England, in Griffiths, 1992: 11)

If it is difficult to define a magazine in general terms – how can a 'specialist' magazine be pinned down? Professor David Abrahamson (1996b: 28) came up with a useful definition in his study of postwar periodicals in America: 'specific information in a specific form that can be expected to appeal to a definable segment of readers'. Abrahamson, an academic with the background of a practising journalist, locates this definition within the commercial context of 'delivering' those readers to 'a group of manufacturers or distributors with the means and willingness to advertise their products and services' to them.

It seems unlikely that there was a group of manufacturers or distributors in 1693 waiting for a vector to access the women's market, but the *Ladies Mercury* established the principle of distinguishing between groups of readers and making a particular appeal to their interests. Once this had been demonstrated to work it could and would be adopted by other publishers, so that the 'beginning of the reign of Queen Anne saw the periodical press firmly established, both in respect of newspapers and the periodicals of entertainment and instruction to which Cave had given the name of magazines' (Clair, 1965: 180). The variety was increasing too, for in the early half of the eighteenth century 'specialist publications mushroomed ... ranging from trade papers to political periodicals, literary journals to publications centring on gossip, scandals and manners and moral instruction' (Williams, 1998: 23).[4]

Magazines frequently acknowledged as landmarks in this period include the *Tatler* (April 1709) and the *Spectator* (March 1711). Samuel Johnson launched two different titles, the *Rambler* (1750) and the *Idler* (1758). If he followed his own advice – 'No man but a blockhead ever wrote except for money' – we may assume that his ventures were profitable. Addison's *Spectator* certainly was: 'My publisher tells me', he wrote in the tenth issue, 'that there are already three thousand of them distributed every day; so that if I allow twenty readers to every paper, which I look upon as a modest computation, I may reckon about threescore thousand disciples in London and Westminster' (Plant, 1939: 57).[5]

Part of this success must be attributed to Steele and Addison's social awareness and commercial nous. According to Harold Herd (1952: 52–53), the *Tatler* 'invented a new kind of periodical journalism that was to develop into the modern weekly review ... a two-page, thrice-weekly paper intended to reflect in particular the more urbane outlook and interests of those who frequented the coffee-houses', while the *Spectator* 'daily reached a wide audience ... by means of a new and enlightened type of journalism that revealed keen observation of the contemporary scene'.

These titles were among the successes, but there seem to have been plenty of entrepreneurial publisher-editors willing to take the risk of launching their own magazines. Names that do not have the same sheen of longevity

---

[4]As Ian McBride, a lecturer at King's College, London, notes in a book review published in the *Financial Times* of 19 July 2003, 'Georgian society was, like our own, an information society: the newspaper, the novel and the periodical were among its successes' (p. 5).

[5]It is worth noting that in discussing the size and growth of the reading public during the eighteenth century, Ian Watt questions this figure, which, as he points out, is 'not disinterested'. Watt believes that 'the real proportion was probably no more than half of this', giving a reading public of less than one in 20 of the population (Watt, 1974: 39).

include *The Parrot* (1728, four issues); *The Bee* (1759, eight issues, edited by Oliver Goldsmith); *The Poetical Magazine; or, the Muses Monthly Companion* (1764, one issue); *Terrae-Filios* (1764, two issues); *The Trifler. A new periodical miscellany by Timothy Touchstone, of St Peter's College, Westminster* (1788, one issue); and *The Wonderful Magazine, and Marvellous Chronicle; or, New Weekly Entertainer* – which survived from 1793 to 1794, perhaps because of its all-bases-covered title. A quick scan of Muddiman's *Tercentenary Handlist of English and Welsh Newspapers, Magazines and Reviews* (1920) turns up scores of others.

'By this time' James Playsted Wood (1956: 8) notes, 'England had about 150 periodicals'. One of the material conditions that permitted and encouraged this expansion of titles and circulations was a doubling of the country's printing capacity; according to Marjorie Plant (1939: 86), in 1724 there were 103 printers in Great Britain (28 in the provinces and 75 in London) and by 1750 there were some 248 (120 and 128 respectively).

The actual number of magazines published is an important consideration in the history of the form because in the next era, that of industrialisation, specialisation and consumerisation, there was an explosion in volume, even if this was not recognised at the time.

William Poole, the Victorian librarian who gave his name to *Poole's Index to Periodical Literature*, believed it would be useful to catalogue periodicals because:

> Every question in literature, religion, politics, social science, political economy, and in many other lines of human progress, finds its latest and freshest interpretation in the current periodicals. (1882: iv)

Poole's intention was to provide an index to articles appearing in British and American magazines – or, to be more accurate, those in 'a list of periodicals *which it was desirable to index*' (p. iv, emphasis added). This clearly implies strict, and unstated, criteria although we can make a good guess at these from the list quoted above. Clearly even a restricted listing would be an almost impossible task for one man to achieve within a reasonable time, so he recruited voluntary help among his fellow librarians. Even so there were only 25 English serials included in the plan for Poole's book, and of those only eight were eventually included in the first volume. One of the reasons for this, in Poole's dry opinion, was that the typical English librarian would not, or could not, 'give up for several weeks or months his hours of rest and recreation. Perhaps the climate and social customs of England are not so favourable as they are in America for night work' (p. vi).

By the time the Sixth Supplement to *Poole's Index* appeared in 1908 the total number of periodicals covered had risen to 190, not many more than the 150 Playsted Wood identified as existing at the end of the eighteenth century. This does not seem right, and when we discover that Vann and

Van Arsdel (1978: x) cite a figure of 16,000 periodicals published in the Victorian era, and that they note the *Wellesley Index to Victorian Periodicals* was revising the figure upwards, it can be seen that Poole's pool was but a highly selective drop in the ocean.

Even then, the *Wellesley Index* covers only a fraction of the published periodicals in any depth, restricting its analysis to literary, philosophical, political or religious titles. This leaves a massive gap in titles aimed at both domestic and business markets, a point noted in the *Encyclopedia of the British Press*:

> There were many other kinds of periodical publication which were aimed at particular sections of the public. One was the magazine for home reading for the middle-class family. Some had existed before the beginning of the century but they grew in numbers and popularity in the 1850s and 1860s. Early Victorian newspapers carried little in the way of features or reading matter designed for women and the family. Such material was provided instead by publications such as *Household Words* (1850), *All The Year Round* (1859) and others ... Yet another area in which there was a massive growth in the second half of this period was in the great range of specialist journals. They were the publications which served to keep the members of a sect or an economic interest or a profession in contact ... (Dr Lucy Brown, 'The British Press 1800–1860', in Griffiths, 1992: 29)

The principle underlying the choices made by both William Poole and Walter Houghton (editor of the *Wellesley Index*) seems to reflect the traditional stand-off between high and low culture, with literature and politics in the former camp and popular titles like those edited by Charles Dickens in the – unindexed – latter. This may have contributed to the situation noted by Lionel Madden and Diana Dixon:

> ... the more weighty studies of individual periodicals have tended to be devoted to the more obviously 'major' or 'significant' titles ... it is clear that the attention of students of the nineteenth century has tended to concentrate upon a relatively small number of frequently studied titles rather than upon the whole diverse field of Victorian periodicals ... Michael Woolf's comment in 'Charting the Golden Stream' (in *Editing Nineteenth-Century Texts*, ed. John M. Robson, 1967) still has applicability for the student of Victorian periodicals: '...what one must generally conclude about the current use of the periodicals is that scholars' needs have been met and that familiar evidence has been extracted only from familiar sources.' (*Histories and Studies of Individual Periodicals*, in Vann and Van Arsdel, 1978: 117/118)

Such an attitude certainly informs the comment by Richard D. Altick that:

> The higher journalism—there is no better term for it—was an art indigenous to the Victorian periodical edited for the intelligent lay reader. Its forte was the treatment of a subject of interest to the educated mind, in a manner that was serious but not heavy, urbane rather than facetious or sedulously 'bright.' The writers in that genre discovered

a happy middle way between vulgarization and pedantry, an art almost lost today
because evidently there is no demand for it. (1974: 67–68)

Given that much academic study of magazines – such as there has been –
has tended to focus on a given set of 'familiar sources', it must make sense
to look for fresh material. With at least 16,000 magazines to choose
between there should be plenty of new titles and even whole sectors from
this period of rapid expansion waiting to be investigated. And indeed there
are, as Muddiman's *Handlist* shows (1920).

One of the reasons for the growth of periodical titles in the Victorian
period was, according to John S. North, 'the fascination of the public with
newspaper and magazine reporting of rapid developments in technology
and science' (*The Rationale: Why Read Victorian Periodicals?*, in Vann and
Van Arsdel, 1978: 4). Analysis of Muddiman for the five year period 1890
to 1895 shows 141 titles that can easily be identified as covering such developments. These include both trade and leisure/hobbyist magazines that
were influenced by scientific or technological developments but exclude
others, such as farming and stock breeding, which would also have made
some claim to scientific influence. Examples of titles are *Electricity* (1890);
the *Engineering Review*; the *Humming Bird: a monthly magazine scientific,
artistic and industrial review* (both 1891); the *Phonographic Herald* (1893);
Hardwicke's Science Gossip (launched in 1894 and extant until 1902); and
Technical Journals Review, Technical Papers Advertiser, and *Technical Press
Review* (all 1895).

Vann and Van Arsdel (1994) look at this area in *Victorian Periodicals and
Victorian Society.* They state in their Introduction that they aim to 'identify
the ways that periodicals informed, instructed and amused virtually all of
the people in the many segments of Victorian life' (p. 3) and their sampling
does indeed open up areas not previously examined, breaking away from the
Poolean version of periodicals 'worth studying'. However it can be argued,
with conviction, that this does not go far enough in identifying new specialisations and new publishing sectors. For example, the chapter on Transport
(pp. 179–198) covers railways, canals, roads and coastal shipping. with never
a mention of the automobile. In fact, authors John E.C. Palmer and Harold
W. Paar note: 'Thus road transport, like the canals, appears to have generated
little or no specialized periodical literature' (p. 197). (As Palmer was a historian of early British railways and Paar a research officer for the Railway and
Canal Historical Society it is perhaps not surprising that this area received
such scant treatment.)

However, it does not take much thought to see that, of the modes of transport mentioned above, that which has had most impact on the world, never
mind the UK, is road – bicycles, cars, motorcycles, lorries, buses. These have
become everyday modes of transport, bringing with them a range of social,

industrial, military and environmental issues; road transport has ensured the decline of most of the other forms covered by Palmer and Paar. And far from generating 'little or scant' specialised literature, the bicycle alone inspired numerous periodicals in the last third of the nineteenth century and the motor car benefited from a weekly magazine dedicated to its cause – a magazine, *Autocar*, that thrives to this day – at a time when there were still only a handful of horseless carriages in the country.

To illustrate one sliver of this phenomenon further, by counting the number of cycling titles in Muddiman's *Handlist* it is possible to see that between 1875 and 1900 a total of 31 cycling magazines were launched. Numerous reasons can be ascribed post hoc:

- once John Kemp Starley's design for the Rover Safety model (1886) had standardised bicycle manufacture, marketing and advertising became necessary to create distinctions between brands, and specialised magazines provided excellent opportunities to reach potential markets;
- bicycle-based sporting and leisure pursuits expanded or split into specialised fields and these specialisations fostered magazines to cater for them;
- increasing numbers of people had sufficient disposable income with which to buy a bicycle and the leisure time in which to use it;
- a 'supervening social need' of the type posited by Brian Winston (1998) in *Media Technology and Society* created the conditions that made ownership and use of a bicycle acceptable, desirable and necessary.

The overall result was nine cycling titles launched between 1874 and 1879; another nine in the following decade; and 13 in the 1890s (Stewart et al., 1955). There was evidently at least one magazine to meet each social need – and it is a phenomenon worth noting that when one magazine is successful competitor titles will rapidly appear in that same sector of the market.

Such levels of activity indicated a force that was working strongly on the social, cultural, commercial and economic life of the country, one that helped to shape the world we live in today. The best sources for finding out how that force was viewed at the time (pace Poole, Houghton et al.) and how it helped to define the very phenomenon it was serving (pace Ohmann, 1996) must be the specialised periodicals of the day: as John S. North observed, 'Civilisation may never again have so sensitive an instrument for registering its course as the Victorian periodical press' (Vann and Van Arsdel, 1978: 5).

Indeed so – or, to put it another way: 'That's what magazines are so good at; they harness change as it's happening'. Sarah Bravo, then editor of *Real Homes*, produced this quote in the *Observer* Business Section (20 July 2003, p. 6) , however she was not referring to Victorian periodicals. To chronicle the development of magazines in the twentieth century would be a substantial volume of its own, a volume that would need to chart the development of new specialisms, new hobbies, new technologies, new trades, new professions, and whole new magazine sectors to serve new cultural phenomena.

The first 25 years of the new century saw the launch of *John Bull* (1906), a general interest weekly that would become Britain's biggest magazine; they also witnessed Condé Nast buy *Vogue* (1909); the birth of *Woman's Weekly* (1911), a cornerstone of IPC's rise to the top of British magazine publishing; and the foundation of the *New Statesman* (1913), *Vanity Fair* (1914), the *Reader's Digest* (1918), *Good Housekeeping* (1922), the *Radio Times* and *Time* (both 1923), and the *New Yorker* (1925). If we squeeze in one more year we can encompass the launch of *Melody Maker*, one of the first magazines to cover the new wave of popular music.

Taking these headline titles alone we have a patriotic but anti-establishment journal that supported the hard-done-by British private soldier (founded and edited by Horatio Bottomley, who also founded the *Financial Times* as a means of promoting his investment schemes); the epitome of high fashion; the epitome of a mass women's title; a standard-bearer for middle-class leftwing political thought; a chronicle of high society; a modern version of the 'miscellany' periodical that blazed a trail for brand extension into money-raising activities; the nonpareil of what has come to be known as the 'shelter' sector; a listings magazine for the new era of mass communication; the classic model for all news weeklies; the waspish literary journal; and the harbinger of a new period in popular music culture.

Alongside such launches there were technological developments in the improving quality and diminishing price of woodpulp-based paper, the perfection of the rotogravure printing process that eased and improved the reproduction of photographs, and the increasing adoption of colour plates, as well as commercial developments such as the institution of the Audit Bureau of Circulation (1914) that began to formalise methods for measuring a magazine's reach and readership for the benefit of advertisers.

During the twentieth century the magazine industry as a whole became increasingly skilled at adopting both technological and commercial developments and harnessing them to make and market attractive products that could address the particular needs of a particular readership. On the one hand, this could mean the desire amongst women aged between 20 and 30 to be kept informed of fashion trends in the high street: on the other, it could mean serious mountain bikers' need to know about new chainsets. Similarly, it could mean architects' requirement to be kept abreast of new developments and regulatory restrictions: on the other, it could mean the desire by advertising account managers to have a publication in which their photographic portrait might one day appear.

In *Magazines That Make History* (2004), Norberto Angeletti and Alberto Oliva identify a 'canon' of influential magazines from the twentieth century (or just before): *National Geographic* (1888), *Reader's Digest* (1922), *Time* (1923), *Life* (1936), *Paris Match* (1938), *¡Hola!* (1944), *Der Spiegel* (1947), and *People* (1974). The majority of these are news-based titles, specialising in summary and analysis, but even within that genre it is instructive to note the change of emphasis from the straightforward 'hard news' of the earlier titles to the more people-, and specifically celebrity-, based news of the later ones. All of these titles, however, can be categorised as 'mass' interest, which is typical of magazines in the first half of the last century: publishing companies followed the general pattern of industrial development, which was focused on large corporations, and in this specific industry the costs of printing and paper meant that expenditure had to be amortised over a long print run. And just as importantly, personal identity was bound up in a fairly limited number of hobbies and interests.

Abrahamson (1996b: 19) identifies the 1960s as the key period for the expansion of magazine offerings in the USA: 'During the 1960s, the American consumer magazine industry completed a major transformation: a shift away from general-interest mass-market publications toward more specialized magazines'. Johnson and Prijatel (1999: 54) agree: 'In the 1960s, audience specialization became the name of the magazine game, with four new magazines appearing for every one that folded'. Abrahamson draws on Jean-Louis Servan-Schreiber's work to draw out the socio-psychological reasons for the expansion of personal interests - and this is examined further in Chapter 7 (*Theorising The Field*) - but there were also relatively straightforward political-economy factors at work as everything became cheaper and more plentiful. Falling costs for paper, printing, typesetting, page composition, and colour reproduction combined with a decline in the power of the craft unions to lower the barriers of entry to accomodate new or short-run magazines.

A common adage in the British magazine publishing industry predicts that where the USA treads, the UK follows five years later. Like most commonplace sayings there is an element of truth to it, although British post-war development took somewhat longer to get into full swing. Paper was rationed until 1950, general rationing stayed in force until 1952, and the magazine world remained somewhat greyish until the 1970s or even 1980s, following which time it blossomed into a multi-coloured phantasmagoria. As in the USA, the increasing emphasis on individual identity and subcultural tribalisation (pace Marshall McLuhan's statement that 'our new electric culture provides our lives again with a tribal base'; see McLuhan and Zingrone, 1995: 127) combined with an increase in specialist consumption and technological changes to the material conditions of production to create a fruitful time for magazine publishers both large and small.

Although printing and production technology made significant advances in the 1960s and 1970s, it was not until 1985 that the introduction of postscript-based software (such as Aldus *Pagemaker* and Adobe *Illustrator*, running on Apple Macintosh computers that could output to increasingly cheap laser printers) heralded the advent of desktop publishing (DTP) and revolutionised the production of magazines and newspapers – a revolution that could not have occurred without first Eddie Shah and then Rupert Murdoch defying, and destroying, the power of the print unions. Two years later Quark launched *XPress*, which rapidly overshadowed *Pagemaker*. Once in place, the 'holy trinity' of magazine publishing software (*Quark, Photoshop* and *Illustrator)* running on Apple Macintosh hardware must have given rise to more magazine projects than any other advances in print technology.

2

THE POLITICAL ECONOMY OF MAGAZINES

Anyone in the UK can publish a magazine. This statement might seem self-evident but it is worth noting because this is not the case everywhere in the world and it undoubtedly has had, and will continue to have, a material effect on the shape of the magazine industry in this country. Any potential publisher of a print title needs nothing more than enough cash (or credit) to pay a paper merchant, printer and, possibly, the people who will supply the content. Getting the magazine distributed might not be quite so straightforward and there's no guarantee that anyone will buy it even if it does get onto the newsstands. However the principle is clear – anyone in the UK can publish a magazine: you don't need a licence, a permit, or any kind of qualification. Publishing a magazine in digital form, on the web or as a mobile application, reduces the barriers to entry, and the costs, even further, as doing so requires no paper and minimal distribution costs.

That said, as with all media forms, magazines operate within overlapping spheres of political, commercial, and cultural influence. Taken together, these spheres define the political economy of the industry and they overlap because like many industrial fields – but particularly those involving communications – political and legal frameworks affect the practice of commerce, and commercial factors may also affect the consumer response (assuming consumers are the practitioners of culture). There is also a general culture of professional journalistic practice and within that a specific culture of magazine practice (see Chapter 3 for more on this), both of which exert a material influence on the industry.

Or rather we should say *industries*, because while the magazine market is commonly regarded as a unified entity even the most cursory analysis reveals that it is divided into three major sections – Consumer, Customer (also known as contract), and Business to Business (B2B). According to industry figures that were current at the time of writing there are 3,366 Consumer magazines in a market worth £2.98bn; 563 Customer magazines in a market worth £904m; and 5,108 B2B titles in a market worth £3.3bn (data from the Periodical Publishers Association and the Association of Publishing Agencies).

These sectors intersect and diverge at significant points and the relationship between them is evolving in interesting ways, but general analyses of the media tend not to take these aspects into account. It is not widely acknowledged, for example, that while there are relatively few Customer magazines compared with Consumer, the former dominate the circulation statistics for non-business titles. *Sky: The Magazine* was number one overall because it is sent to every BSkyB satellite tv channel subscriber as part of their package; in some eyes this did not quite count because the magazine was not *paid for*, although price does not necessarily appear to be a barrier since many Customer periodicals are actively bought. Even though the circulation figures in this sector can put many famous Consumer titles into the shade, there have been few studies of the companies that produce these magazines despite the number of intriguing questions that could be raised. For example, what are the relationships between the company that commissions them, the company that produces them, the people who work on them, and the people who buy them? (Lynda Dyson addressed some of these issues in her contribution to *Mapping the Magazine*, 2008.)

In terms of sheer numbers, the B2B sector is larger than the Consumer sector by a factor of almost two to one. In addition, the basic rules of economic behaviour dictate that titles tend to be clustered around significantly profitable business sectors such as management, medicine, financial services and, inevitably, property. Specific commercial sectors may be subject to general upturns and downturns but management consultancies, pharmaceutical companies, venture capitalists, and real estate seem to be highly resilient whatever the economic conditions. This creates a situation that has a number of implications, including the potential to influence policy and employment within the industry.

As a result, although the word 'magazine' is likely to conjure an image of something glossy like *Vogue* or entertaining like *Take A Break*, as we have seen in the previous chapter the historical development of the magazine publishing sector within wider social, cultural, and economic contexts has created a reality that is a great deal more complex than has been allowed for in such a simple characterisation.

Following Cave's eighteenth-century adoption of the word 'magazine' to describe his periodical (see Chapter 1) this came into general use to describe a type of publication that was different from a newspaper, inasmuch as it was not focused entirely on news, contained a miscellany of material and not just political intelligence, and targeted a specific rather than a general readership. Over the last three centuries the content of all categories of magazine (Consumer/Customer/B2B), and of individual magazines within those categories, has become more narrowly focused as professional communities, commercial developments, and personal identities have become more specialised or reliant on more specialised information.

At the end of Cave's century it has been estimated there were about 150 magazines in regular publication (Wood, 1956: 8); 100 years later there were 2,097 (Curran and Seaton, 1997: 37). Today there are estimated to be between 8,000 and 9,000 magazines published in the UK. The Periodical Publishers Association (PPA) lobbies for the magazine publishing industry and has a membership of 300 publishing companies, a significant but not comprehensive representation. According to PPA research undertaken in 2008, on average 350 new magazines are launched each year, but these launches must be balanced against the number of closures and failures: indeed, the ease of publishing a magazine (as referred to above) makes failure a statistical likelihood. General economic conditions and consumer confidence will also have a direct bearing on the number of launches and closures.

Two major forces have driven this expansion of titles – specialisation and commercial development: the specialisation of consumer interests and the increasingly specialised nature of business, professional, and commercial practices. According to Harris and Lee, these factors came to the fore in the 1850s and created a tension between opposing concepts of the press; on the one hand it was seen as a vehicle of instruction and on the other as a reflector of popular interests:

> Though it is difficult to generalize when faced with the extravagant range of material produced during the later nineteenth century, modifications in the content of the periodicals and newspapers were broadly characterized by the interconnected processes of 'specialization' and 'diversification'. Each reflected the shifting relationship between the press and readers as commercial pressure hastened the move away from the provision of precept and instruction toward the gratification of a range of established tastes. (1986: 109)

There has been a third force at work too – the need for capitalist enterprises constantly to grow. The latter applies not only to magazine publishing enterprises themselves but also to the need for marketing/PR that large, and particularly shareholder-owned, companies have. Under the current economic system a business that is not actively expanding is considered to be contracting and is thus also ripe for a takeover or even annihilation. The magazine form has been drawn into this constant struggle, with companies using its community-relationship-building characteristics to attract potential, and retain actual, customers. It is important to remember that in this context there are customers on both sides of the publishing equation – readers *and* advertisers.

This creates an obvious tension with, if not an actual contradiction of, the magazine's trusted position as the 'reader's friend' (Hermes, 1995; Beetham, 1996; Korinek, 2000; Consterdine, 2002). There is no simple way to resolve or diminish this tension but it can be explained to a certain extent by referring to the economic theories of Ferdinand Tönnies (2001), which use the concepts of *Gemeinschaft* and *Gesellschaft*: individual magazines tend towards the condition of *Gemeinschaft* (feudal and small-scale, with power deriving from personal and social relationships), while the businesses that publish them tend towards the condition of *Gesellschaft* (corporate and impersonal, with power deriving from economic relationships).

Looked at in this light, it becomes easier to understand how individual magazines can continue their pseudo-personal relationships with readers while the companies that publish them are bought and sold in the international marketplace. A good example of this is the rise and fall of Emap.

Emap started as a publisher of local newspapers in the East Midlands. Looking for ways to lessen the downtime of its printing presses in 1953 it ventured into specialist titles that were printed like newspapers – *Angling Times, Motor Cycle News, Garden News*. When these proved successful it ventured further down the specialist path and began to launch or acquire magazines. Through the usual mixture of luck and judgment this policy succeeded so well that by the end of the 1990s Emap was the second largest magazine publisher in the UK, with divisions that covered consumer and B2B sectors. The company then expanded this success further to cover radio stations and tv channels. But in 2007 it all came to an end, for reasons that have not yet become fully transparent but which include the lack of a sound digital strategy, a hangover from a disastrous venture in the USA, and intense sensitivity to the value of its shares. The family-owned German publisher H. Bauer bought the consumer titles and radio stations (with Mr Bauer himself, the anecdotal evidence has it, literally writing a cheque for £1.14bn) while the B2B titles had a brief independent existence before being absorbed into the Guardian Media Group.

Yet despite this high level and potentially disruptive impersonal *Gesellschaft* action the magazines continued to communicate with their readers on the *Gemeinschaft* basis of 'friendship' and 'community'.

But whereas Emap failed for reasons that seem to include the perceived lack of a clear strategic vision that affected its share price and old-fashioned management practices, *Reader's Digest* in the UK has suffered from a very different large-scale effect of the political economy of a big corporation: the pension fund. In February 2010 the company publishing the UK version of the magazine was placed into administration by its board because it could not reach agreement with the pensions regulator over a £125m deficit in its fund; this, in turn, was triggered by the US parent company, the Reader's Digest Association, filing for Chapter 11 protection from its creditors. Given that *Reader's Digest* was at this time still the largest selling magazine in the world and its UK edition had an audited circulation of 465,028 a month, it becomes all too clear that size alone does not guarantee continued success within the political economy of magazine publishing. (Happily, the value of the brand was recognised by Better Capital, a private investment firm that rescued the UK edition in April 2010.)

Revenue models

All of the above might naturally lead us to ask 'So where does the money come from?' and at the same time to find that factor missing from Johnson and Prijatel's (1999) definition of a successful magazine (see Chapter 1). When Edward Cave published the *Gentleman's Magazine* and Addison published the *Spectator*, there was only one important source of revenue: the readers. With economic developments and industrialisation came another source of revenue: advertisers. This arrangement lasted for more than a century, giving publishers a very stable business model that could be adapted in order to favour one source of revenue over the other as specific conditions required. For example, consumer magazines have tended to derive a greater proportion of their income from reader sales than B2B magazines: historically, the division has been 49 per cent cover price/51 per cent advertising revenue for monthly consumer magazines, 40/60 for weeklies and 18/82 for B2B titles (Wharton, 1992: 3).

This business model also allows for shifts of emphasis within the general arrangement: magazines in the USA have focused on selling cheap subscriptions to drive up circulations and attract more advertisers (in many instances actually guaranteeing a minimum level of circulation), whereas in the UK sales became focused on attracting readers at the newsstand, a process that the railways and W.H. Smith's nationwide retailing business (founded in 1848 but with a history going back to 1792) assisted enormously.

This model was captured almost perfectly by David Abrahamson (1996a: 28) when he noted that the editorial (*Gemeinschaft*) side of a magazine offers 'specific information in a specific form that can be expected to appeal to a definable segment of readers', while at exactly the same time the commercial (*Gesellschaft*) side is 'delivering those readers to a group of manufacturers or distributors with the means and willingness to advertise their products and services to them'.

Although differences in revenue distribution between the categories of magazine (Consumer, Customer, B2B) will lead to important distinctions in production practices (in the treatment of front covers, for example: see Chapter 3), all three still need to attract paying advertisers and this commercial necessity has the potential to induce conflicts and pressures. The classic description of the advertiser/magazine/reader trichotomy as articulated by Abrahamson assumes that the editorial division of the magazine will act as an autonomous body. Although editors would generally insist that editorial and advertising are separated by a 'Chinese Wall', many critics (McRobbie, passim; Curran and Seaton, 1997; Currie, 1999) would also assume that one way or another advertisers will hold sway at particular junctures; there have also been suggestions that retailers may be inclined, or actually able, to influence the content or treatment of certain subjects. In 2004, for example, the *Observer* reported that Tesco had asked a number of publishers to change their covers before allowing the magazines to go on display. As the titles concerned were ladmags this concern may have been understandable and it is certainly mild compared with Wal-Mart's actions. The US retailer 'reportedly asked publishers of women's magazines to remove cover lines flagging up features on abortion or sex tips' (www.guardian.co.uk/business/2004/nov/28/observerbusiness.tesco#_jmp0_).

There can be no doubt that multiple opportunities exist by which the exertion of pressure through commercial or revenue threatening decisions can be attempted. However, it is worthwhile to remember here that '[o]nly through the growth of advertising did the press achieve independence' (Williams, 1957: 51) and the ability to set newspapers free from direct political patronage (Herd, 1952: 64), as well as allowing magazines to lower their prices and increase their readership among the less well off.

According to Theodore Peterson (1964: 7), the 'big revolution in the magazine industry came ... in October 1893' when Frank A. Munsey reduced the cover price of his eponymous magazine from 25 cents to 10 cents and an annual subscription from $3 to $1. This was possible once the publisher had realised 'one could achieve a large circulation by selling his magazine for much less than its cost of production and could take his profits from the high volume of advertising that a large circulation attracted'. As with most innovations, there was also a backlash. Munsey was called a magazine 'manufacturer' rather than a publisher by the more higher minded of his competitors and some publishers 'were reluctant to jump on the advertising bandwagon, preferring to keep their magazines unsullied by advertising' (Johnson and Prijatel, 1999: 36).

British publishers were initially deterred from including too much advertising by the Stamp Duty Act of 1712 that imposed a tax of one shilling (the equivalent of 5p) on every advertisement. Although Stamp Duty was amended several times over the years, the advertising tax was not abolished completely until August 1853. After that, publishers were as free as their American colleagues to include as many ads as they desired and many saw the inclusion of advertising as a positive bonus for readers. Harold Herd quotes nineteenth-century publisher Daniel Stuart to this effect:

> Numerous and various advertisements attract numerous and various readers, looking out for employment, servants, sales, and purchases, etc etc. Advertisements act and react. They attract readers, promote circulation, and circulation attracts advertisements.

(D. Stuart (1838) 'Anecdotes of Coleridge and of London Newspapers', *Gentleman's Magazine*, 10: 25; in Herd, 1952: 152)

Munsey's name has been attached to this innovation in the political economy of periodical publishing but he was not the only one thinking this way; Cyrus Curtis (who may have been the originator of this scheme with his *Ladies Home Journal* and later the *Saturday Evening Post*) and Samuel McClure (*McClure's Magazine*) adopted similar policies at around the same time, until up to 80 per cent of their publishing revenue came from advertisements (Morrish, 2003: 7). Was this a result of synchronicity, historical inevitability, copycat capitalism, or a combination of all these possibilities? Whichever, the profits that publishers achieved demonstrated the effectiveness of the method and lo! – a business model was born, based on a virtuous circle: low cover or subscription prices led to more readers, more readers led to more advertisers, more advertisers subsidised the production costs, and subsidised production costs led to low cover or subscription prices.

This model took American magazines into the twentieth century in good health and Theodore Peterson (1964: 13) identified four factors that characterised mass circulation ('popular') titles of this period:

1 magazines had become low in price, and thus within reach of more people;
2 low price, mass production and mass distribution combined to achieve 'undreamed-of circulations'; where 200,000 had been a good figure in the nineteenth century, the *Ladies Home Journal* was nearing 1,000,000;
3 advertising had become essential for profitability and manufacturers needed national markets;
4 'magazine content had become "popular" as publishers and editors reached new audiences ... Then, as now, magazines were edited for little publics within the population as a whole; but they were discovering new publics to which to appeal.'

In the UK the model worked differently inasmuch as consumers were far more resistant to taking out subscriptions. In a much smaller landmass, with a large proportion of the population living in cities and well-established distribution, wholesale and retail systems that put magazines within easy reach of most people (geographically at least), the focus was much more on increasing sales at the newsstand, and this in turn led to a greater emphasis on magazine craft – creating covers that would appeal to the target readership and planning the publication so that a potential reader flicking through would be attracted by the layout and the rhythm of the content (American magazines still tend towards packing the front of the book with nicely laid out material and then using rather functional turn-to pages at the back of the book to complete stories). The same imperatives have also led to more of an emphasis on marketing campaigns and free gifts (often cover mounts). That said, some British newspapers and magazines in the 1920s and 1930s promoted their subscriptions very hard, canvassing house to house as well as offering benefits such as free insurance. George Orwell gave some insight into this in the first chapter of *The Road To Wigan Pier* (1937), where a number of his fellow boarders in the Brookers' lodging house were canvassers.

There was, however, one thing that could turn this virtuous business circle into a vicious one – an economic recession. When both reader-consumers and advertiser-producers had less money to spend, things went bad very quickly, since the costs of production were no longer being subsidised to the same degree and the equation no longer balanced. At times like these (the Great Depression after World War One; the global financial collapse that started in 2008) publishers needed deep pockets and steady nerves to survive, but the fact that so many established titles have come through several wars and several recessions demonstrates clearly that a good magazine brand is a very robust commercial entity.

That said, even the most robust of commercial entities will not thrive without constant attention and more forward-thinking magazine publishers will formulate strategies to counter predicted threats. In 2004, for example, BBC Magazines looked at the potential for disruption posed by aggressive retailers (specifically supermarkets and Tesco in particular), a downturn in the advertising market, and growing use of the internet. Peter Phippen, the managing director, and Nick Brett, his deputy, came up with a deceptively simple four-point strategy:

- they would publish only strong brands that attracted passionate communities;
- they would publish global brands that had international potential;
- they would boost the number of subscribers significantly, getting closer to the readers and cutting out the middlemen;
- they would invest in and launch titles that could harness digital potential.

A consistent application of this strategy has seen BBC titles exported all over the world and taken BBC Worldwide to first place in the UK for subscribers (overtaking National Magazines), thus allowing the business to rebalance its income to 20 per cent subscriptions, 30 per cent advertising, and 50 per cent cover price. Brand extensions for the most popular titles include live events, websites, internet tv channels, apps for tablets and smartphones and, potentially, branded goods.

When it comes to subscriptions, Nick Brett readily acknowledges the insight of another publisher – Felix Dennis: his tripartite mantra states that subscribers must benefit from an unbeatable price, they must get the magazine first (before it reaches the shops), and the subscription must not seem like a life sentence (so it's easy to pull out).

Dennis achieved success from very small beginnings and as the PPA's figure of 350 magazine launches a year shows, there are plenty of people and companies that still believe they have a good idea for a new magazine. These ideas will usually arise because their originators think something is *missing* or something has *changed*. As John Wharton (1992: 4) notes, 'Markets, tastes, interests, educational standards, technologies change at an ever-increasing rate and in order to survive a magazine must change as well'.

The 'something missing' genre of launches can be exemplified by *Promise*, which appeared in the mid-1990s (there are a few magazines with that title). The people behind it believed that true Christianity was missing from most children's upbringing and they could do something to rectify the situation. For example, the first issue contained a feature telling parents why they should not allow their children to take part in Halloween festivities. The world is still waiting for the second issue.

When it comes to 'something changed', there are three main subcategories:

- A new readership – or an old readership that has been taken for granted. The former can be exemplified by *Loaded*, which identified a new generation of young men who wanted a different kind of multi-interest magazine, paving the way for *FHM*, *Maxim*, *Men's Health*, *Front*, *Boy's Toys*, *Petrolhead*, *XL for Men*, *Deluxe* and *Eat Soup*. The latter is the reason why German publishers decided to launch *Bella*, *Best*, *Prima*, etc., in the UK; IPC had become lazy with its women's weeklies, leaving an opportunity to appeal to a younger generation.
- A new trend – such as with the generation of women who grew up reading *Cosmopolitan* and *Company* and then grew out of them but didn't want to grow old with *Good Housekeeping*. New titles such as *Frank*, *Eve*, *Red* and the second iteration of *Nova* were launched in the late 90s to cater to the 'middle youth' demographic. Sometimes this can be accomplished by relaunching an existing title as NatMags did with *She*, obliterating the original 1955 concept (that had itself been frequently relaunched) and replacing it in April 2006 with a completely new concept using the old name: as launch editor Matthew Line explained to *PR Week*: 'It's not a relaunch – it's a totally different magazine … it was decided that *She* would go and the new magazine would take its name'.
- New advertisers – who could be serving new trends or new technologies. Felix Dennis founded his fortune on the rise in popularity of kung fu and the attendant increase in kit, accessories, classes, books, and so on. Technology is changing all the time (think of phones, personal music systems, computers) but a classic example of this category is the Tamagotchi craze of the mid-90s, which was served by a number of short-lived magazines.

As can be seen from some of the examples above, it is common for a new launch to be rapidly joined by competitor titles in that sector of the market: for example, in January 2004 *Nuts* and *Zoo*, two leading examples of the lads' weekly, were launched virtually simultaneously.

Towards the end of the last century magazine publishers began to discover other sources of revenue that could be spun off from, but still closely associated with, any given title. Conferences or exhibitions could be branded with magazine names; B2B magazines could easily claim this as an extension of their professional operations, whereas consumer magazines had to be careful to present such developments as special opportunities for their readers, or as a chance to 'meet the team' behind the magazine. As publisher, poet, and author of *How To Be Rich* Felix Dennis remarked, 'If young magazine journalists want to know their business they must understand the importance of events' (personal conversation).

Once the idea of a brand extension had been found to work in one field, it did not take long for it to be applied to others. Hence the American version of *Maxim*, a men's magazine published in several editions around the world (by Dennis Publishing, as it happens), developed plans for a casino and hotel in Las Vegas – it was seen to fit with the girls-and-gambling interests of the readership. This particular idea proved hubristic when *Maxim*'s circulation plummeted so far that the publisher pulled the plug on the print edition, but the principle behind it lives on: at the time of writing, *Rolling Stone* is in the process of launching a bar/restaurant and *Playboy* is seriously considering re-establishing a worldwide chain of Bunny clubs. Other magazines, such as *Elle*, have also licensed their logos to ranges of clothing and housewares.

There is one other category of magazine that must be mentioned here – the part work. Part works are, as the name suggests, intended for collection and they tend to be either an encyclopedia-like publication that builds into a comprehensive work about a particular subject or a vehicle for delivering sets of collectables. The market has traditionally been dominated by publishers who specialise in this genre (Marshall Cavendish, who claim to have pioneered it, Eaglemoss, and De Agostini, who claim about 50 per cent of the worldwide market), but in 2009 BBC Worldwide entered the sector with *Top Gear Turbo Challenge*, leveraging the popularity of the television series and the print magazine with (mainly) boys. Every issue featured content adapted from television, came with a set of collectable trading cards, and was highly integrated with the accompanying website. The part work has its own business model – intense research into the market, a highly publicised launch with a television campaign that lasts for perhaps two weeks, and the newsagents flooded with copies; there then follows a scaling back of distribution, followed by subscription-only availability until the end of the run.

Recently a new phenomenon has been observable and although it could be considered a form of vertical integration – the business practice by which companies attempt to form a virtuous circle of stable consumption – or a variation on brand extension, it is worth noting as a novelty in the political economy of the media. Boomerang Plus is a television production company based in Cardiff. It makes a programme for Channel Four called *Freesports on Four* that includes a section on snowboarding; associated with this is Freeze, a major snowboarding festival in London. So far, so good, but more can be added to this nice mix including a specialist snowboarding magazine.

Thus, on 15 September 2009 Boomerang acquired *Method* magazine and its associated website and internet tv channel. The new corporate entity was presented as Boom Extreme Media, established to collaborate 'with key publishing brands, help drive and develop multimedia concepts and build a digital media portfolio within the extreme sports space using the group's existing infrastructure and expertise' (www.walesonline.co.uk/business-in-wales/business-news/2009/09/15/boomerang-acquires-extreme-sports-multimedia-firm-91466-24688088/).

In the 1980s some British publishers began to develop a profitable line in syndicating material published in the UK editions of their magazines to overseas publishers. This, of course, meant that contributors were required to sign over all rights in their original work and publishers' contracts began to include wording to that effect; writers and photographers were expected to allow the publisher to sell their material wherever they saw fit and also to allow it to be reproduced in any medium the publisher chose. For a brief period before the internet became mainstream CD-Rom computer disks were thought to offer a multimedia digital future for magazines. In 1995 IPC produced *UnZip* on disk, which claimed to be the first interactive title in the UK, while Felix Dennis launched *Blender*, a music title. Tony Quinn's *Magforum.com* lists the last known launch on CD-Rom as being *Enter* (a lad mag) in 2000, but research for this chapter uncovered *Virtually*, a Canadian title that claims to be 'the world's first Naturist/Nudist magazine published on CDRom', with a mission to 'bring the wonderful world of Nude Living to every Computer'. However, as its website was last updated in November 2006 it too may have gone to the great CD rack in the sky.

The next step beyond selling contributed material overseas was to sell the title itself – or rather, since overseas sales were usually already factored into circulation figures (often as a very soft element), to sell the right to use the title. In other words, publishers developed new revenue streams by licensing the rights to overseas publishers who would then create localised versions. In itself this was not a new idea – *Reader's Digest* launched a UK edition in 1938 and *Vogue* before the First World War. Transnational publishing houses such as Condé Nast (owned by the Newhouse family) and National Magazines (owned by Hearst, the US newspaper giant) have leveraged the value of brands such as *Vogue, House & Garden* and *Cosmopolitan* wherever they could and the phenomenon of localising publication has been the subject of a major study by Van Leeuwen and Machin (2005: 577–600). It is also worth noting that licensing is not limited to companies based in the USA or UK; the Swedish company Bonnier has made successful efforts to extend its titles into the new states of the Baltic and eastern Europe.

In the second half of the twentieth century, this idea took hold rapidly and publishers of any size with a successful title could look to license it overseas: Emap (before it became Bauer) took its men's magazine *FHM* around the globe and BBC Worldwide continues to do the same with *Top Gear*. A brief look at any issue of the FIPP's house journal *Magazine World* underlines the point – the Q4 2009 edition reveals that *Hello!* has been licensed to Ambracom in Morocco, *FourFourTwo* to Plus One Media in Thailand, and so on.

Although profitable, one of the costs of such ventures is eternal vigilance: licences come with strict requirements to guard the core brand values and licensers must constantly police licensees' products to ensure such requirements are being met.

The trend to licensing can be, and has been, attributed to many factors. It fits neatly with theories of globalisation and the development of the public sphere that tend to accompany the development of a bourgeois class (Habermas, 1989). Although Habermas did not directly address the simultaneous rise of a consumer culture, this issue has been examined by Richard Ohmann (1996), whose study of the rise of a business and professional class establishes very clear connections between such a social and economic evolution and the rise of both business and consumer magazines. Thus an increase in the number and variety of magazines being published in a country offers an indication of social and economic changes (as hypothesised in the General Theory, Chapter 1).

There is, however, a distinct difference between aspiration (a word that consumer magazine publishers love) and the economic or cultural ability to realise that aspiration. It is one thing for a family in, say, India to aspire to own a car but quite another for that family to be able to afford to buy one. A complex chain of socio-economic factors has to be forged for that possibility to come about: general economic growth, the development of car manufacturing and distribution industries, growth in personal and disposable incomes, notions of the social and cultural acceptability of possessing a car, infrastructural considerations (having roads to drive on and rules to drive by, not to mention a reliable supply of fuel). All of these things must be in place before widespread car ownership and a car culture become possible – and until these conditions are at least in sight there will be no market for a magazine that fetishises the car in the way that *Top Gear* does. Even a magazine like *What Car?*, which ostensibly offers the sensible consumer advice embodied in its title, will not fully succeed until there is a reasonably wide range of cars from which to choose. (Although it should be noted that a recent visit to Chennai demonstrated new car sales are healthy, and both BBC Worldwide and Haymarket report strong sales for *Top Gear* and *What Car?* respectively in India.)

The point here is that although licensing titles overseas has become an important element in any major publisher's revenue portfolio, it is by no means a straightforward process, relying as it does not just on the licensee's craft proficiency and financial probity but also on much less predictable global economic trends and specific national, cultural, commercial, and legal developments. In some territories it is more advantageous, or legally necessary, to set up a joint venture. Anyone wanting to publish in China, to take one potentially massive national market, must find a local business to work with, and not just any old local business but one with the correct form of publishing license. *Rolling Stone*, for example, partnered with the publisher of *Music World*, so that the first issue of *Rolling Stone China* was also issue 240 of *Music World*. When *RS* founder Jan Wenner's latest baby was shut down after that premiere issue (for official reasons that included the *Rolling Stone* name appearing too prominently on the cover), the Chinese music magazine was able to continue publishing.

After a long period of protectionism, the Indian government opened up its markets to 'foreign direct investment' in the 1990s. Since then the rules have been further liberalised, encouraging media companies to establish joint ventures with counterparts on the subcontinent (although news publications are subject to stricter regulation). One of the first companies to set up was BBC Worldwide, which formed a new joint venture with the *Times of India* in 2004. The original portfolio included the native titles *Femina* and *Filmfare*, the biggest names in the women's and Bollywood sectors respectively. Since then Worldwide Media has launched Indian editions of *Top Gear*, *Good Homes* and *Lonely Planet*, and has itself licensed the right to publish both *Hello!* and *Grazia* from their respective Spanish and Italian owners.

While this kind of geographical spread can help to 'normalise' global revenue flows – the recession is different from country to country; growth in India and China has slowed down rather than stopped – current conditions have also seen some multinationals looking closer to home too. For example, in March 2010 *Advertising Age* reported that *Elle* had teamed up with 'local' Californian lifestyle magazine C in the search for more advertising:

> The deal means *Elle* can offer its big national advertisers the chance to 'heavy up' in both *Elle* and, using C magazine's resources, key California markets such as Los Angeles or San Francisco. 'If you run a handful of pages in *Elle* but not with C, for a slight increase in your total spend, you're able to increase your presence in *Elle* and layer on C,' said C publisher Lesley Campoy. (adage.com/mediaworks/article?article_id=142785)

Although all of these diversifications add both to the revenue portfolio and to the burden of management on publishers, they each derive from the same basic economic law, a law that Karl Marx would have identified in an instant: the power to control the use and supply of a scarce resource.

The barriers to entry for publishing a national magazine have long been much lower than trying to launch a national newspaper, and have become lower each time a technological development such as desktop publishing (and its associated hardware) has come along, yet the act of making and distributing a magazine on a continuous basis still requires financial and business capital. Very few magazine publishers used to own and operate their own printing presses or even colour reproduction facilities (although colour repro is now an in-house job), until recently they have only been able to control or at least influence key areas of the industrial process.

In particular, negotiating the bottlenecks of national distribution and retail availability posed a massive problem for smaller or new publishers. Physical distribution itself was a lesser problem, because there were (in the final quarter of the last century at least) any number of businesses dedicated to shifting bundles of paper around the country. It was where they shifted them to and in what numbers that posed the bigger problem. When WH Smith was the major outlet for newspapers and magazines, a publisher or would-be publisher would have to convince the chain's chief buyer that stocking their title was a good business decision; if the buyer said no, the chances of a successful launch would almost certainly be scuppered. Even though there were still large numbers of independent newsagents all over the country, negotiating with them en bloc was almost impossible.

When big supermarket chains began to add a substantial range of magazines to their stock this might have offered one opportunity to solve the problem: more outlets would equal more chances of retail exposure. In fact, the reverse became the case. Supermarkets thrive on a rapid turnover of popular items – a category that has its own acronym: FMCG or fast moving consumer goods. If you had £16m to spend on a launch, as IPC did with its weekly *Closer*, and you could afford a massive television advertising campaign allied to printing a million free sample copies the week before the first issue hit the streets, that was one thing; however, if you were making a super-specialised niche periodical for a select readership that was quite another. In the supermarket distribution chain, a big publishing company with big brands can use the leverage that gives it to dictate terms – or at least use them as a powerful negotiating point.

And this is before taking into account what might be called either restrictive practices or normal business procedure, depending on your standpoint. For instance, a publisher could pay to acquire premium space on the retailer's shelves: that is to say, the magazine would be guaranteed a highly visible position on the end of a display unit or would be given a large area to itself. In short, a well capitalised and well organised publisher could ensure that their title could dominate a large amount of retail display area for a specific time, and that time might well coincide with a rival publisher's launch plans.

There has, of course, always been a radical alternative to the arrangements described above that has remained open to publishers: to give your magazine away. This phenomenon has a long history in local newspaper publishing and has recently been theorised as a distinct economic policy, a trend perhaps best represented by Chris Anderson's (2009) book *Free: The Future of a Radical Price*.

In the magazine world 'free' has been adopted with apparent success by a small number of titles (if we assume 'apparent success' to mean the ability to continue publishing for more than a year). One of these is *Shortlist*, the brainchild of Mike Soutar who, having first made his name as a successful editor, left a well-paid and well-respected position as head of the magazine division at IPC-Warner to pursue his idea of a men's magazine that did not rely solely on images of naked females to appeal to its readership and would be given out on the streets by trained vendors.

Shortlist may be free to the consumer but it is not cheap to produce. Soutar sourced financial capital from a number of investors to fund the start-up but as with almost all 'free' publications there was a hidden cost – a massive reliance on advertising and the need to keep those clients happy. *Shortlist* does an honourable job of flagging its advertorials clearly but the issue of 21 October 2010 demonstrated this problem. It appeared to have two front covers, one dominated by the massive image of a TAG Heuer watch and the other that looked like a news story about Las Vegas. The latter, however, was the start of a four-page advertorial about a new computer game, while the former (the 'real' cover) was flagging up an 'Essential Watch Guide'.

Soutar's move may have been personally and professionally brave (and he even risked ridicule by starring in a training video for the distributors of his magazine, showing them how to approach their targets: http://www.youtube. com/watch?v=hZXrc3QqNmk), but he was following a trend (more like a micro-trend) that had been established by *Vice* magazine. *Vice* was founded by Suroosh Alvi, Shane Smith and Gavin McInnes, in Montreal, Canada, to cater for their unmet needs for a bullshit-free magazine that addressed a hedonistic lifestyle of pop culture and general slacking. It would be free and it would be distributed in the places where their potential readers hung out – street clothing shops, skate shops, surf shops, and slacker shops.

As it turns out, the founders have proved more hyperactive than slack: *Vice* is now not only published in 19 international editions, the brand has also been extended into a multimedia website, an internet protocol television channel that shows the documentaries made by *Vice* journalists, a record label, a feature film production company, and an advertising agency.

Yet for all its go-ahead diversification and adoption of digital trends, in one important respect *Vice* had an old-fashioned start-up – it was printed on paper, an artefact that would meet with approval from Professor Samir Husni (see Chapter 1) in all but its pricing. In 2010 it is perhaps more likely that a new magazine would be launched as a digital entity, in the manner of *PistonHeads*, which would allow the publisher to avoid the heavy industrial elements of paper, print, and physical distribution. Costs for production and reproduction are slashed, distribution becomes much more of a level playing field on which individuals or companies with clever ideas about how to promote their products can outwit larger and better-funded rivals; being able to commandeer acres of display space in WH Smith or Tesco counts for nothing in cyberspace, where a video that goes viral or a social media policy that harnesses the power of the network will depend more on capital funds of creativity and savvy than cash.

In short, the relationships that exist between publisher, consumer and advertiser – the tricotomy referred to above – are currently going through a radical shift in the balance of power.

Given all this activity (and there's more to come), it is no wonder that Mel Nichols, former Editorial Director of Haymarket Media's magazine division, lamented: 'This used to be such a beautifully simple business, but now it's unbelievably complicated' (personal conversation).

The former simplicity was this: the publisher owned the means of publishing and could extract revenue from readers on one side and advertisers on the other – the classic Abrahamson model of 'push' publishing. Additions to the revenue stream all depended on the ownership of capital (financial or intellectual) and although they made the management task more time-consuming, they still fell into the traditional 'simple' format. This model was subject to the cyclical ups and downs of normal economic activity but had still shown itself robust enough to come through several recessions (although it may be worth noting that when Elsevier did decide to sell off its B2B arm Reed Business Information, one of the reasons given was to reduce the overall exposure to cyclical effects).

It is difficult to pinpoint exactly when the magazine publishing business moved from simplicity to complexity but it is quite easy to see the factors involved: computers, data in digital form, desktop publishing, the internet, the world wide web, web design programs, blogging platforms, smart mobile phones, social media widgets, and the desire shown by those people formerly known as readers (to adapt Dan Gillmor's famous (2004) phrase) to become writers. In short, the world wide web, and the software tools developed to access it in ever simpler ways, gave any individual the power to publish and, in principle, to communicate with masses of other individuals all over the world: *push* publishing, where the publisher has the power, became *pull* publishing, where the power can flow the other way.

Much, or perhaps most, of the resultant cacophony of communication has proved to be of poor quality; millions of blogs have been started and abandoned, millions lie unread in cyberspace, social media platforms like Twitter are full of inane 140-character comments about nothing. But there remain four very important factors that are overlooked or ignored at a publisher's peril:

1   There are thousands more publications (to use the term broadly) competing for your potential readers' time and attention.
2   Now that it is possible to have a two-way conversation with readers, power relations have changed and it has become clearer that journalists or their magazines are not necessarily the main or best sources of information or opinion.

3　Among the dross there are some diamonds that can pose a real threat to publishers' hold on an interest group (or community).

4　Your advertisers now have the power to become your competitors.

Point 1

The first point was addressed succinctly by Stevie Spring, CEO of Future Publishing, on Radio 4's *The Bottom Line* business programme. Asked by presenter Evan Davies about the main challenges her company faces, she said: 'Publishers used to be able to define their competitor set. My competitor set is now infinite' (first broadcast 25 February 2010). This chapter began by stating that anyone in the UK is *allowed* to publish a magazine, but now literally any one of us *has the power* to publish a magazine. You no longer even need a computer to assemble content; an Apple iPhone is more than capable of doing the job and publishing it as well (although a computer might be cheaper).

Point 2(a)

There are many examples of the second point in action but two will suffice. The first of these concerns television rather than magazines. On the 8 September 2004 edition of *60 Minutes* (a current affairs show broadcast by CBS) veteran news anchor Dan Rather declared that typewritten documents critical of President George W. Bush's service in the Air National Guard were authentic: by this action he lit a fuse that eventually resulted in the show's producer losing her job, his having to resign, and CBS having to issue a public apology. A backlash to the allegations began almost immediately on right-wing blogs and websites – the documents were thought to be fakes because they used anachronistic typefaces, which indicated they had been composed on a computer and not a typewriter. The story was picked up by the more established right-wing press, by the Associated Press wire service, rival television networks, and major American daily newspapers. Further investigation showed that the initial authorisation process undertaken by *60 Minutes* had not been conclusive, following which CBS stopped defending itself and admitted it should not have used the material in the way it did. The final result was the fall of an almost legendary American journalist.

Point 2(b)

The second example demonstrates how a specialist print magazine can harness the power to publish for a positive effect. When *Trail* magazine ran content that was critical of lightweight equipment (and thus by association, critical of the lightweight hiking/camping community), it found itself on the receiving end of a tongue-lashing by Peter MacFarlane (aka Petesy of www. petesy.co.uk), a key and influential figure in that community. Rather than having such an enemy sniping at the magazine from cyberspace, *Trail* demonstrated an understanding of the shift in power dynamic between magazine and reader that is still beyond the comprehension shown by a significant number of other magazines. Editor Matt Swaine takes up the story:

> We recognised that this was someone with genuine enthusiasm for the subject matter and a really good understanding and experience of walking. So it wasn't a need to 'keep your enemies closer' but rather a sense that we had to find a way of channelling the expertise and enthusiasm that he had into our editorial pages. He continues to be a growing brand in his own right with increasing involvement and influence among readers and manufacturers and that is in part due to our championing of his work ... he brings a credibility to our coverage of lightweight topics that we simply don't have.

> Another interesting point is that the controversy that surrounded our first article got people talking on websites and caused the first big jump in sales on *Trail*, so we actually quite welcome people ranting about us on forums and we'd in no way wish to stop that.

> (Personal Communication)

Point 3

This example above could also, to some extent, serve to illustrate the third point, but we can see a better one in Appendix 1 regarding *PistonHeads*. Mel Nichols, quoted above, was one of those most closely concerned with incorporating this title into the Haymarket Media Group, which is itself a good example of a complex magazine publishing business.

Point 4

In March 2010 Arnaud de Puyfontaine, CEO of NatMags, gave an interview to *MediaGuardian* (29/3/10) in which he pondered the future of some of the magazines in his charge. Advertising was unlikely to return to its previous high levels and could not be relied on to fund digital publishing, he thought; the future would involve a lot of data mining and creating opportunities to develop e-commerce but titles such as *She*, which had suffered from falling circulation, could be rescued with the right kind of attention. Taking the example of a fashion brand that became a little too popular with the wrong sort of customer he said:

> Think about Burberry. Burberry was a brand a while ago on which some people would not have spent a penny. But after the fantastic job done by Angela Ahrendts and the creative director, Christopher Bailey – what a success. I do see an analogy. (http://www.guardian.co.uk/media/2010/mar/29/arnaud-de-puyfontaine-natmags-interview)

By a strange coincidence, Andrew Losowsky, who writes about magazines for the *Wall Street Journal* and at *losowsky.com*, had used the Burberry analogy just three days before, but for very different ends. Considering whether the Apple iPad and its apps might or might not be the saviour of magazines he noted that newspapers and magazines had lost their monopoly on communication with potential consumers:

> However, on the internet, and now through iTunes as well, companies can talk directly to their consumers, and create their own experiences, be they editorial or otherwise, without the interference of editorial independence or ads for competing brands. *The Art Of The Trench* isn't just a natty website – it's also where Burberry's advertising dollars went, and fashion magazines felt the pinch. Others will follow... iPad magazines may soon find that the ads they carry will be in the form of links to other applications, this time created by brands – all of which compete with the magazine itself for the iPad user's time. (www.losowsky.com/magtastic/2010/why-everybody-needs-to-calm-down/#ixzz0jlymgXLl)

A few months after de Puyfontaine voiced his thoughts about the structural change in advertising, Condé Nast announced a similar change of emphasis in their business model. Robert A. Sauerberg, previously group president for consumer marketing, would become president as the company looked, according to chief executive Charles H. Townsend, to move 'beyond the magazine'. This seemed to mean a desire to acquire more subscribers across more platforms and charge them for more items. In an interview reported by the *New York Times* on 23 July 2010, Mr Townsend said:

> We have been so overtly dependent on advertising as the turbine that runs this place, and that is a very, very risky model as we emerge from the recession, Mr. Townsend said on Friday. 'In a company like ours where 70 percent of our margins are generated on the advertising side, we must develop a much, much more effective financial relationship with the consumer.' The goal of the overhaul, is to transform Condé Nast into a business that relies less on advertising revenue and more on the income it makes from charging consumers to read its products on both digital and print platforms. (www.nytimes.com/2010/07/24/business/media/24mag.html)

Some media commentators became very excited about this, claiming it as a clear indication that the advertising revenue-based model was broken (Jeff Jarvis summarised the situation pithily as 'Advertising is fucked' – www.buzzmachine.com/2010/07/24/advertising-is-next/). However, in reality it has *not* been the end of advertising, which will continue to be with us as long as there is a market in goods, but a rebalancing of the company's revenue portfolio: Condé Nast, like every other big publisher, has numerous sources of income and they now need to find ways (not *a* way) to tweak the non-advertising sources. As Catharine P. Taylor noted more sanguinely on BNET:

the days of over-reliance on advertising are over ... It's about licensing Condé Nast titles in every way they can be leveraged, and also building deeper, more lucrative bonds with consumers ... It's easy to picture the company experimenting with exclusive house tours to subscribers of *Architectural Digest*, previews for *Vogue* readers of the fall collections, and exclusive screenings of movies from *Vanity Fair* — for a fee of course ... like everyone else, the company is going to have to figure out pricing strategies for digital products like its iPad apps ... For Condé Nast, or any magazine company, to be less reliant on advertising, it's going to have to get creative about discovering ways to get people to pay. And that's not just about content.(www.bnet.com/blog/new-media/conde-nast-will-reach-out-to-consumers-8212-in-more-ways-than-you-think/5695)[1]

If anything, Condé Nast has shown more faith in advertising than, for example, Reed Elsevier, which put B2B giant Read Business Information (RBI) up for sale precisely in order to avoid the cyclical nature of advertising revenue.

B2B magazines

As a case study Haymarket (see above and Appendix 1) contains all the elements of modern magazine political economy but as a company it is perhaps too eclectic to be representative of the B2B sector, which has come to be dominated by large specialised businesses like Reed Business Information.

However, like Haymarket, Reed has had a varied history that has included ownership of both the *Daily Mirror* and IPC (the UK's largest consumer magazine publisher); a history that is linked together by paper as detailed in Appendix 1. Reed International's purchase of the IPC-Mirror Group newspaper and magazine conglomerate sounds as though it should have been an unholy mess of contradictory interests and indeed, according to Cynthia White in her classic (1970) study *Women's Magazines 1693–1968*, this proved to be the case. Before the Reed purchase, IPC had called in McKinsey & Co (who had also reviewed Condé Nast before the change of policy outlined above) to try and rationalise the situation, especially the 'tough, internal competition' (1970: 294) that saw Fleetway, Newnes, and Odhams all fighting it out in the same marketplaces.

---

[1]And sure enough, on 5 August 2010, Condé Nast announced that they would be opening, or licensing, restaurants branded with their upmarket magazine titles. Chairman Si Newhouse said: 'Restaurants are a natural way to extend our brand values and to reach our customers while championing the highest standards of quality'.

'We can do so in our magazine markets and in countries where for one reason or another, we don't publish'. (www.mediaweek.co.uk/news/1020783/CondE-Nast-open-GQ-Vogue-restaurants/)

Further rationalisation took place in 1974 when IPC and Mirror Group Newspapers were separated into discrete publishing operations. Ten years later Reed quit the national newspaper business, selling the Mirror Group to Robert Maxwell but continuing to acquire specialised business publishing companies as well as exhibition organisers. The most important deal in this phase was the merger with Elsevier, a Dutch publisher noted for its scientific and medical journals, in 1993.

After the subsequent disposal of non-core businesses, Reed-Elsevier was left with a strong core of scientific, medical, and legal publishing together with Britain's largest stable of B2B magazines, the latter coming under the aegis of Reed Business Information. RBI publishes in sectors ranging from Aerospace to Utilities, and claims to bring 'over 100 market leading brands to an audience of 30 million decision makers worldwide through its multi-platform media of web products, magazines, exhibitions, conferences and industry awards' (www.rbi.co.uk/rb2_about/rb2_about_profile.htm). However, while the risk of cyclical economic downturn in advertising and subscriptions was spread through 20 business sectors it was still too great for Reed-Elsevier and the main board opted to sell off RBI in February 2008 (but not, interestingly, the exhibition businesses associated with the magazines). With an asking price of over £1bn this turned out to be very bad timing; even when the decision to sell was announced on 21 February, the *Financial Times* reported a competitor as saying, 'They're probably a year too late for this' (www.ft.com/cms/s/0/517e9d86-e0bb-11dc-b0d7-0000779fd2ac.html). The prediction proved correct when Reed-Elsevier abandoned the sale in December of the same year, citing the worsening state of the economy and poor credit market conditions. Since then RBI has cut jobs, closed a number of titles, and reported substantially lower profits for the 2009 financial year with almost everything (print advertising, online advertising, and subscriptions) down and predicted worse times to come (reports.reedelsevier.com/ar09/business/reed-bus-info-fin-perf.html). By contrast Reed-Elsevier itself has remained surprisingly profitable.

And if RBI, with some of the best titles on the market, has suffered so badly, its market competitors cannot have escaped. Yet it remains a fact, as noted earlier, that there are still almost twice as many B2B magazines published as Consumer titles and the sector still generates substantial financial returns.

There are a number of factors that may contribute to this:

- B2B magazines are generally less expensive to run inasmuch as they are less exposed to the need for large marketing budgets that affects the top end of the very competitive consumer press;
- B2B magazines will generally cost less to produce as, for example, they do not need to commission expensive photo-shoots and can be printed on less luxurious grades of paper;

- B2B magazines will very often have smaller, and more controlled, circulations than consumer magazines, reducing paper and print costs and wastage; only 30 per cent will have a cover price, with the rest being distributed via controlled circulation (a select mailing list) or direct to members of an organisation;
- some sectors of the business press have traditionally been awash with promotional, marketing, and advertising money: there are two main reasons why the medical sector attracts so many titles (633, or more than 10 per cent of the entire B2B output according to the *PPA Handbook*) – one is the degree of specialisation in the health sector, the other is the amount of money pharmaceutical companies will spend on marketing and advertising;
- the nature of B2B magazines allows publishers to employ the castle-and-outlier strategy; this is a business policy that sees the establishment of a main title (the principal cash generator), which is then ring-fenced by smaller titles that can cater for a very specific niche. Doing this protects the principal title by absorbing the readership and potential advertisers, thus simultaneously raising the barriers and costs of entry to any potential rivals while driving down potential revenue; it does, however, depend on the economy of that sector being healthy enough to ensure positive returns on the outliers.

For any combination of the reasons above, it should in theory be easier for an individual or small enterprise to launch a B2B title but the fact is that many B2B magazines are concentrated in a few large enterprises; RBI we have looked at and others include United Business Media, Incisive Media, and Centaur.

However, because B2B publishing tends to be increasingly specialised, individual titles whether part of a big stable or not are also vulnerable to the well-connected organisation or individual starting up an online information service. Likewise, the development of new business sectors and the evolution of old ones offer nimble journalist-entrepreneurs with a good understanding of the situation opportunities to come in under the wire. Two good examples of this can be found online: *PaidContent* and *TechCrunch*.

PaidContent.org is one of four specialist B2B blogs published by ContentNext, an enterprise founded in 2002 by the American business journalist Rafat Ali, who spotted a need to:

> chronicle the economic evolution of digital content that is shaping the future of the media, information and entertainment industries. Our belief is that in the near future, all media will be digital media, and we are helping define sustainable business models and innovation within this sector. (paidcontent.org/about/)

The other sites cover the media industries in the UK and India, with the final one dedicated to mobile content. ContentNext was bought by the Guardian Media Group in July 2008 for £4m.

TechCrunch.com started up in June 2005 as a blog 'obsessively profiling and reviewing new Internet products and companies'. Since then it has grown into a global network of specialist sites and, most importantly, the annual, sold-out, heavily sponsored, TechCrunch50 conference with tickets at nearly £3,000 a pop. The European site has been named as one of the top 10 blogs in the UK and, worryingly for RBI, also voted the best Web2.0 and Business Blog in the UK by readers of *Computer Weekly* (an RBI title). A *Financial Times'* profile of TechCrunch founder Mike Arrington published in December 2006 highlighted the speed at which reputations can be established in the online B2B world:

> An out-of-work entrepreneur just a year and a half ago, Arrington was researching other start-ups in search of his own next business idea when he decided to write about what he was seeing. A boom in interest in new internet companies to rival the late 1990s quickly followed. 'I clearly found the parade and got in front of it,' he says. 'I was lucky.' (www.ft.com/cms/s/0/f7cbee36-9617-11db-9976-0000779e2340.html)

As a kind of *Through The Looking Glass* appendix to the above, a number of long established B2B titles are no longer able to support the costs of print and paper and have been obliged to migrate to online only. Among them are the journalist's weekly *Press Gazette* and Haymarket's *Media Week*, both operating in roughly the same field as *PaidContent* and *TechCrunch*.

Yet big companies can get along fine in this arena too: Informa, which publishes *Lloyd's List* among many other titles, reported a decline in revenue but improved profits for the financial year 2008–2009 and took the opportunity to announce that 72 per cent of its publishing revenues were derived from digital formats (ar2009.informa.com/highlights). RBI, the giant of B2B, has among its staff a 'Head of Blogging' whose job is to make sure that the company's journalists are making the most of opportunities to communicate with their readers in as many and as effective ways as they can. For example, there are blogs to complement certain titles, such as the Big Lorry Blog (www.roadtransport.com/blogs/big-lorry-blog/), an extension of RBI's *Road and Transport* website as well as other publications from their road transportation strand. The *Flightglobal* website aggregates content from *Flight International, Airline Business, ACAS, Air Transport Intelligence,* and *The Flight Collection,* and includes daily news updates, searchable directories, blogs (readers are invited to set up their own), and reader forums; it can be found and followed on Twitter, YouTube, LinkedIn and Flickr. The result is a multitude of new ways to source and distribute news, to engage with a wider community of readers, to consolidate old revenue streams such as subscriptions, and to invent and establish new revenue streams.

Customer magazines

Customer publishing concerns those titles that are published on behalf of other enterprises. This could mean shops and supermarkets (*Sainsbury's Magazine*, Debenham's *Desire*), finance corporations (American Express's

Expressions, Royal Bank of Scotland's *Sense*), or Government departments (*Early Years*, *Governors* for the Department for Children, Schools and Families).

Although this activity could be considered a branch of public relations or marketing, and some scholars do categorise this type of magazine as a 'public relations magazine' (Johnson and Prijatel, 1999: 2), it has become increasingly important to the political economy of the magazine industry as a whole. One indication of this is the fact that, until recently, customer magazines were produced by specialist customer publishers like Redwood, John Brown, and Cedar. Thanks partly to the high editorial and production values that these publishers have made the norm (thus giving the sector an air of professional legitimacy) and partly to the levels of profitability within the sector, these specialists have in recent years been joined by some unlikely companions such as Condé Nast (the upmarket publishers of *Vogue* and *Tatler* have joined forces with Great Universal Stores, the ultimate owners of discount giant Argos, to produce what are essentially mail order catalogue/magazine hybrids) and BBC Worldwide (the commercial arm of the BBC, which produces *About The House* for the Royal Opera House); also, as Appendix 1 documents, Haymarket and Dennis have customer publishing arms. These companies are vying for a market share of a sector that turns over £904m, a figure that Mintel predict will rise to £1bn by 2013 (Mintel: The Customer Publishing Industry, 2008 www.apa.co.uk/knowledge/research/).

How are such alliances as Condé Nast and Argos brokered? At the heart of the Customer sector is the Association of Publishing Agencies (APA), a representative body that sets standards, undertakes research, and acts as a point of contact for potential clients (it used to be part of the Periodical Publishers Association but became an independent, though still affiliated, entity at the start of 2010).

According to Sara Cremer, editorial director at Redwood, most business contacts come via APA, which will help clients to form briefs by working through what they hope to achieve and then creating a shortlist of suitable publishers. The publisher will usually have a fortnight after this to prepare a pitch that will answer the client's needs – in other words, they will have a mere two weeks to come up with a completely new magazine concept. 'As you can imagine', Sara observes, 'this can become a bit frantic'.

Sometimes business will come in directly, and sometimes existing clients will decide to expand their offering, for example if they are thinking of marketing a product to a different consumer segment or demographic. The publisher may also have an idea that fits well with something already being produced for a client; for example, Boots already had their *Health & Beauty* magazine, but Redwood spotted the opportunity to create a 'parenting club' that has since developed into a massive site in its own right.

Customer publishers will also be proactive, taking their ideas directly to potential new clients, and they have found that online and social media now form very important elements of most new offers. Sara Cremer has observed e-zines (electronic magazines) taking off in a big way – but these do have to be done properly, with a good understanding of the medium. 'We very definitely don't do the paper magazine in an electronic format', she says. 'It's a completely different experience. They're a very interactive experience, very video rich, lots of games'.

Sara further notes there is one type of organisation for which e-zines are exceptionally well suited – those with something to sell: 'They work well for retail brands because you can click through to buy'.

And what of third-party advertising within customer magazines? There are two ways of looking at it – either jam on the bread or the bread itself. Most Customer publishers will work for a fee, sell advertising into their magazines, take a commission on the sale, and then return the rest to the client. This rarely covers the costs of production but may be a useful way to offset these. In the FAQ section of its website the APA offers the following advice: 'We always make it clear to prospective or reviewing clients that third-party advertising should at best be viewed as a contribution or a cost offset, rather than providing full funding for a customer magazine'.

The full funding (the 'bread itself') method requires a suitably healthy advertising market to support the production costs of the magazine and still leave a profit for the publisher. Clearly this is a business model that would be attractive to cost-conscious clients – they will get a promotional title for free. Unfortunately, the last publisher to attempt this model on any scale came a cropper. In 2007 Publicis Blueprint trumpeted the possibilities of ad-funded magazines for clients such as the video rental store Blockbuster and the De Vere hotel chain. In April 2008 the publisher revealed a £6m hole in its finances, a discovery that led to the resignation of the chief executive, the loss of around a third of the workforce, and a rapid switch from an ad-funded to a fee-based publication. Fortunately for the other two-thirds of the workforce Publicis Blueprint survived and is still active in the Customer sector, servicing such clients as Asda, Renault, and Orange.

Customer publishers do not have a monopoly in this sector – sometimes a company will do the job in-house. A successful, and interesting, example of this was found at TalkSPORT, the radio station once run by ex-*Sun* editor Kelvin McKenzie. After being taken over by Ulster TV, changes in 2008 included the decision to complement broadcast output by launching a magazine, just as the television sports channel ESPN has done in the USA. However, rather than investing in print and paper TalkSPORT followed the electronic route to an e-zine (using Sara Cremer's definition). The title's Ceros page-turning software replicated the feel of flicking through a magazine but used the potential of the medium to overlay the pages with videos, live links, and interactive quizzes.

TalkSPORT magazine complemented the radio output and the station's website. It used some of the station's broadcasters and aggregated plenty of material from the internet, but it was also edited by Bill Borrows, a magazine professional with a track record that includes *Loaded, Esquire, Time Out*, and much more. From an editorial perspective, this helped to give the title an existence in its own right. From a commercial perspective it allowed UTV to offer advertisers extended coverage.

In a separate but related move, UTV demonstrated its belief in magazines by rescuing *Sport*, a free weekly distributed mainly in London, when its original owner Sport Media & Strategie went into administration in 2009. It is currently available in print and as an e-zine, and while the latter has similarities with *TalkSPORT* magazine, the two are run as separate entities and UTV has no current plans to rebrand *Sport*; they do claim, however, to have returned it to profitability.

In general terms, this strategy is similar to that of the Boomerang Extreme Media outline earlier in this chapter – the core proposition is the radio station supported by the e-zine, with an element of horizontal integration added by *Sport* magazine.

A rather more complex business that attempted to bring its Customer publishing in-house was News Corporation – or rather its subsidiary News International and *its* part-owned subsidiary BSkyB. News International set up News Magazines Ltd late in 2005 and the new venture published its first title in February 2006 – the real life *Love It!* – which was soon joined by *Inside Out* (about interior design) and a planned women's weekly (known as Project Dannii, which might hint at its proposed content). At that time *Sky: The Magazine* was being produced by John Brown Citrus and the contract was coming up for renewal. News Magazines Ltd bid for the business and won it; as noted above this magazine possessed the highest circulation in the UK and was a pretty big deal. However, News Magazines discovered that the magazine market was possibly even more competitive than the newspaper market; the women's weekly was never launched, *Inside Out* was closed in January 2007, and *Love It!* was sold to Hubert Burda Media UK in December 2008. Now, rather than going through an intramediary, BSkyB's magazine really is produced in house at BSkyB's headquarters in Osterley, London.

Electronic magazines

Some aspects of the effects of digital production and consumption have been considered above, but there are others that touch on the current and future political economy of magazines, and we cannot leave this chapter without mentioning them. Tony Quinn has compiled a very useful timeline for digital developments (at Magforum.com) that places the start in 1982, when *Acorn User* was perhaps the first magazine to use email and an online bulletin board. As technology and global standards developed, the world wide web and html simplified both the production and consumption of online material and in 1994 the *Daily Telegraph* published its first online issue. *Loaded* and *NME*, both IPC titles, were the first mainstream publications to establish themselves online, with *uploaded.com* and *nme.com* respectively. The sector gained commercial respectability when the Audit Bureau of Circulation established ABCe to audit online figures.

Digital moved on through facsimile editions (page-turning e-zines using software by Ceros, Zinio, and Olive), editions for mobile phones and online-only publications (*Monkey* by Dennis Publishing, *Jellyfish* by NatMags, and any number of small independents), but revenues could not keep up with technology. In brief, the cover revenue dropped when it became possible to read content without paying for it because many people preferred the free version, and advertising revenue dropped because of a global recession and client unfamiliarity with digital media.

One of the basic problems was that 'online' had come to mean 'free': very few people proved willing to pay to look at magazine (or newspaper) websites. Mobiles offered an opportunity to remedy this as using a mobile phone has always had a cost attached and therefore customers had been 'trained' to pay. There was also the advantage that this cost was usually invisible or disguised – the bill would come later or the cost would be included in the monthly contract or top-up fees.

However accessing the web on a mobile phone was a slow and clunky procedure and not a very satisfactory visual experience – until Apple launched the iPhone and its associated app store. Suddenly the mobile experience was transformed from being an inferior version of browsing on a computer into becoming a cool, sleek experience of its own (or at least enough people believed this to be so in a short enough period of time for a tipping point in this perception to be reached). Apps then began to be seen as a way for magazines to raise revenue because, just as with iTunes, people would pay for downloads – but this new form also presented new challenges for designers (and programmers) who had to incorporate the look and feel of a magazine into a new digital form.

Apple's next piece of kit, the iPad, enjoyed a hyperbolic welcome from the publishing industries, with many in the business proclaiming it as a saviour (try Googling 'iPad will save publishing' for a typical sample), mainly because it offered both a way to recapture the willingness to pay for content and a new opportunity for advertisers to connect with consumers.

Perhaps typically, Richard Branson found a way to jump aboard this bandwagon by announcing in July 2010 that Virgin would launch an appazine (iPad app magazine) called *Maverick* later that year. Overseen by his daughter Holly, the title would 'aim to encapsulate the spirit of the

Virgin brand by focusing on entrepreneurial endeavours and highlighting new creative, business, travel and technology ideas, targeting an upscale international audience' according to *AdAge* (adage.com/globalnews/article? article_id=144967).

There was, however, some magazine grit to be found in this Virgin froth – Anthony Noguera, former editor of *Arena* and *FHM*, was to be involved on the editorial side through his business Accelerated Intelligence and online experts Seven Squared had been contracted to supply the tech input for the app. As expected from Branson, there was a sharp business angle: whereas publishers with print products would try to avoid undercutting them with their app versions, Virgin, with nothing to lose, aimed to produce *Maverick* (launched as *Project*) for a lower cost than its rivals.

There was also speculation that Virgin would use this opportunity to expand into magazine publishing more generally, with some commentators saying that Branson wanted to compete with Bauer and IPC; anyone who remembered Virgin Cola might have regarded this idea with a degree of scepticism.

Shortly after Branson's announcement came another, for an iPad app called Flipboard that would take an individual's social media connections and, for example, follow the links on Twitter feeds and turn them into a personalised publication. As BBC technology correspondent Rory Cellan Jones explained, it

> turns your Twitter and Facebook activity into an instant magazine. You set up your feeds, then find your friends' Facebook photos laid out as if in the pages of *Vogue,* or the links your Twitter mates have posted turned into an edition of the *Economist.* (www.bbc. co.uk/blogs/thereporters/rorycellanjones/2010/07/uk_tech_is_anyone_listening. html)

Those who have tried Flipboard have certainly liked the all important 'look and feel', which has a degree of typographic sophistication lacking in other readers. Martin Weller, a professor of education technology at the Open University, said, 'I think it's an example of how a good UI (user interface) can make you read content differently, or at least pull you into content you might skim otherwise'.

But Flipboard will not be the last application of this type, the iPad is not the only tablet-sized reading device, and Apple's is not the only operating system. It may well prove to be the device that establishes the potential of this sector and it may also prove to be dominant, but at the time of writing competitor platforms such as Android (Google), Ovi (Nokia) and BlackBerry (RIM) have been upping their games, and a tidal wave of tablets from numerous manufacturers, running several different operating systems, is now gathering momentum.

Apart from the hardware, there are numerous pieces of software, either installed or in the cloud, that will impact on the political economy of magazine production. To cite just three as exemplars:

- Issuu.com – the pro/am version of page turning software that allows anyone to upload digital magazines to a virtual magazine rack (and offers a free mobile option too);
- MagCloud.com – an initiative by printer giant Hewlett Packard that allows anyone, anywhere, to print any number of professionally finished magazines, or to optimise their magazine for the iPad;
- Flipboard – as discussed above.

Whether any of these or their successors will have a lasting effect remains to be seen. Barry McIlheney, chairman of the PPA, thinks that while platforms may multiply, the underlying essence of a magazine will remain the same:

Types of launches may change. The old FMCG-style multi million pound TV and print launch extravaganza for a print-only product is probably not now the way forward. But we will see more launches, and we will see print-led offerings across multiple platforms. Because the starting point, irrespective of platform, remains the same: a really clever idea that will turn people on by appealing to their passions. And while there will be a growing need for technical people within publishing, there will still be a strong need for people with journalistic skills, creative ideas, flair, spark and – of course – consumer understanding. (www.inpublishing.co.uk/kb/articles/barry_mcilheney_interview.aspx)

Our own predictions are as follows:

- print will remain an important part of magazine publishing but will concentrate at the top (glossy) and bottom (pulpy) ends of the market and around special titles like the first issue of *Vintage* (November 2009), an independent title that played with different qualities of paper and binding as part of its aesthetic;
- mobile, in its widest sense, will be an important element of the political economy, especially outside Europe and the USA, but quality will improve as devices evolve and coverage expands;
- apps (for whatever platform) will develop their own aesthetic and design rules, partly because large publishers will want to standardise production processes;
- advertising will continue to be an important component of revenue, especially for specialised titles and those that can offer well targeted customer data that have been harvested ethically;
- customer publishing will continue to expand until it replaces PR as the 'dark side' to which magazine journalists defect – in this chapter alone we have seen that editors of the calibre of Sara Cremer, Bill Borrows, and Anthony Noguera are working in this sector; this will happen because advertisers will increasingly value the direct communication with consumers and global corporations will value the universal appeal of a good magazine;
- and finally, the magazine – in its many forms and iterations – will continue to be the most successful media form.

3

THE MAGAZINE WORKFORCE

Sometimes the simplest questions can be the hardest to answer. For example, what is journalism and who are journalists? Of course, the real question for this book should be who are *magazine* journalists, but it will be helpful to have the full context for journalism before looking in more detail at the specifics.

It's not as though attempts to answer these questions have not been made already. Many distinguished academics have tried to do so, and here is just one small sample:

- In journalism there is no single clear 'core activity'. (Tunstall, 1971: 10)
- Journalism is many things, and often different things to different people. (McNair, 2005: 42)
- ... journalism is not an undivided field, but consists of a variety of subgenres or domains, each with its own rules and values. (van Zoonen, 1998a: 124)

A smattering of media knowledge and a brief look around even a small newsagent's are enough to confirm this. In the former case, producing an item of 'journalism' is a team activity: someone to write it, someone to provide photographs, someone to get the words and pictures on the page, someone to print it. As McNair points out, this means journalism can at one and the same time be considered a set of technical skills, a craft, a noble profession that defends democracy, and a creative art form. All of these activities are part of the journalistic effort.

In the latter case (looking around the newsstand), it is not hard to see that the types of publication (genres) will range from upmarket newspapers to magazines about soap operas and that they will fulfill different functions and expectations. Trying to fit all of these roles and outputs into a single definition is therefore mightily difficult, even without bringing national and cultural differences into the equation.

Because of this complexity many attempts at defining journalism will become highly selective, and most will also focus on what we can call 'Fourth

Estate' journalism. This definition goes back to 1855, when Henry Reeve, editor of the *Edinburgh Review*, coined it. Reeve believed that the press were more representative than parliament, that they could act to redress individual wrongs and that they could correct official information which might be wrong (Boyce et al., 1978: 23). However, in order to undertake this role journalists had to be professional and dedicated and Reeve believed that British journalists had been so since the start of the nineteenth century:

> Journalism had been taken out of the hands of 'mere hack writers' and had been placed in those of 'men of fixed opinions, of consummate knowledge and deliberate purpose' who sought a connection with journalism 'as others sought a seat in parliament or an office under Government, for the sake of influencing their age and country, of promulgating their own sentiments.

> ... the special value of the function which journalism exercised, the remarkable talent with which it was habitually conducted, and the 'generally high and pure' character which it maintained, meant that journalism was not the instrument by which the various divisions of the ruling classes expressed themselves; it was rather the instrument by means of which the aggregate intelligence of the nation criticises and controls them all. It is indeed the 'Fourth Estate' of the Realm: not merely the written counterpart and voice of the speaking 'Third'. (Boyce et al., 1978: 24)

Thus much of the literature examining the question of what journalism is should be read with a health warning in mind – is this about *all* journalism, or just a part of it that the writer has privileged above others? To add to these difficulties, a significant element of research into journalism involves referencing other research data to build into a 'global' picture, making it even more important to ascertain whether the various methodological bases are compatible. Most of the time, most of the data will manage to avoid non-Fourth Estate journalism – but not always.

In their large-scale research on first-year journalism students, a uniform study that ranged across 22 countries around the world, Slavko Splichal and Colin Sparks devoted considerable time and effort to teasing out the simple questions that we started with. As far as the first is concerned, they decided:

> Journalism is an unstable and fluid occupation which is particularly responsive to social and technological change, and, consequently, the concrete content of *journalism* varies from one historic period to another and from one country to another. (Splichal and Sparks, 1994: 20)

And if the category of journalism is so self-evidently variable (as our glance around the newsagent's would have shown), what about those involved in its creation? The second chapter of Splichal and Sparks' work considers at some length the vexed question of who could be counted as a journalist before concluding that 'it is unfortunately not possible to give an exclusive and exhaustive definition to the category journalist ...' (p. 30). Further, because definitions of those considered to be journalists vary so much, 'it has not been possible for us to make any detailed comparisons between the occupations in different countries' (p. 30).

In this inability to reach a definitive decision, they echo those who came before and after, like David Weaver, whose works should be read with the caveat that it is not made clear who is being surveyed or what definition of 'journalist' is being followed, just 'US journalists':

> The question of who journalists are has never been definitely answered, in part because journalists themselves don't want to be licensed, certified or classified by any official authority or by anyone outside journalism, and in part because there is no specific body of knowledge that journalists must master to practice their craft. (Weaver, 2005: 44)

Liesbet van Zoonen acknowledges the same point while adding a feminist perspective:

> It seems obvious that in contemporary studies of journalism and journalists it has become impossible to take the field as an undivided whole and consider journalists as a homogeneous group ... our comprehension of contemporary journalism and journalists is arguably limited to a modest understanding of the workings of institutionally oriented, 'masculine' journalism. We know comparatively little about audience-oriented journalism either aimed at the women's or men's market, nor of institutionally oriented journalism practised in a 'feminine' context. (Van Zoonen, 1998a: 138)

Note that she also introduces the concept of 'audience-oriented journalism', which is particularly relevant to magazines. However, in traditional terms it is often seen as a very bad thing because despite Henry Reeve's flattering view of journalism as the Fourth Estate, what actually happened when the legal restrictions on publishing (stamp duty, paper duty, advertisement duty, all of which restricted commercial development) were lifted was this: 'the way was open for the press to become big business ... this attracted people whose interest lay, not primarily in enlightening or informing public opinion, nor in criticising public policy, but in making money by giving the public what it wanted – or, at least, what it was supposed by the entrepreneur to want' (Boyce et al., 1978: 25). In other words, content that readers wanted to read was being created because they would buy it.

Van Zoonen acknowledges her debt to the grand-daddy of sociological researchers into journalism when she notes the tension between Institutional Goals (which she characterises as masculine) and Audience Goals (feminine). These terms were first used by Jeremy Tunstall in his pioneering (1971) study *Journalists At Work*, although he chose to list three rather than two: (i) the advertising revenue goal; (ii) the audience (or sales) revenue goal; (iii) the non-revenue (or prestige) goal. He explained that 'certain types of specialist newsgathering are seen as having a primarily advertising revenue goal (such as motoring and fashion), others as having a primarily audience revenue goal (such as crime and football) and some as having a mixture of goals (such as aviation, labour and education)' (p. 7). In terms of journalistic status, the tension he observed arose between the 'serious' journalists who undertook non-revenue/prestige work and those journalists whose work pandered to either the audience or the advertisers. This also translated into a hierarchy of critical evaluation:

> Journalists tend to rate journalists in other sub-fields in terms of the prevalent level of criticism. National journalism aimed at general audiences is generally believed to be the best and the most critical. Journalism which is either local or aimed at specialized audiences is believed in most cases to be less critical and of lower quality. (Tunstall, 1971: 11)

All of this implies a certain approach to the job of journalism. As Meryl Aldridge states, 'Being a journalist is held to be a vocation, to which practitioners have a passionate, almost compulsive–if ambivalent–attachment' (1998: 111). Once again, this has to be read with the health warning that her study concerns 'serious' news journalism but it also resonates strongly with one aspect of magazine journalism – which is that a significant proportion of magazine journalists did not set out to become journalists per se, but had a depth of specialised knowledge that led them to the job. Matthew Swaine, editor of *Trail* magazine and director of training at Bauer Consumer Media's Peterborough offices, notes 'these tend to be the real enthusiasts who have something to offer beyond their journalistic qualifications or experience', who have 'got into the industry through different paths, rather than college or long work experience placements' (personal communication).

In her piece quoted above, van Zoonen adds ideas that help to illuminate this idea of journalistic vocation and passionate attachment to a subject (*passion* is a word much bandied about in magazine circles). Noting that journalists 'working for women's magazines ... have hardly ever been deemed worthy of research' (p. 125) she observes that one of the few such studies that does exist (Ferguson, 1983) emphasises the way women's magazine editors rely on intuition, but that '... on closer examination this intuition can sometimes be seen to be the individual translation of various known audience and market imperatives, it is quite clear that a thorough knowledge of and feeling for "the world of women" is necessary for women's magazine editors' (p. 133).

Compare this with what Angela Phillips has to say about the cliché concerning a news reporter's ability to sniff out a good story: 'That mythical "nose for news" is in fact a finely tuned understanding of the culture and the particular power nexus in the subject or geographical area in which we work' (2005: 231). It does not stretch one's incredulity, or even take any great leap of the imagination, to find a correlation between the two. (Although it is a shame that Phillips then goes on to deliver a massively back-handed compliment: 'Of course not all our journalism students will end up working for news organisations. Today people with journalism training are to be found everywhere: they produce magazines ...' (p. 232).

Perhaps, then, it would be safe to say that one important characteristic of a magazine journalist is that he or she must have a keen sense of audience and market imperatives and a finely tuned understanding of the culture and power nexus in a specific subject matter. There is also the matter of the power nexus between producer (journalist) and consumer (reader), one that has changed very considerably since the days when Jeremy Bentham and John Stuart Mill laid down the philosophical principles around which editors and journalists coalesced in the early part of the nineteenth century, around which the myth of the press as defender of freedom and champion of political representation came into being, and as a result of which Henry Reeve could state his vision of the press as the Fourth Estate: 'The press ... was not just a channel of opinion, but a guardian, with its own ideas and attitudes' (Boyce et al., 1978: 21).

Such a view requires journalists to be like the priesthood, with a secret and arcane system for gathering information and access to a rare ability to publish it. In 1855 this might have been the case (although the history of the unstamped or pauper press found in E.P. Thompson's *Making Of The English Working Class* (1968) strongly suggests otherwise), but by 1955 the popular view of journalists and journalism had changed (these high and mighty philosophers had become the heavy-drinking newshounds of Fleet Street) and in the second decade of the twenty-first century this whole system has been blown wide open by digital technology giving widespread public access to information and the ability of any person with an internet connection to transmit it.

This brings us to another vexed question: if everyone has access to information and if everyone has the power and ability to publish it (regardless of whether anyone reads it), what is the difference between a journalist and any other person? This conundrum often manifests itself as a question about whether journalists can be construed as professionals or whether it is true, as Meryl Aldridge asserts, that 'Journalism in the UK has none of the institutional characteristics associated with the "profession"'? (1998: 124).

This debate can be traced back to the late Victorian period, if not before. Writing in 1933, Carr-Saunders and Wilson noted that in 1890 the Institute of Journalists had attempted to formulate the idea of journalism as a profession, although 'the impulse towards association was rather a desire to copy the organization of established professions rather than any spontaneous movement towards coalescence'. The Institute was intended to 'obtain "for journalists as such formal and definite professional standing"' and one of the main aims was 'testing the qualifications of candidates for admission to professional membership of the Institute by examination in theory and practice ...'. Unfortunately a considerable majority of those employed as journalists felt that it was more important to secure better working conditions and wages and preferred to support the National Union of Journalists (founded 1907). Even more unfortunately for journalism as a profession, journalists themselves 'have no monopoly of a technique indispensable to the proprietors who are in a position to go their own ways, whether or not the existing journalists are willing to work for them' (Carr-Saunders and Wilson, 2001: 39, 40).

Yet as Anthony Delano, who has for many years studied how journalists are educated and whence they are drawn, observes, 'A majority of British journalists now believe that their occupation is a profession rather than a trade or a craft', even though, 'anyone may still embark on this enticing career with no credentials whatever' (2000: 264). The same situation obtains in the USA, where one American researcher (Goldstein, 1985) was told: 'You become a journalist when you declare that you are one, and you remain a journalist as long as you keep declaring you are one' (Delano, 2000: 265). Chambers et al. reflect journalism's undefined status and the importance of the craft element when they note 'its more ambiguous origins in a liminal state between middle class profession and trade ...' (2004: 91).

This concept of liminality is also to be found in Marjan de Bruin's survey of work in the field. First she notes that the very idea of what should be included in the scope of a professional is subject to constant change: 'What ... this profession at the practical level was supposed to be, in the eyes of the professional, was not at all clear. Values, supposed to be crucial to the profession, were continuously under scrutiny – objectivity versus subjectivity; detachment versus advocacy; observer versus watchdog ...' (2000: 221). She then makes a very useful distinction between 'professional identity' and 'organizational identity' before drawing on Benedict Anderson's (1983) concept of the imagined community to reinforce the point:

> Organizational identity ... is a framework of beliefs, values and feelings. Not a stable, fixed, completed collection, but rather a changing schema with a range of varieties forming multiple identities ... 'Organizational identity' is connected to a cultural and spatial 'territory' – in this case the (news media) organization – and is carried by those who form part of the organization, as long as they belong to it. 'Professional identity' refers to a wider frame of reference – an ideology – not so much carried by the members of a clearly identifiable organization, but rather by an imaginary community that stretches across organizations. (2000: 229)

As we will see, neither the values nor the imagined community of journalism are stable or even agreed between all of those who claim to be journalists.

Jeremy Tunstall, the editor of the compilation in which Carr-Saunders and Wilson were republished and, as we have noted previously, a key figure in the debates around the social status of journalists, appears to agree with the idea that journalism is a somewhat mixed occupation when he states that, 'Media "professions" do not exist in a form comparable to medicine or law (which have a long period of training, formally controlled entry, a high degree of autonomy, and a recognized, and expanding, body of expert knowledge)' and that '... in both press and TV the most senior "professionals" also require much "craft" expertise' (2001: 17, 18).

In this he echoes what Oliver Boyd-Barratt wrote in an earlier compendium: 'It can be argued that journalism as it exists does not constitute a profession, and that its structure does not allow for appreciable advance in professionalization' (1970: 181).

Since Boyd-Barrett wrote this four decades ago, it could be argued that subsequent changes in the way journalism is organised and executed have only weakened its ability to advance professionalisation – on the one hand, news outlets have been aggregated into fewer corporate hands, giving employers more power over who to employ and how they should do their work; on the other hand, the rise of citizen journalism and a widespread belief that 'we are all journalists now' have diminished whatever aura of professionalism might have existed.

Nevertheless, it is instructive to follow Boyd-Barrett's reasoning further in order to provide any examination of journalism's status with a rational basis. He cites the five attributes that Ernest Greenwood (1966) used to define a profession: it must have

- a systematic body of theory;
- professional authority;
- community sanction;
- ethical codes;
- a professional culture.

He concludes that as far as journalism is concerned, 'these five attributes are either non-existent or exist only to a very limited degree' (p. 181). There is no 'system of abstract propositions to which new recruits are exposed and without which they cannot practice'; there are no professional-client relationships; journalism has 'no power by law to license members or to confer a professional title (p. 182); there is no universal binding code of ethics; and 'finally, there is little evidence of a formal professional culture characterized by institutional settings and professional meetings which stress rationality' (p. 182).

Neither the Press Council (later the Press Complaints Commission), the Institute of Journalists, the National Union of Journalists (NUJ), nor the National Council for the Training of Journalists (NCTJ) in and of themselves provide the conditions for the professionalisation of journalism. Although the NCTJ's objective was (and still, to judge by recent actions, is) 'to embrace all recruits to editorial journalism', it was in practice forced to focus on provincial, regional and local newspapers because 'these have been the most co-operative' (p. 188) and only a restrictive agreement between the NUJ and the Newspaper Publishers' Association prevented new entrants without degrees from joining national newspapers without first working through their indentures in the provinces. (Although as Boyd-Barrett then points out, 'this still leaves open some important channels of entry: magazine entry, for example ...'(p. 188), and educational norms have changed since then, as we will see.)

With the main argument above in mind, it is instructive to examine in more depth the purpose of a 'profession'. Kaarle Nordenstreng (1998) applies two theoretical analyses to the concept of professionalism – that of Emile Durkheim (for whom professions bring a 'much-needed social cohesion and new morality into the process of modernization' (p. 125)) and Max Weber (for whom professions are the 'bastions of narrow and elitist interests' that serve in modern society 'as repressive mechanisms which undermine democracy and turn active citizens onto passive consumers' (p. 126)). Furthermore, in this view, professions are intended to gain a monopoly position for certain social groups, and social developments suggest that 'what is crucial to professions for a market monopoly position are narrow intellectual techniques and a narrow specialization' (Konttinen, 1989: 176)' (p. 126).

Referring to Weber's conception, Nordenstreng declares that journalism 'fits perfectly into this overall picture' and considering that both the NCTJ and the newspaper proprietors who are served by that body stress a very narrow range of intellectual techniques – boiling down to a knowledge of law, of local government, and especially of shorthand, which is almost fetishised – there seem to be strong grounds for agreement.

His solution, which reflects his personal journey from journalist to academic, is to propose that rather than journalists and the media being seen as the 'owners of communication rights and freedoms', it is 'citizens and their civil society that should be seen as the ultimate owners of freedom of information' (p. 127), although that takes us into rather a different debate about 'public journalism'.

Perhaps it also takes an outsider's perspective to bring clarity to the question of whether journalism is or is not, *can or cannot be*, a profession. According to cultural theorist John Hartley it cannot be, for one very simple reason: journalism is a 'craft defined principally by its practice (a practice that cannot be professionalized since journalism remains a trade where the employer regulates entry)' (2000: 39). Without labouring this point, someone who studies to be a doctor and qualifies *is* a doctor, and someone who studies to be a lawyer and qualifies *is* a lawyer, regardless, in both cases, of whether they have a job. But as far as journalism is concerned, there are two contradictory axioms that hold true at one and the same time: i) anyone can be a journalist; ii) no-one can be a journalist until an employer has given them a job.

In addition to this, according to at least one researcher, it is not uncommon for journalists to have a completely different ambition from being a journalist, whether or not it can be classified as a profession. Aleksander Matejko offers an interesting combination of the professional and the literary in his study of Polish newspaper staff:

> It often happens that the newspaperman's ambitions extend beyond journalism to the creative, literary sphere as well. This is because the journalists have many and wide contacts with other people in the creative arts and the professions, such as scientists, academics, artists, writers, engineers, physicians, etc. The journalists want to raise their prestige to the level of those professions, and therefore try to make their work look as creative as possible. (1970: 170)

In his classification (applied to the specific context of Poland in 1970), Matejko assigned journalists mostly to the 'intelligensia' (p. 171) but found they felt insufficiently trained, which gave rise to jealousy about other professions, and attracted them to the 'social model of the literary man' because it is not too difficult to achieve compared with 'alternative roles of professor, politician, or social worker' (p. 177).

It is a widespread joke that most journalists, Polish or otherwise, will have a novel stashed away in the bottom drawer of their desk. However, it is a joke that has some substance to it, as the roll-call of journalists-turned-litterateurs shows: Michael Frayn, Sebastian Faulks, Wendy Holden, Julia Gregson – this is an extremely short and selective list of bestselling authors who previously plied their trade on newspapers and magazines.

It is also a tradition with strong historical roots, particularly as regards magazines – we have already seen that Daniel Defoe founded an early magazine (the *Review*, 1704), and Harold Herd goes so far as to call him 'the first professional journalist of major standing ...' (1952: 46). In 1750 Dr Samuel Johnson launched the *Rambler* and Raymond Postgate tells us that as a periodical 'it was merely admired, but when it was reissued in volume form it gained a popularity whose immensity astounds us' (1969: 14). That popularity extended beyond the British Isles, for in 1784 Johnson told his friends, 'The Empress of Russia has ordered the *Rambler* to be translated into the Russian language: so I shall be read on the banks of the Wolga' (p. 294) – an early example of the syndication discussed in Chapter 2. As Postgate confirms, the *Rambler*'s 'publication ensured for Johnson an eminence among English writers which was the first step to the dominance he was soon to achieve' (p. 14) but he was far from alone. The *British Magazine* of 1760 was edited by Tobias Smollett and his novel *Sir Lancelot Greaves* was the first to be serialised in a magazine (Bonham-Carter, 1978: 21). The *Edinburgh Review* (launched 1802) attracted writers like Hazlitt, Scott, Carlyle and J.S. Mill; the *London Magazine* (1820) included Charles Lamb and Thomas De Quincy among its contributors; Oscar Wilde was appointed as editor of the *Lady's World* in 1887 (and promptly renamed it *Woman's World*).

There can be no doubt that these were literary figures and that the connections between literature and magazines were strong both in the UK and the USA. James Playsted Wood notes:

> For such writers as Lowell, Hawthorne, Cooper, Irving, and those others now recognised as classic American authors, the magazines ... offered an attractive vehicle for their work, extended and added to their reputations, and provided a financial means of subsistence. (1956: 64)

Edgar Allan Poe even 'invented the term "magazinist"' (loc cit) to describe those who wrote for magazines and was one himself. Tumber and Prentoulis summarise this period thus:

> Through the eighteenth and nineteenth centuries, the writing trade was too small to sustain aspiring writers. In the absence of a dividing line between journalists and writers such as novelists or political theorists, journalistic writing was regarded as part of a wider literary tradition with its practitioners simultaneously engaged in different 'genres' of writing, for example literature, political theory or journal articles. (2005: 61)

When Victor Bonham-Carter set out to examine how exactly writers had made a living down through the centuries he used 'no arbitrary distinction between authors and journalists, partly because the categories overlap, partly because journalism can hardly be identified as a separate profession before, say, the 1700s ...' (1978: 5), a point amplified by Laurel Brake, who 'has demonstrated that it was only in the late nineteenth century that journalism and literature became distinguished as separate fields of endeavour ... in the mid-nineteenth century there was no hard and fast distinction between the broad categories of journalist, politician, and scholar' (Hampton, 2004: 7).

Bonham-Carter also pointed out the cross-fertilisation that this encouraged: 'The growth of journalism [in the 18th century] promoted interest in other *genres*. Histories, biographies, and even critical editions of admired writers of the past ... were a natural extension of the same impulse' (1978: 18).

In addition to the literary names mentioned above, Bonham-Carter reminds us of others who owe a considerable amount to magazines. Thomases Carlyle and Macaulay, William Makepeace Thackeray, and Charles Dickens all 'began their writing careers as journalists, and it was through journalism that they made their reputations as leading men of letters' (p. 56), and in Dickens's case we must remember that he was editor of several magazines: *Bentley's Miscellany, Master Humphrey's Clock, Household Words* and *All The Year Round*. This tradition continued into the twentieth century, when some 'highly talented writers, revelling in the openings offered by popular journalism and mass publishing, reached first rank ...', for example, Arnold Bennett and H.G. Wells. While Wells wrote avidly for newspapers and magazines, Bennett was actually a magazine journalist; he won a competition for a staff position on *Tit-Bits* (Alfred Harmsworth's popular magazine) and then became assistant editor and finally proprietor of *Woman* (which Bonham-Carter characterises as a 'mildly militant periodical' (1978: 180–181).

Given the historical precedents and the long association of magazines with literature, it comes as no surprise to learn from many studies that when students on journalism courses are asked why they want to be journalists one of the most important factors that surfaces is that they love to write:

> When respondents were asked to say why they had chosen journalism as a career the answers were: Non-routine, non-conventional, sociable career (35%); Most desirable career available (29%); Creative occupation (16% but 'additional evidence here shows that well over three-quarters of the sample wished to write a book' of fiction). (Boyd-Barrett, 1970: 196)

> In being drawn to journalism as a career, British journalists showed much the same kind of pattern as found in the case of Australian journalists ... The largest proportion (29%) became journalists because of their writing skills, whereas almost one in four [23%] were attracted by the perceived excitement and interest of the occupation. (Henningham and Delano, 1998: 145)

> In 1992, the most common answer centred on a love for writing ...our 2002 survey data suggests that a love for writing is still the most common answer ... (Weaver, 2005: 45)

> ... the lack of much change in motivation data suggests that, within differing personalities, particular motivations were deeply internalised before these students arrived at university, e.g. the proportion referring to journalism as creative/accommodating a love of writing is remarkably similar in both samples [27% and 28%]. (Hanna and Sanders, 2007: 413)

The other factor that consistently scores highly is the belief that journalism is a non-routine, non-conventional career; the kind of job that lends itself to a maverick or rebel. This chimes well with the conventional idea of artistic creativity and also helps to shed a little more light on the question of professionalism. Discussing the findings of his survey Boyd-Barratt says, 'The stress given by respondents to the unstructured, non-conventional nature of the occupation is indicative of their hostility towards any form of organisation'. In other words, the type of person who wants to be a journalist does not want to be a 'professional'! Or as Boyd-Barratt puts it, 'a deep commitment to freedom from control, to maximization of individuality, would make the establishment of professionalism more difficult than in occupations in which such values did not rank so highly' (1970: 196).

It also seems worth pointing out that Hanna and Sanders' survey, which was conducted with students at the beginning and end of their courses, showed clearly that for 'both the arrival and completion "maybes" and "sures" the most popular career goal was in magazines' (2007: 416). As understandable as that is to the author and as relevant as it is to the subject matter of this chapter (and book), there are two things that give pause here: the first is a health warning and the second is a question.

The *health warning*, and this is relevant to what will follow, is similar to the one given above: very little research has been undertaken into magazine journalists. Many of the surveys quoted above ignore this sector, either overtly or by unstated omission. Henningham and Delano provide an example of the former: 'many who contribute to the media in Britain were thereby excluded from the survey – including the growing number of freelance journalists, plus those employed by popular or special interest magazines ...' (1998: 145). In their recent survey of graduates from Scottish journalism programmes, Frith and Meech acknowledge that journalists who work on magazines – and even those who specialise in feature writing – are 'a neglected group in occupational research and our difficulty in contacting them does suggest that they are part of different networks than those connecting newspaper or broadcast news journalists' (2007: 147).

The *question*, as usual, is why? Why are magazines the most popular career goal? Hanna and Sanders did not pursue this in their survey but other researchers have, even inadvertently, made some useful suggestions over the years:

> In Britain, the number of newspapers has been falling over the century. On the other hand, the number of magazines in the UK is rapidly rising, thus the balance in journalism is clearly away from newspaper employment towards the magazine sector. (van Zoonen, 1998b: 39)

> According to government figures the periodicals and journals sector of the UK publishing industry provided employment for more than 53,400 people at the end of 1996 compared with the newspaper industry which employed around 47,000. (McKay, 2000: 5)

> More than half the journalists in the UK are actually employed on magazines, and magazine publishing is a bigger industry than newspaper publishing (and a growing rather than declining sector). (Frith and Meech, 2007: 161)

Perhaps just as importantly, magazines offer people with particular interests the opportunity to turn these into careers. That very specialisation we have seen 'routinely despised' (Hartley, 2000: 39) or belittled by the serious journalists surveyed by Tunstall and others not only works to the advantage of magazine journalists, it is also an essential quality for anyone wanting to work on the kind of publication ignored by Delano and others. However, it is not just this specialisation that is important; there is another characteristic that we have already seen described as 'a nose for news' and 'intuition', qualities closely aligned with paying attention to the readers' needs, which is yet another thing that aroused suspicion in the serious male journalists occupying Tunstall's 1971 newsroom. Liesbet van Zoonen has a clear, if not simple, explanation for this:

> ...organizational identities in the context of institutional 'masculine' journalism are quite different from those in the audience-oriented, 'feminine' field. Whereas involvement, loyalty and a desire to please audiences would distinguish, for instance, the women's magazine journalist, the political reporter would stand for detachment, critical distance and a desire to examine the quality of the political process. (1998b: 138)

This is not a simple matter of men being thought to be better at one thing than women or men being thought to be better at a different thing to women. According to van Zoonen, large-scale surveys of male and female journalists at work 'found only one – albeit quite a revealing one – significant difference in role conceptions: women are indeed more oriented to audience needs than men...' (1998b: 37). Put that together with '... according to a recent UNESCO report on employment patterns in the media, women now make up the majority of journalism students, especially in Europe and the Americas ...' (1998b: 38) and the career goal found by Hanna and Sanders begins to make sense.

What does this mean for the magazine workforce? If true, it should mean that there are more women working on magazines than men – and this appears to be borne out by such data as exist. In 2000 Delano reported, 'The female proportion of the entire journalist population is 40 per cent; the ratio in the periodical sector 55.6 per cent' (p. 269) – although just two years earlier he had put his name to an article that stated 'British journalists are predominantly male: Only 25% of full-time journalists are women' (Henningham and Delano, 1998: 147). The later figure is echoed by the most recent large-scale survey undertaken into the journalism workforce; *Journalists At Work* found that while the gender split in the overall workforce was 51 per cent male to 49 per cent female, in the magazine sector this changed to 55 per cent female/46 per cent male (yes, this adds up to 101 per cent but those were the published figures)(Hargreaves, 2002: 4 , 23). Van Zoonen's assertion that 'the magazine sector has always been more open to women than the press and television news sector' (1998b: 39) is thus proved right.

There is a great deal of interesting data in *Journalists At Work* but several caveats must be attached, the most general of which is that it was commissioned by the then extant Journalism Training Forum, which might well have had an agenda that shaped the outcomes; at the very least, the report's statement that '...media industries will face a [sic] increasing demand for trained journalists in coming years. By 2010 there will be between 80,000 and 90,000 journalists – an increase of about 20,000 on current levels. This suggests that the media industries face a large demand for the training of journalists in coming years' (2002: 18) must now be regarded with some scepticism.

More specific concerns arise when the numbers are used to analyse the magazine workforce. The report states, 'The majority of journalists work in a publishing environment, with 41 per cent working in newspapers (30 per cent in regional or local newspapers and 11 per cent in national newspapers), and 25 per cent in magazines (15 per cent in business magazines and 8 per cent in consumer or leisure magazines)' (2002: 18), but Frith and Meech have since pointed out that magazine journalists appear to be connected by networks that are different from those used by newspaper journalists, something which is very likely to make a difference to this kind of survey, and they also note that the 'figures are probably distorted by the self-selected sample of a postal questionnaire with an 11.5 percent return rate' (2007: 139). To underline both points, their Table 6 shows a nil return for magazine journalists in the East Midlands and a small number in East Anglia. Given that Emap (East Midlands Allied Press) had a large establishment of magazine journalists in Peterborough (which is arguably on the border of the East Midlands and East Anglia) this would seem to be a major omission from the data.

The presence of a majority of women in the magazine workforce seems to have two major effects on its demographic and economic composition: age and salary. Table 9 of *Journalists At Work*, shows the following age breakdown:

- Under 25: 12%
- 25–29: 28%
- 30–39: 38%
- 40–49: 13%
- Over 50: 8% (Hargreaves, 2002: 23)

There are two things worth noting about these figures (which must be taken with the previous caveat about completeness): the first is that despite the conventional idea of magazines thriving on fresh intakes of keen young people whose salary expectations will be low, the number of under 25s is relatively small; the second is that the 30–39 year old band is the largest in the print sector. To interpret the data crudely, magazines tend to be staffed mainly by women in their 30s.

As to the question of pay, Delano found that, 'Salaries are most equitably distributed among the sexes in the periodical sector. Of journalists earning £40,000 and above in periodical journalism, 53 per cent are women …' (2000: 270).

Interestingly, and perhaps oddly, some female researchers possess, to judge by their published output, what seems to be a rather ambivalent attitude to the opportunities offered to female journalists by the maga-zine sector. Marjan de Bruin seems to attribute this solely to commercial needs when she offers what could almost be taken as an insult: 'the greater presence of women seems more likely to be decided not by professional judgment but by personal bias and market needs' (2000: 233). Chambers et al., whose work barely mentions magazines at all, say: 'Women are still concentrated in sectors considered to be "soft" news, such as those with an emphasis on "human interest" stories, features and the delivery of a magazine-style of journalism' (2004: 1). We would note that it seems odd, if not downright perverse, to ignore a field of journalism that employs more women than men in a book called *Women And Journalism*; the authors seem to accept the 'masculine' (to use van Zoonen's categorisa-tion) definitions of what constitutes 'serious' journalism – features engage with an enormous range of subjects, hard and soft, and the strategic use of the term 'magazine-style' encapsulates manifold implications or connota-tions that are not necessarily complimentary, although later there is an acknowledgement that, 'In Britain, periodicals played a vital role during the women's suffrage movement ...' (p. 152).

Despite the reservations expressed above, Chambers et al. provide a his-torical context for women journalists that will be seen to have contempo-rary social and educational echoes: the first women 'who managed to enter paid journalism were highly educated, white ... and from middle-class backgrounds' (p. 15). Education and class in the magazine workforce will be examined shortly but there is another implication folded neatly into the sentence quoted above – the fact that it was, however marginally, socially acceptable for a woman to have a career in journalism.

Social acceptability for journalists was not something that could be taken for granted through the centuries. Although J.S. Mill has been cited above as an example of a literary figure who wrote for magazines and periodicals, his opinion of journalists as a category was not complimentary. Raymond Snoddy (1992) reminds us of his forthrightness on the subject:

> our daily & weekly writers are the lowest hacks of literature, which when it is a trade, is the vilest & most degrading of all trades, because more of affectation & hypocrisy, & more subservience to the baser feelings of others, are necessary for carrying it on, than for any other trade, from that of a brothelkeeper upwards. (Taken from *The Collected Works of John Stuart Mill, Volume XII – The Earlier Letters of John Stuart Mill 1812–1848 Part I, 1812–1830*, paragraph 290 available at oll.libertyfund.org/index.php?option=com_staticxt&staticfile=show.php&title=249&search=the+vilest+and+most+degrading&layout=html#a_769678)

Lawyers (true 'professionals') have not always enjoyed universal admiration from the societies they serve but 200 years ago they certainly felt themselves to be superior to journalists. Nevett tells us, 'The low reputation of the profession of journalist and editor persisted well into the nineteenth century, the Benchers of Lincoln's Inn making a rule in 1807 that no one who had written for a newspaper could be called to the bar, and as late as 1846 Charles Mitchell could observe in his Newspaper Press Directory that "English editors, unlike those of their class in France, hold, at best, but a dubious position in Society"' (1986: 153).

This ambiguity of social status, a condition that could perhaps be described as anomie, continued through the Victorian period and beyond, as according to Lee, 'The poor remuneration of the rank and file was compensated in part by a "middle-class" status ... As F.H. Rose, one of the prime movers of union organisation amongst journalists, remarked in 1906, they had the status of receiving 'a "salary" instead of "wages", and of accepting an "engagement" rather than a "job". Yet in terms of respectability and security, the journalist held a low position amongst the professional men of whom he claimed to be one' (1976: 112).

Even denizens of the bohemian demi-monde, many of whom wrote for, or even published their own, journals and reviews, held journalists in a certain contempt. Dante Gabriel Rossetti's advice to a relation considering a career in journalism was, 'I do not think it a sphere suited to anyone who has health, gifts, and an inclination for an active life ...' (Brake, 1994: 29), despite the fact that his brother William Michael had founded *The Germ* (*floreat* January to April 1850) to promulgate the Pre-Raphaelite Brotherhood and Dante Gabriel had contributed to this.

Journalism's status as a calling that was neither whole-hearted art-and-craft nor fully figured profession was perhaps an important factor in this, as was the apparent social division between magazines and newspapers. To understand the social composition of British magazine journalists, it may help to revisit the first publication to use the word in its title: the *Gentleman's Magazine*. That sent a pretty clear class message about who it was created for and, given the educational norms of the day, who it was likely to have been created by. Sir Richard Steele's *Tatler* (1709) and *Spectator* (1711) were targeted at the aspiring middle classes; the *British Magazine* was subtitled *Monthly Repository for Gentlemen and Ladies*; the magisterial *Edinburgh Review* was founded by a group that included Lord Murray. The *London Magazine*'s editor John Scott died as a result of a duel with John Gibson Lockhart of *Blackwood's Magazine* – and duels were definitely the province of the gentlemanly.

Laurel Brake makes a telling observation in this respect when she summarises Leslie Stephen's view of 'working journalists', which indicates not only the social difference between classes of men involved in different aspects of the business, but also a significant cultural difference between newspaper and periodical – for Stephen was the well-educated editor of the *Cornhill Magazine*, a literary journal founded in 1860:

> The contempt of the leisured wealthy for the working journalist is more explicit in the hierarchy of the profession, contempt that emerges in his account of 'journalists pure and simple' who are 'men who have no other occupation or position in life than those they derive from newspapers, and no other prospects than those which lie in their success'. They are often of low beginning and 'without much other education than the newspaper itself supplies'. (1994: 89)

We will return to education shortly, but given this kind of snobbish attitude it is not surprising that 'serious' journalists eventually armed themselves against attacks with the 'prestige goal' that Tunstall identified (1971: 7) and counter-attacked with withering contempt for the dilettantes who specialised in audience-oriented publications. Nevertheless, it took some time – and a generational shake-up of social attitudes – for opinions to change. Delano notes that in 1928 'journalism was not seen as a particularly desirable or distinguished calling' (2000: 263), but 40 years later there had been a complete reversal. Peter Cole, who has been both a distinguished journalist and a professor of journalism at Central Lancashire and Sheffield universities, confirms this social shift in an anecdotal piece published in the *British Journalism Review*:

> Journalism became more middle class during the time of the youth upheaval in the late 1960s. It became fashionable at the time business became unfashionable, and suddenly considerable numbers of graduates from the finest universities, who had until then over-whelmingly aspired to the traditional graduate professions (law, finance, medicine, teaching, and engineering) wanted to be journalists. (Cole, 2003: 56)

Various reasons have been given for this sea-change, including Vietnam-inspired baby-boomer contrarianism (that rebellious streak again) and Woodward and Bernstein's Watergate investigations (although this had been in the 1970s). However, Delano convincingly identifies something that looks both backwards to the literary tradition of journalism and forwards to both the expansion of higher education and its new fields of study – cultural studies, media studies and journalism itself:

> The transformation of the image and status of the journalist first became apparent in America during the 1960s, an era vigorously explored by the impressionistic and inter-ventionist 'New Journalism' that was personified by Tom Wolfe and other writers in Clay Felker's *New York* magazine … … Their extensive exposure to higher education (Wolfe left Harvard with a Masters degree in American Studies) imbued those innovative American journalists with a keen appetite for distilling high culture out of low; high, at any rate, as the readers of *New York* and its advertisers saw things. (2000: 263)

The appeal of low culture to educated writers is, of course, nothing new. Writing about the careers of Frederick Greenwood, George Augustus Sala, and Edmund Yates (all of whom 'helped to give form and shape to the New Journalism' – the Victorian version of New Journalism, that is), Joel Weiner tells us, 'All three men ... were strongly influenced by the bohemian atmosphere of London in the 1850s and early 1860s. They helped to define the concept of a journalistic bohemia ... where novels and light verse and satirical paragraphs for comic magazines were hatched (1988: 63-64). It could be argued that this 'journalistic bohemia' developed in several directions, one being the boozy ambience associated with old Fleet Street and another the persistent dream of the novel in the bottom drawer.

Nevertheless, an obvious, if unintended, consequence of journalism's renewed appeal is that it has become a middle-class occupation. The various surveys cited above are unanimous on this, even if their specific percentages vary, and anyone who teaches on a university-based journalism course will also confirm this, although even here there is an evident difference between undergraduate and postgraduate courses. Cathy Darby, who runs the PTC-accredited magazine courses at the University of Central Lancashire, thinks 'the undergraduate route is more diverse both ethnically and by class' but 'postgraduate courses could be defined as middle-class courses given that the majority of students have a first degree and have to find the additional funding for a second one' (personal communication), which more or less echoes the JTF survey:

> ... the need to have wealthy parents to fund courses, or the willingness to face considerable debt, may be deterring potentially good students from entering journalism ... new entrants to the journalism profession are much more likely to have a parent from one of the highest occupational orders than would be expected given the distribution of all employment in the economy ... This finding is common to men and women, to journalists from white and non-white ethnic groups and to journalists employed in all sectors. (Hargreaves, 2002: 25)

Seven years after the JTF had done its work, and drawing on its data, even politicians noticed the imbalance. When Gordon Brown commissioned a report examining barriers to social mobility in Britain the resulting document, *Unleashing Aspiration*, found that 'Between the 1958 and the 1970 birth cohorts, the biggest decline in social mobility occurred in the professions of journalism and accountancy. For example, journalists and broadcasters born in 1958 typically grew up in families with an income of around 5.5% above that of the average family; but this rose to 42.4% for the generation of journalists and broadcasters born in 1970' (Milburn, 2009: 19). Patrick Wintour, political editor of the *Guardian*, summarised this finding thus: 'journalism has become one of the most exclusive middle-class professions of the 21st century'.

My co-author, Liz Nice, established the magazine journalism courses at Sheffield University after a successful career on women's magazines and her take on the issue, which also touches on ethnicity, is unambiguous: 'In terms of class, most [students] were "middle class" and few could really claim to be "working class", although I certainly worked with more journalists/students who defined themselves as working class than I did journalists/students who weren't white' (personal communication).

In addition to class, there is a second theme that unifies all surveys of journalism and its practitioners in the last 20 years, which is that most journalists now have undergraduate degrees and an increasing number also have postgraduate degrees. *Journalists At Work* (Hargreaves, 2002) puts the figure at 98 per cent with an undergraduate degree, 43 per cent with a postgraduate degree (and 58 per cent with a qualification in journalism), and although Frith and Meech (2007) point out the methodological shortcomings of this survey, they still agree that it confirms the general trend identified by Henningham and Delano (1998) who found that 69 per cent of journalists had been to university.

In one sense this is completely unsurprising – it is part of a broader social trend that started with the provision of universal child education following the Elementary Education Act of 1870 and has since included more people going to university as the provision of higher education has expanded with the establishment of 'redbrick' universities in the early twentieth century and the post-Robbins Report 'new' universities of the 1960s (East Anglia, Sussex, York, Essex, Warwick, etc.) and then the conversion of polytechnics to universities following the 1992 Further and Higher Education Act. According to national statistical data, around 10,000 people were awarded degrees in 1900, rising to 90,000 by 1993 (Hicks and Allen, 1999: 10). In 1970/71 there were 0.6 million students in higher education and by 2004/05 this had risen to 2.5 million (Self and Zealey, 2007: 31). It was inevitable that the number of journalists with degrees would rise proportionally. The expansion of higher education coincided, generally, with increasing commercial success for newspapers and magazines as well as the launch of Independent Television News and then Independent Radio News, all of which meant that more journalists were needed. This demand was then fed by graduates from universities with the result that, 'The newcomers of the 60s brought about the first fundamental shift in the configuration of the British journalist since the 1890s. The raw material from which the greater number of journalists had been shaped over nearly three-quarters of a century of commercialized news output became different in background, attitudes and expectations' (Delano, 2000: 264).

While this hypothesis works well as a generalisation there are still differences within the broad field of journalism and *Journalists At Work* (possibly) identifies an interesting distinction between newspaper and magazine journalists, which is that 'The lowest proportion of journalists to hold a qualification work in magazines, where fewer than half (42 per cent) hold a qualification and where very few (two per cent) are working towards one' (Hargreaves, 2002: 34). This issue of 'qualification' is an interesting one, with ramifications that extend into the skill set required of magazine journalists in particular, even though there are other data within the same report which set up an intriguing tension that will be examined in the next chapter.

One thing that can be said with some certainty is that journalism does not compare well with most graduate careers when it comes to pay. Surveying journalists' salaries and conditions of employment in the inaugural issue of *Journalism Practice*, Stephen Cushion noted that although competition to get a job in the sector had never been higher, '… one of the most striking findings is how rates of pay have actually decreased over the last five years' (2007: 121). It seems here that either the attraction of a non-conventional, creative career overrides material rewards or would-be entrants are poorly informed, but in their survey of three cohorts of Norwegian journalism students, Bjørnsen et al. found that, 'Neither job security nor high wages attract them to the profession' (2007: 396). (They also found that students were uniformly middle class and ethnically Norwegian.)

This new situation – graduate/postgraduate employees on low wages – benefits the employers in several ways. Most obviously, the salary budget can be reduced since expectations are low; de Bruin noted that 'Two of the now more important factors that correlate are lack of experience and salary … both instrumental in getting or keeping a job' (2000: 232), while Frith and Meech demonstrate clearly that the responsibility for training has shifted from the employing organisation to the would-be employee: 'the industry is now enjoying, in effect, a substantial subsidy from the public purse for its training costs, and the squeeze on costs, particularly in the regional press, means that few editors now have the resources to provide any sort of on-the-job instruction themselves … This new training model certainly suits employers; the costs of access to journalism careers in both the press and broadcasting are now borne, almost entirely, by the trainees themselves' (2007: 141, 157).

Self-funded training has an obvious social effect, which Cushion identifies clearly: 'The extent to which this disenfranchises people from poorer backgrounds is a real concern, as a new generation of middle class journalists is emerging' (2007: 127). However, the effect may not *just* be social, it may well have an deleterious effect on the output as well, as Liz Nice notes: 'More voices should be represented in a medium that has become horribly homogeneous and, let's be honest, for those of us who have been around a long time, rather boring' (personal communication).

If most new journalists are middle-class graduates, it is obvious that the class-based diversity of this workforce will be severely restricted. The same is true of ethnic diversity and nowhere is this more so, according to Weaver's survey of racial and ethnic minority group inclusion in journalism, than in the UK: 'The reported figures are small at best, ranging from 1 to 11 percent, and reinforcing the conclusion of the 1971 U.S. Study by Johnstone *et al* (1976) that journalists come predominantly from the established and dominant cultural groups in society. This seems to hold true especially in Taiwan, Britain and Canada ...' (2005: 48). Henningham and Delano confirm this: 'Journalism in Britain is literally the domain of White Angle-Saxon Protestants' (1998: 148). Their summary of the data relating to ethnicity and religion reveals homogeneity on a massive scale:

- 93% British born
- 1% Indian, Pakistani, Black African or Caribbean
- 46% Church of England
- 16% Roman Catholic
- 10% Non-conformist
- 1% Jewish
- Islam, Buddhism, Hinduism, Sikhism et al. = 1% in total
- 17% no religion
- 72% non-practising

Journalists themselves are not blind to the problems this can cause. Peter Wilby (2008) expressed it very forcibly in a *MediaGuardian* supplement about journalism training: 'Faced with trying to understand, say, the grievances of the Muslim community or what drives inner-city youth to violence or what it's like to have children attending a "sink school", most journalists are lost. They have no contacts and no inside information'. Beyond that, 'In our multicultural and multi-ethnic societies tolerance is of utmost importance. Diverse information on different cultures and different patterns of values, norms and ideas may contribute to mutual respect and acceptance' (van Cuilenberg, 1998: 39).

Given this, it is not surprising that van Zoonen can say with certainty, 'In critical academic analyses, journalists ... are shown to be structurally aligned to particular class interests, patriarchy and white culture' (1998b: 124) and Liz Nice can bemoan the fact that '... the media are saturated with one type of person. White. Well educated. Middle class. Whether this has changed much since the dawn of media time, I doubt' (personal communication).

Once again, it is important to note that the figures above refer to journalism in general and, in this instance, may even exclude magazine journalists. This leads us in two directions – first, why should journalism per se be like this, and secondly, can we say anything more about magazine journalists?

Van Zoonen's statement above suggests there may be an important structural component to journalism culture but in another piece she identifies another potential factor – journalism's occupational mythos, especially the hard-living, hard-drinking stereotype. Looking at masculine culture in newsrooms and how women deal with it, she found 'The high alcohol intake of German male journalists was mentioned as a particular problem ...' (1998b: 33). Meryl Aldridge takes this further in her examination of the mythos of journalism: 'To be "larger than life" appears to be compulsory. In detail the prescribed behaviour is quintessentially macho, involving any permutation of drinking too much, smoking too much, working too much, turbulent personal relationships and bodily excess: in violence of temper, in capacity for sustained shouting, in profanity of language, in appearance' (1998: 116). Incidentally, that piece was inspired by the sudden death of a *magazine* journalist – Michael Vermeulen.

Looking at this occupational attitude, it would be easy to construct an argument that in itself it provides a sufficient condition to restrict interest from ethnic/religious minorities (perhaps especially from the older generation who may be subsidising both university study and early-career), not to mention many non-macho individuals. On the other hand, memoir-like books such as *Secrets Of The Press: Journalists on Journalism* (Glover, 1999) are full of former Fleet Streeters bemoaning the demise of the liquid lunch and 'traditional' journalism culture: perhaps there is still a perceptual hangover from this golden period when the road of excess led to the palace of wisdom.

It is also worthwhile recognising that not all research has reached the same conclusions. For example, after analysing student enrolment on London-based courses, Anthony Delano was optimistic (at the time of writing anyway) that things were not perhaps as bad as had been painted:

There is a widespread empirically and anecdotally based impression that journalism is racially exclusive but in reality the journalism population may accommodate, in proportion, more ethnic elements than the general working population of the United Kingdom ... A typical 2000 graduating class of BA and HND journalism students includes 5 per cent black British and 5 per cent British Asians. (2000: 270)

Sadly, the Journalism Training Forum took a short, sharp axe to this green shoot of optimism: '... the profession is predominantly white (96 per cent). Representation from the minority ethnic groups is lower than needed for them to be fairly represented in the occupation' (Hargreaves, 2002: 21).

As far as magazines are concerned, it might be possible to take Oliver Boyd-Barrett's idea (cited earlier), and argue that the magazine industry has, institutionally, been more open to a diverse intake than the newspaper industry because whilst the NCTJ aimed to embrace *all* editorial recruits, it *actually* kept a very tight rein on the intake for provincial newspapers and restricted the flow of journalists from the provinces to London, which still left open 'some important channels of entry: magazine entry, for example' (1970: 188). We could also cite van Zoonen's (1998a, b) hypothesis that journalism is becoming 'feminised' as it moves away from straightforward news reporting, and Hartley's (2000) concept of the 'smiling professions', among which magazines feature prominently. All of these ideas could suggest that magazines have done better as far as encouraging diversity is concerned.

But on the whole they haven't. Over the last 15 years several schemes have been launched by publishers, only to disappear after perhaps one year. One honourable exception to this is BBC Magazines, which runs a diversity scholarship that is open to students enrolled on PTC-accredited magazine journalism courses.

In July 2010 the Periodicals Training Council (PTC) and Periodical Publishers Association (PPA) launched a scheme called MagNet, specifically intended to encourage people from ethnically diverse and socially less privileged backgrounds to join the magazine industry. As PTC Director Loraine Davies (2010) explained:

> Ethnic minorities are under-represented within the publishing industry. Fact. We know that Black, Asian and Minority Ethnic (BAME) employees make up between seven and eight percent of the workforce. But whilst this is close to the national average, these figures to be taken in context: 50 percent of our industry's workforce is based in London and BAME groups make up 24 percent of the London working population. Considering there are no barriers to employment for ethnic groups in magazine publishing you'd expect the proportion of BAME employees to be – well – higher. (Data from Skillset: Diversity strategy and disability action plan)

MagNet will be a mentoring scheme, whereby those already in the industry will spend time advising journalism students in addition to providing one work experience opportunity and arranging one networking opportunity. In their turn, students must commit to writing one feature for their mentor's magazine. As Davies is at pains to point out, the scheme is not about box ticking, quotas, or positive discrimination, and nor is it a pure-bred consequence of disinterested idealism. The magazine workforce will be chosen from the best talent available, but 'MagNet will make it easier for employers to engage with talented BAME students. Which we believe – ultimately – is good for our community and good for business'.

So while the magazine industry has been neither much better nor much worse than any other branch of journalism, MagNet *may* help to address *part of* the situation that Liz Nice mentions at the end of her recollection of many years spent working in the sector:

There may have been a slight increase in diversity but not a great one. Certainly that was my experience working in women's magazines anyway. I worked on weeklies, monthlies and a fortnightly and in that time, as I recall, I worked alongside only one black person in the UK and two in the US. This does not seem terribly representative. I don't remember working with many Asians either. All the offices were predominantly white, as indeed were the applicants.

As a lecturer, my experiences were similar. I remember a handful of students who weren't white but it really was a very few.

Class and race seem to be a matter of embarrassment for many journalists. From time to time there is an outburst about the unfairness, maybe even a report is written, but nothing is ever done. 'We don't get many applicants who aren't white,' I've heard that argument a lot. But even if that's often true, does it really let our profession off the hook? (Personal Communication)

4

SKILLS AND POLICY DEVELOPMENTS

In the previous chapter a number of factors that contribute to the formation of the magazine industry's workforce were examined, as part of an attempt to explain its basic shape and constituency. However, the tasks that workforce is allowed and expected to undertake and the formal and informal conditions under which it labours also require analysis if a fuller understanding is to be reached. As Margaret Beetham has noted, the production of periodicals depends on technological advances, on 'the work of producers both of hand and brain', and as the sector 'developed within capitalism … [it] is impossible to understand unless it is situated within the economic system' (1990: 21). Provided the 'economic system' is understood to incorporate regulatory political elements this provides us with a useful template for examining first the material and cultural conditions and then the political conditions of production.

Material and cultural conditions of production

As many of the commentators cited in the previous chapter point out, socialisation is a key element in the formation of journalists, especially as there is no true process of professionalisation. The magazine industry is similar to other media industries in this respect, and like those other industries it has in recent years developed a tendency to demand pre-employment socialisation through the practice of work experience or unpaid internships. However, this development does not appear to be a simple matter of preparing individuals with the skills and habits necessary for participation in the magazine workforce; in many cases there is a clear economic element too, since 'workies' are not usually paid and many internships are expected to be undertaken as a labour of love (or 'passion').

Nevertheless, it is widely recognised that work experience has become a necessary part of any would-be magazine journalist's personal armoury and if it is undertaken in the right spirit on both sides it can be extremely useful as a formative experience. For every workie who finds that working on a particular magazine would be their dream job, there will be another whose eyes will be opened to the possibilities offered by working on a magazine or in a sector they would not previously have considered. Most journalism educators will have a story about the student who came onto the course determined to get a job on (say) a music magazine, only to waltz off with a job on (say) a B2B finance magazine, having discovered a solid metier in the process. It could even be argued that this is a valuable and necessary part of the educative experience.

The other side of the coin here, unfortunately, represents the potential for exploitation. There is little properly documented research into the phenomenon within this specialised sphere of work, but plenty of anecdotal material about young people working for nothing for months on end in the hope of being offered a lowly job. Most of the 'evidence' is said to involve young women hoping to ingratiate their way into working for high-end fashion magazines and young people in general being used as runners by tv production companies. There are employment regulations that cover such situations but given the scenario they are very unlikely to be invoked.

As described previously journalism has largely become a graduate career, but within the overall sector magazines seem to operate slightly differently – at least according to such data as exist. The Journalism Training Forum's survey of *Journalists At Work* found that, 'The lowest proportion of journalists to hold a qualification work in magazines, where fewer than half (42 per cent) hold a qualification and where very few (two per cent) are working towards one' (Hargreaves, 2002: 34), although this seems to run counter to Hanna and Sanders' finding that among the university students they surveyed, 'For both the arrival and completion "maybes" and "sures" the most popular career goal was in magazines ...' (2007: 416). We should remember that Frith and Meech described magazine journalists as 'a neglected group in occupational research' who appear to be 'part of different networks than those connecting newspaper or broadcast news journalists' (2007: 147).

It is also worth restating that many magazine journalists, particularly those on specialist titles, will have entered the sector as a result of their specific knowledge, experience, and contacts rather than because of their skill or training as journalists per se. This diverse group is even more 'neglected' than those who are taken on after completing an undergraduate or postgraduate course but it perhaps accounts for the magazine industry's strong, if still patchy, record of post-employment training. Frith and Meech (2007) made the point that the newspaper industry, for example, has no equivalent of the Periodicals Training Council (PTC), which has a remit to enhance

the performance of people working in magazines and professional media publishing by improving the quality and availability of training ... It is the overall responsibility of PTC to identify and develop courses and qualifications, which are then delivered by PPA Training. (www.ppa.co.uk/jobs-careers-and-training/the-periodicals-training-council-ptc/)

The PTC emphasises the importance of properly structured, non-exploitative, work placements and it is not difficult to understand why. Even after 15 years' experience of running a postgraduate magazine journalism course, it still comes as a surprise that so few applicants take the trouble to find out sufficient details about the industry they want to work in, be it the ownership structures, the different types of job available, the different sectors or even the pay scales. Many, if not most, will only have a vague idea of the subject matter they wish to pursue, beyond the already noted desire to 'write' (which is often mixed up, in the case of those who have formally studied the media, with an idealistic intention to tell 'the truth' or use what they believe to be the immense power of media structures to give readers a proper overview of the world).

The basic hierarchy of a magazine editorial structure runs from the editor, through a deputy, to section editors and then writers, designers and subeditors, with editorial assistants and work experience people at the lower end of the scale. On a consumer magazine, particularly one with any pretence to aesthetic quality, the art editor will play a key role in determining the look and feel of the title, and sometimes even the running order of its content. Above the editor there may be a group editor or a publisher who will oversee the commercial aspects of a number of titles, though a good publisher will contribute to editorial development just as a modern editor is expected to participate in the commercial life of a magazine.

Advertising managers and staff will be of equal importance, given their contribution to the financial wellbeing of the magazine, but they will also tend to have a separate hierarchical organisation. It used to be usual for a person from an advertising background to be promoted to the publisher role, but this has changed in recent years and people from editorial or production backgrounds are now commonly found doing the job.

Something else that has become subject to considerable variations is the physical disposition of the workforce. Whereas before all specialised members of the editorial team (writer, subeditor, designer) would be together in the same office, now a number of companies will operate separate production studios where one person may be responsible for overseeing a number of titles through the 'assembly' process. (Incidentally, once the general principle of in-house outsourcing has been accepted, there is no theoretical reason why production could not be outsourced to an offshore contractor and in some cases, usually where deadlines are not so pressing and creativity is not so important – for example academic journals – this has indeed happened.)

These are very general descriptions and the specific formations will vary from company to company. Specific job descriptions will also vary and are likely to continue to do so as production technology continues to evolve and corporations continue to seek workforce efficiencies. It is generally true that larger organisations and larger titles will have more people doing specialised jobs (e.g. writers who write and subeditors who sub) than smaller ones, but there is currently a general trend towards combining roles where possible. Contracts (and job descriptions) are much more likely to be negotiated with (or dictated to) individual workers than be the subject of a house agreement with a union, and surveys (with their limited data) indicate that the magazine sector is generally less unionised than other print or broadcast media.

Patterns of recruitment have changed considerably in recent years. There used to be three main sources of jobs – *Press Gazette, MediaGuardian,* and the grapevine. The latter was only really useful for people already in work but the other two were the 'bibles' of recruitment. They were however expensive, particularly *MediaGuardian*, and recruitment costs also became a subject of concern among publishing executives. So when the internet offered alternative opportunities these were suitably embraced. Every major publishing company now has its own corporate website that includes job opportunities and other sites such as *Gorkana, journalism.co.uk*, and even *Press Gazette* online, make a feature of their free job search pages. The grapevine does still operate as well and is another strong reason why work experience placements are popular – you are more likely to hear about jobs if you are on the spot. An electronic grapevine is also emerging as social media like Facebook and Twitter become increasingly popular for formal and informal recruitment. The actual number of jobs available will vary with the general economic cycle – in good times existing magazines will increase their pagination and new titles will be launched, but in bad times these will shrink and close.

The skill set demanded of new recruits has also changed over the past 15 years. Whereas before the ability to come up with a story and bash it out on a typewriter, or correct the spelling and grammar in a story written by someone else, were sufficient qualities, today's new journalist is expected to be able to operate sophisticated software and connect with readers across a range of communication platforms. The material conditions of production have been in flux ever since Friday 24 January 1986, when Rupert Murdoch moved the newspapers he owned to a new site in Wapping and started to produce them without the involvement of the traditional print unions.

For the first time in recent history journalists were able to key their copy straight in to computers without it having to be keyed in again by a compositor. A complicated and wasteful process became simple and straightforward – and also cheaper. Inevitably, it was not a matter of journalists 'being able to' key their copy in, they had to. After that they had to be prepared to do a certain amount of other production work, up to and including layouts, with the result that it is common for magazine journalists to have to load copy and pictures on to a website using a content management system – copy that has been prepared specially for the site and pictures that have been cropped, sized, and captioned – and then promote it to readers via Facebook, Twitter, or online forums.

However, it is generally true to say that people who work on magazines have been, and would prefer to be, closer to the creative side of production than journalists in other print media. Margaret Beetham observes that one of the difficulties faced by scholars trying to theorise the magazine is that 'Periodicals are heterogeneous in that they are made up of different kinds of material' (1990: 24): text and pictures, certainly, but also different kinds of text (body copy, headlines, standfirsts, captions) and different kinds of pictures (monochromatic photographs, colour photographs, illustrations, charts, diagrams), and Beetham is perceptive about the medium on which these elements are carried as well – the substrate, the paper that conveys the aspects of 'texture, size and weight which are so important to what a periodical means' (p. 23). (One of the great difficulties faced by magazine publishers is trying to convey the same 'meaning' on a digital platform.) When all these different materials are brought together in the pages of a magazine the effect can be stunning, but its power depends on all of the elements working in harmony: a single line of a Bach partita can be sweet and moving but it does not have the same capacity for catharsis as the St John Passion.

Achieving such a result requires individual abilities being deployed within a team and the skill set required of a modern magazine journalist was set out by Matthew Swaine, editor of *Trail* magazine and training co-ordinator at Bauer Consumer Media, in a presentation to the PTC's Academics and Industry Forum 2010.

Above all else, in Swaine's canon there comes the traditional mantra of magazine journalists: know the reader. This does not just mean being able to recite the demographic targets of average age, median income or social categorisation, it also means knowing what readers want from that particular magazine. Swaine's advice to would-be magazine journalists applying for a job is to 'analyse magazines in terms of the readers' needs. This is especially true of special interest magazines where readers come to the magazine for very functional reasons … Good feature ideas come from understanding reader needs not reader demographics'. Encouragingly he believes that, 'Great feature ideas are the most essential thing a new writer brings with them'.

However, the feature idea – the story, the narrative, the structure – is not sufficient on its own because, 'Good writers need to be able to visualise exactly what a feature is going to look like … They need to be able to brief photographers when out on a job. They need to get their ideas across to designers. They need to write with a clear visual end result that they are working to. The pictures need to tell the story as much as the words'. This aspect is of even greater importance now that print is under such competitive pressure from other media platforms – a great story in a great layout with great pictures on great paper (each one being an element of what is known as magazine craft) can remind readers of what they like, or love, about print and reinforce the special qualities that only print has.

On the other hand, print *is* under pressure, it is not the only medium and, despite its potential to achieve great things, the reality is that magazines are digital entities as well. Therefore it is essential that magazine journalists grasp the importance of digital output and its potential to communicate with readers in new or different ways. This should be easier for young entrants, who are likely to be Digital Natives (to use Mark Prensky's term), but they need to be able to harness their techo-savvy to the basic mantra. As Swaine puts it, 'digital and print media need to have very different functions and aims. What you do with them and the way they work together will be different for each magazine and your strategy needs to be guided by an understanding of your readers' (2010).

Finally, a new buzzword has joined 'passion' in the lists of must-have attributes for magazine journalists – 'entrepreneurialism'. Like digital technology, no-one is quite sure what this is, what it means, or what to do with it. In some cases it means the ability to create brand extensions (for example, special supplements that cover specific aspects of a hobby or sport), while in others it means the ability to dream up new forms of communication with an extended community of interest (there is a growing number of social media editors), and at the far edge it means the willingness to go it alone and set up your own business. A number of universities, particularly in the USA, are running courses in Entrepreneurial Journalism, including CUNY's two-year MA devised and overseen by Jeff 'What Would Google Do?' Jarvis.

Given all of these attributes that are expected of magazine workers, it is scarcely surprising that *Journalists At Work* found '... over three-quarters of journalists (76 per cent) had undertaken some form of learning activity in the last 12 months ... Journalists who work for the magazine sector are most likely to have undertaken a learning activity in the last year (82 per cent having done so)' (Hargreaves, 2002: 39–40). The locale of the learning activity is not revealed but is it most likely to have been either an in-house course or one laid on by the PTC. Although the reasons for needing the training are not reported either, two broad categories suggest themselves here. The first is the need to improve understanding of the commercial side of the business, catered for very effectively by the PTC's range of diplomas and certificates; the Diploma in Publishing is particularly worth mentioning in this respect as it was endowed by Felix Dennis, the independent magazine mogul, and encouraged by the PTC's chairman Nicholas Brett – an excellent example of the magazine industry investing in its own future and a stark contrast to the situation in NCTJ-designed newspaper training identified by the National Union of Journalists:

In an industry increasingly dominated by graduates (an estimated 80 percent of new entrants into journalism are currently graduates), the NCTJ's resolutely apprenticeship-based approach seems outmoded. But if NCTJ accreditation arguably fails to address the issues of journalism at an appropriate level for highly educated individuals, it also appears to undervalue the need for flexibility and constant upskilling that marks today's journalism. (NUJ, n.d.)

It is also worth considering this in connection with the finding in Frith and Meech's survey of early career journalists – mainly those in newspaper and news broadcast media because very few in the magazine workforce participated – that 'few respondents had had any further training at all. This is clear evidence that the majority of journalist employers do now assume that journalism training will take place in academic institutions' (2007: 153).

The second major reason for magazine workers recognising the need for training was identified by John Tulloch when he noted the 'main source of the innovations in the publishing industry that created the modern popular press was magazine and periodical publishing ...' (2000: 139) and confirmed by Matt Swaine above – magazines are constantly reinventing themselves in order to take advantage of the advances in technology, culture, and aesthetics. Magazine workers will be well aware of the need to be competent in new software, technology, and modes of communication with the communities of interest that comprise their readership/audience. *Journalists at Work* found that 63 per cent of magazine journalists perceived a need for training in new or additional skills, second only to television journalists at 72 per cent (Hargreaves, 2002: 43).

All of the foregoing can be applied across the three sectors of the magazine industry – consumer, customer, B2B – but there will be different emphases within them and different interpretations of how magazine craft should be applied. Consumer magazines fetishise the front cover because it is so important at the point of sale, determining both the direct income and circulation, which can then stimulate the advertising income. There is a pseudo-science (or at least a broad strand of magazine craft) connected with the creation of a strong cover and many editors will claim to spend hours or days trying to get everything just so. It is certainly true that a poor cover can affect sales drastically. When *Word* magazine put the singer Dido on the cover of its September 2003 edition, the result, according to Editor Mark Ellen's colourful description, was that it remained 'both nailed and glued to the shelves ... metric tonnes of unsold copies were recycled to make confetti, the rest bulldozed into giant landfills all over Kent and Suffolk'.

B2B magazines, on the other hand, have something of a tradition of selling their front covers to advertisers. They do not rely anything like so heavily on individual sales and so do not all have to make the same effort, though it is worth noting that B2B magazines at the 'consumer' end of the scale, and those based heavily on news reporting, will often create brilliant and compelling covers. But what B2B readers seem increasingly to demand is data they can mine for themselves – and that is usually best done in digital form.

Customer magazines incorporate most of the elements of consumer magazines in that to fulfil their function they must encourage people to read them and then think well of them. However, workers on these magazines must also be extremely sensitive to the needs and feelings of the corporate body that is paying for them, the client whose magazine it is.

Workers in all three sectors seem likely to be attached to their part of the industry in general, their magazine in particular, their job within the editorial hierarchy, and their ability to exercise magazine craft by the 'organizational identity' recognised by Marjan de Bruin – 'a framework of beliefs, values and feelings. Not a stable, fixed, completed collection, but rather a changing schema with a range of varieties forming multiple identities ... connected to a cultural and spatial "territory" – in this case the (news media) organization – and is carried by those who form part of the organization, as long as they belong to it' (2000: 229). Bourdieu's concept of *habitus*, as applied to journalists by Bjørnsen et al. (2007: 385), also seems to be relevant in this respect.

Political conditions of production

In general, the magazine industry is regulated by

- those laws and bodies that affect commerce and business, such as the Communications Act, the Competition Commission and the Advertising Standards Authority;
- the laws of Great Britain and Scotland that govern the press in general, such as libel and contempt of court;
- the laws of Europe that bear on the press, particularly those that concern issues of privacy embodied in the European Convention of Human Rights and the Human Rights Act of 1998;
- the bodies that have specific responsibility for overseeing press content in the UK, which largely means the Press Complaints Commission (PCC), although the Teenage Magazine Arbitration Panel (TMAP) has been established by magazine publishers to arbitrate on complaints against content considered unsuitable for young people.

In theory magazines fall under the Communication Act of 2003 inasmuch as they constitute 'other media enterprises' as mentioned in the Preamble to that Act. However, the Act is principally concerned with the ownership of television and radio stations, and national and local newspapers – in other words, the ostensible suppliers of 'news'.

Ofcom clearly spent some time thinking carefully about what ownership means. Its statement on the subject, issued at www.ofcom.org.uk/

consult/condocs/media2/statement/ is supplemented by a 12 page document (stakeholders.ofcom.org.uk/binaries/consultations/media2/statement/ media_statement.pdf) that considers the minutiae of what exactly constitutes a 'majority interest' and the difference between 'de facto' and outright control. There is, however, no legal definition of what constitutes a newspaper attached to the Act.

The Newspaper Society, a body founded in 1836 that represents the interests of Britain's local and regional media, has researched legal definitions of newspapers and lighted on the Newspaper Libel and Registration Act of 1881:

> The word 'newspaper' shall mean any paper containing public news, intelligence, or occurrences, or any remarks or observations therein printed for sale and published in England or Ireland periodically, or in parts or numbers at intervals not exceeding twenty-six days between the publication of any two such papers, parts or numbers. Also any paper printed in order to be dispersed, and made public, weekly or oftener, or at intervals not exceeding twenty-six days, containing only or principally advertisements. (Section 1)

and the Defamation Act of 1952:

> ... the expression 'newspaper' means any paper containing public news or observations thereon, or consisting wholly or mainly of advertisements, which is printed for sale and is published in the United Kingdom either periodically or in parts or numbers at intervals not exceeding thirty-six days. (Section 7(5))

before coming up with its own definition that radically reduces the intervals between publication

> Any publication in written form on newsprint or a similar medium, published in the British Isles (excluding the Irish republic) at regular intervals not exceeding seven days and available regionally rather than nationally (ie, not available throughout all or most of the British Isles). It contains news and information of a general nature, updated regularly, rather than being devoted to a specific interest or topic. (www.newspapersoc.org.uk/ Default.aspx?page=2524)

Formal definitions of a magazine are equally hard to come by, as we have seen previously. The Periodical Publishers Association's version seems more concerned with describing what a magazine does than with what its essence, or even its content, may be:

> The word 'magazine' describes branded, edited content often supported by advertising or sponsorship and delivered in print or other forms. Traditionally, magazines have been printed periodicals which are most commonly published weekly, monthly or quarterly. These may be supported by printed one-off supplements and annual directories. Increasingly, magazines exist online where content is available through websites or in

digital editions, or delivered by email as an electronic newsletter. Many magazine brands also deliver tailored information services to their audiences. Magazine brands also engage with their audiences face-to-face by organising exhibitions, conferences and other events. (www.ppa.co.uk/all-about-magazines/what-is-a-magazine/)

Given this situation, what would prevent a newspaper proprietor intent on circumventing Ofcom regulations from reclassifying those properties currently called 'newspapers' as 'magazines', in much the same way that in 1816 William Cobbett reclassified his *Political Register* as a vehicle for opinion rather than news to avoid taxation?

Be that as it may, magazines are evidently not seen to be an official element of plurality in the media landscape: apart from a reference to Emap's ownership and subsequent disposal of its *Smash Hits* radio station, there is no further mention of magazine publishers in Ofcom's 2006 Review of the ownership rules. (Ironically, *Smash Hits* radio was a brand extension (see below) that outlived both the original print magazine brand and, as of 2007, the original publishing house too.)

Newspapers are specifically bound by a combination of Acts, including sections of the Enterprise Act of 2002 and the Fair Trading Act of 1973, but magazines seem to be regarded as more generically commercial operations that fall under the general rules for business and competition. A trawl of the Competition Commission's past enquiries reveals that in 2001 a proposed merger between Reed Elsevier and Harcourt (both publishers of science, technical and medical journals) was referred, and in 2005 the enquiry into the proposed acquisition of Highbury House by Future (both consumer magazine publishers) was cancelled when the deal was called off. Similarly a deal between IPC Media and Horse Deals was on the slate and then cancelled in 2006. The huge deals between IPC and AOL-Time Warner (2001) and Bauer's acquisition of Emap (2007) do not feature in the commission's list.

Clearly the 'official and traditional' Fourth Estate is considered more influential than the magazine sector, yet both politicians and researchers have identified magazines' ability to influence and affect debates in the public sphere. In 2005 Viviane Reding, European Commissioner for the Information Society and Media, 'praised the magazine sector as a key element of making a stronger Europe. She said: "Magazines are an enormous influence and an important growth sector. We need magazines in order to construct the family of Europe"' (PPA).

In his critical history of journalism, Martin Conboy notes, 'The journalism of women's magazines has shaped a debate around the public and private visualization of the female, constructing a network of imagined communities for their readers. To this extent they constitute an important aspect of the public sphere ...' (2004: 128), while later on he adds, 'Magazines, in all their variety, produce a range of social and cultural knowledge which is not specifically, but implicitly, political' (p. 163).

Writing of *Votes for Women*, a magazine published by the Women's Social and Political Union from 1907 to 1918, Chambers et al. state, 'Despite its radicalism, it reached a national circulation of 40,000 and was able to attract advertising revenue, in part, due to a strong sales campaign with a large number of women involved in promoting and selling the paper. Thus, *Votes for Women* is an example of a periodical that managed to combine a commercial strategy with radical political objectives ...' (2004: 153). Moving from a specific example to the more general effect of radical magazines, they write:

> Obviously all these periodicals were partisan to a degree not seen or admitted among the mainstream news media ... But the fact is, these efforts sustained and nurtured the community of new women that these periodicals dramatized ... they circulated the news to women who were geographically isolated, thereby motivating and encouraging them, and keeping the movement and its ideas alive. (p. 156)

Interestingly, Chambers et al. also note that, 'A further difficulty for women's alternative media in Britain has been distribution' (2004: 165), because unlikely as it seems the distribution of magazines has become a highly political issue. Not just in the expected sense brought about by the recent (and ongoing) Office of Fair Trade investigation which sought to decouple the rules governing magazine and newspaper distribution, nor plans to privatise the postal system which may affect the cost of subscription delivery, but more endemically in the manoeuvering which surrounds special distribution arrangements. It is part of the marketing of every new launch from a big company that special positions will be bought: these might take the form of a column of magazines all facing outwards with unobscured covers on the normal shelving or a prestigious 'end bay' or 'solus' display. All of these have become not insignificant money earners for retailers such as WH Smith.

However, WH Smith itself has come under increasing pressure from evolving distribution arrangements, with the big supermarkets playing an increasingly important role in making magazines available. Indeed, there are those within the industry who believe that distribution in supermarkets has had an effect on the shape of the industry itself, encouraging the recent tranche of high-turnover weeklies.

This loop between publisher and retailer may also even be leading to a diminution of risk-taking in the bigger titles. Certainly, in women's magazines, there is an increasing sense that any editorial experimentation is struggling in the face of this relentless commercial drive. Anna Gough-Yates (2003: 153) talks about the 'anxieties' experienced by publishers and advertisers as they struggle to find the right balance for their targeting of young, middle-class women, who are, she says, essentially 'unknowable'.

Despite this perception of reduced risk-taking, from time to time a moral panic will be whipped into existence about one kind of magazine or another. In recent years, titles aimed at teenage girls have been the focus of several such panics, usually because of their sexual content. In 1996 Peter Luff, as MP for Worcester, proposed to introduce a private members' bill requiring magazines to be age-rated in the same way as films. Although this never got anywhere near a serious implementation, the industry responded by forming the Teen Magazine Arbitration Panel (TMAP). This has a strong family resemblance to the Press Complaints Commission (PCC) in that it is an industry-dominated body but it has still proved sufficiently resilient and rigorous to deal adequately with complaints against specific issues of magazines. Examining the role and judgements of TMAP could provide a useful model of an effective response to political pressure; annual reports are available at www.tmap.org.uk but the most recent is dated 2007. The panic and the panel can now be put into a different context because just as the market for teen girl magazines has collapsed, really quite suddenly, the Qualifications & Curriculum Authority, following a laudatory speech by Margaret Hodge, has recommended that teachers 'should use titles such as *Sugar, Bliss* and *CosmoGIRL!* [now defunct] to help pupils discuss their problems ...' (*Press Gazette*).

Morality and ethical behaviour have also been brought into focus by the Human Rights Act 1998 and the interpretation of its privacy clause by the judiciary (mainly through Mr Justice Eady, until September 2010 when he was replaced as the senior libel judge by Mr Justice Tugendhat). High profile judgements have been made against newspapers more than magazines, but clearly the gossip and celebrity magazines are likely to be affected by either their apprehension of action under the law or actual lawsuits from celebrities who feel their privacy has been breached by, say, a photograph that has claimed to show their cellulite.

Other legal and political restrictions that affect magazines can be found in taxation and advertising. The imposition of VAT on reading material has long been a source of contention, and publishers have so far been successful in protesting against a 'tax on knowledge'; perhaps the history of newspaper Stamp Duty is useful in this instance. There are restrictions on alcohol and tobacco advertising that the magazine industry must adhere to, but they are not exceptional in this.

When the Periodical Publishers Association appointed a new chief executive in January 2010 (Barry McIlheney, who has a very strong background in magazine editorial and management) he quickly identified a number of key policy areas that the organisation should engage with: VAT, alcohol and tobacco advertising, and the environment. Like other industries, the magazine sector has had to agree recycling targets with the government, in this case to raise the level of post-consumer magazine recycling to 70 per cent by 2013. The target was exceeded in 2008 with a level of 72 per cent but the PPA intends to raise these levels further and publishers are being advised, for example, to use the official Recyclenow UK campaign logo and encourage readers to recycle their magazines rather than send them to landfill.

There is also a movement to use paper that has been responsibly or sustainably produced, environmentally friendly inks, and so on. The PPA is also looking at ways whereby distribution of magazines can be made more efficient and thus reduce the number of unsold copies that need to be recycled or otherwise disposed of.

Apart from specific instances of policy affecting the conditions of production mentioned above, the magazine industry appears to enjoy considerably more freedom than the newspaper and broadcast industries. On the whole this might be taken as an indication of its general compliance with legal, ethical and political norms – but one positive outcome is that magazines can continue with their function of 'reinforcing the individual consumer within a fragmented social world as the dominant political actor of the post-bourgeois public sphere' (Conboy, 2004: 164).

5

CONTEMPORARY PRACTICES

A career working in the magazine industry is glamorous, exciting, and generally more fun than decency allows. As *Golf Monthly* editor Mike Harris, who won Editor of the Year (specialist interest and current affairs) at the annual BSME (British Society of Magazine Editors) awards, in October 2008, acknowledges:

> My job is fantastic. I get to do all the creative stuff that is the best thing about working in magazines and I also get to play golf during work time. It doesn't get much better than this. (Harris, 2008 Personal Communication)

For most magazine journalists, it is an opportunity to do what you love and get paid for it, whether that's writing, editing, interviewing interesting people, designing beautiful layouts, sourcing fabulous pictures, or indulging your passions – perhaps as a fashion editor on a lifestyle magazine or as a reviews writer for *Official Playstation Magazine* or *Total Film*. For Harris it has meant realising that a great way to really get to know his readers was to challenge them to a game of golf, so part of his job now actually involves travelling to golf clubs all over the country so that readers can '*Challenge Golf Monthly*': 'We get a DPS (*double page spread*) out of it every month and readers love to see themselves in the magazine'.

It's not exactly arduous for the editor either.

Pay in the magazine industry is generally better than in newspapers; the government estimates a starting salary of between £18,000–£25,000 compared to £15,000 in local newspapers (Careers Advice online, 2008). And it's great for treats as well, whether that's meeting the celebrities most people only read about (though, in the case of many so-called 'celebrities', journalists tend to enjoy this reservedly), going on 'press trips' to exotic destinations, or receiving piles of free goods from press officers desperate for you to feature their clients' products in your magazine. Says Margi Conklin, editor in chief of *Page Six Magazine*, the *New York Post*'s supplement: 'The only time in my adult life when I actually went out and bought a lipstick was a short period in 2006 when I was working from home as a freelance journalist. You forget how much free stuff comes into magazine offices' (Conklin, 2006 Personal Communication).

However, putting all the perks aside, life in the magazine industry can also be exhausting and all consuming. Marie O'Riordan, who resigned as editor of British *Marie Claire* in October 2008, found that her job so took over her personal life, she began to feel as though the part of her that wasn't engaged in producing, living, and breathing *Marie Claire* had all but disappeared:

> One of the reasons I decided to leave was that I had no head space left for the rest of my life. I couldn't think about my home life, or what I wanted to do in the future beyond the magazine. Magazines are so seductive but over time I began to want more delineation between work and me and I realised that the only way to retrieve something of myself would be to leave. People talk about the glamour and I wouldn't disagree but I don't think they understand how emotionally draining it is. I gave every ounce of my being to my staff, advertisers and readers. You become very passionate about the delivery of this quite unique product but at the same time I was really starting to wonder if I had anything left. (O'Riordan, 2008 Personal Communication)

This idea of journalistic exhaustion is rarely considered by academics writing about contemporary practices in journalism. Indeed, there have been very few studies of magazine *practice* at all, partly because academics in general have trouble getting into magazine offices (Gough-Yates, 2003: 22) and partly because of a tendency among many journalism academics to 'feel they (do not) have to bother' (Hermes, 1995: 149) with magazines, a view that may well be sexist in origin: although some academic study of men's magazines has been undertaken (e.g. Jackson et al., 2001; Benwell, 2003; Crewe, 2003), much of the best known magazine research has focused on the women's media and this has generally come from a feminist perspective (see Chapter 7).

Magazine journalists themselves aren't much keen on shining the torch on their own practices either. In his book *Flat Earth News*, which rails against the decline of journalistic standards in a spin-driven media, Nick Davies wasn't writing about magazines specifically but might as well have been when he argued that journalists 'dig into the world of politics and finance, sport and policing and entertainment. We dig wherever we like – but not in our own back garden' (2008: 1).

This chapter however aims to get its hands as dirty as possible by reviewing magazine practice in more depth, exploring the activities of magazine journalists in an ever changing media landscape and considering the implications of current practices for the health of the magazine profession.

Magazine practice: a new landscape

A day in the life of magazine journalist, Will Cooper, a 2003 graduate of Sheffield University's MA Web Journalism programme, is 'all about being able to adapt to a multi-platform environment'. Cooper, who works as deputy news editor for *New Media Age*, has to put five news stories online by lunchtime, send daily email alerts to magazine subscribers, and take a microphone with him everywhere he goes; 'We have to "think podcast" at all times,' he says, 'which means if someone we're interviewing says something interesting, you have to whip out the microphone and ask them to say it again so you can put it on the website'.

Cooper's online duties, of course, are on top of the writing, staying in touch with contacts, and researching he has to do for the print version of his magazine. 'You have to adapt to the media you're in and have the agility to skip between formats', he says. 'So, it's no good just recycling the news in print – you know the readers will be looking for the breaking news online. We've just re-launched (the print version of the magazine) with a different way of thinking about our magazine stories. We're trying to be thought-leading; leading the way the industry is approaching important issues and highlighting stories such as McDonalds using MSN to get around government guidelines which stop junk food advertising to children. It's all about lobbying where necessary and trying to change the way things work' (Cooper, 2008 Personal Communication).

Of course, it's nothing new for magazines to think of themselves as campaigners. *Cosmopolitan*'s 'lipstick feminism' was revolutionary in the early 1970s and the magazine for 'fun, fearless females' still campaigns against domestic violence, the low rate of convictions for rape, and the pay gap (Seal, 2007). Similarly, the UK's biggest selling women's weekly, *Take a Break*, always has a campaign running; in 2008 *Mums4Justice* was urging the government to provide better protection for mothers following plans to close the Child Support Agency (CSA), while *chums4mums* aimed to support mothers suffering depression and *Mums' Army* was trying to tackle antisocial behaviour. What is new however, as most magazines now attempt to provide online content to complement (or even outdo) their print offerings, is the conception that magazine journalists now need to think across platform and adapt their content to the medium they are using. Print cannot afford to sit still; it has to be continually aware of what *it* is offering that readers can't get elsewhere. Will Cooper argues:

Online is all about breaking the exclusives while print is about developing the big stories and moving them on. And because of your readership, you need to have a global perspective online, whereas our print product must find the UK angle on the big global story. It's still journalism, uncovering the stuff that people don't want you to uncover, but you're just learning how to do it in lots of different, platform-specific ways. (2008 Personal Communication)

Giles Barrie, editor of *Property Week*, agrees, although he believes big news exclusives still have a place in 'print': it's simply a matter of exploiting print's unique attributes – the ability to use beautiful photography and to explore issues in more depth than is comfortable for readers to consume online.

I really don't believe in getting our biggest [story] off the print pages. We had a massive shopping centre opening in White City and ran that over six pages with lots of pictures. You just can't do that online. I've got news reporters who work weekly, daily, hourly. They like writing big news stories; they like emailing in stuff on their BlackBerries for the web. They are all gagging to do everything and that's how they need to be. (2008 Personal Communication)

Barrie believes that 'although people have become used to getting their information in quick bursts, good print is irreplaceable, good journalists will always do well, and information isn't journalism'. However, students of magazine journalism who think they are going to make their names in the industry writing beautiful, Will Self-esque copy could be surprised to learn that Barrie now believes his newly created 'web editor', 'may well be the most important person in the office.'

He's a mix of subbing skills, navigating his way around the CMS (content management system), using html and marketing skills, and working with Google and people like that to make sure your number of hits goes up. He's all about pushing up traffic, counting the number of people accessing our breaking news alerts, negotiating with Google as to where our news sits in the pecking order, and constantly checking the Omniture [web analysis] machine, which records how many visitors come onto the site. The technology is amazing: for the first time ever, editors can get instant reader feedback which can actually be quite addictive – if you do a breaking news alert, you can't help wanting to see how many people are reading it. (2008 Personal Communication)

What the web has changed for journalists

Omniture web analysis isn't the only new addiction for magazine practitioners since the internet explosion. Talking to readers via forums, blogs, or email can be another occupational hazard, particularly among editors, who, urged on by their publishers and advertisers to be the chief fountains of all knowledge about their readers, can become so obsessed with 'understanding their readership' that they find talking to them daily becomes an irresistible urge, leaving them oblivious to the piles of proofs accumulating on their desks and the ire of their increasingly hard-pressed production editors who now often have to worry not just about print content but also about their magazine's online offerings as well. Editors and other staff members can also find themselves regularly appearing in videos and podcasts, although magazine guru David Hepworth, Editorial director of Development Hell which publishes *The Word*, sounds a note of caution on this, reminding them that producing material they are not well trained to provide, such as video, can have a negative effect on their brands if it looks like 'cheap telly'.

Magazines doing video – they've got to unlearn an incredible amount of TV language. They still produce a lot of video that looks like cheap telly. Audio is the most flexible, direct way of communicating complicated subtle things to people. There's immense talent within magazines that can be turned towards that. [But] the industry ought to be ... selling people harder on the actual experience of reading a paper product. I look at my own children and they don't read magazines. We need to sell the idea of: wouldn't you like to be in your kitchen on Saturday reading that thing? (McNally, 2008)

Such warnings aside, the online medium offers magazine employees ever more irresistible ways of communicating with their readers. Giles Barrie at *Property Week* now holds *'webinars'* for readers, which are sponsored online seminars offering a detailed look at technical issues of interest to those working in the property sector, such as: *What will the new Homes and Communities Agency mean for you?* Others use the web to ask readers to vote on everything from whether to do a particular feature to who should grace the front cover.

'We gave readers a list of five celebrities and were shocked that Kate Moss ran out the overwhelming winner, even beating J-Lo', said Margi Conklin of her time editing the British women's glossy, *New Woman* (2004–6). 'We imagined that Kate was too cool for our readers but we listened to what they said and used her on our January cover, meeting our sales target in the process' (Nice, 2007a).

The idea that readers can influence magazine content has been disputed by some academics (e.g. Oates, 1999), who claim that magazines – which use ostensibly reader-generated material such as readers' letters, photographs, problems and real life stories – create no more than an 'illusion of reader participation'. This is arguable anyway: writers and editors will inevitably tweak reader contributions to fit the house style but readers' letters aren't generally fabricated and their photographs can't be (Nice, 2007a). But with the rise of the citizen journalist in the online age, user-generated content, particularly for magazines' online provision, is likely to become increasingly addictive to staff who are being required to produce more and more material across multiple platforms. Some experiments are already in place for magazines to be produced entirely from user generated material, such as *Everywhere* magazine (produced in San Francisco by 8020 Media) and *Greece* (Merricks Media) which recently ran what it billed as 'the UK's first User-generated magazine', with a special issue called *Your Greece* produced entirely from reader contributions.

Naturally, many journalists are expressing alarm at the march of the citizen journalist, concerned that this may put them out of a job:

> We are surely moving towards a situation in which relatively small 'core' staffs will process material from freelancers and/or citizen journalists, bloggers, whatever (and there are many who think this business of 'processing' will itself gradually disappear too in an era of what we might call an unmediated media). (Greenslade, 2007)

However, as magazines have always worked fairly closely with their readers the fit may be more comfortable for them than is the case for other media. Magazines have always been, at least ostensibly, about empowering readers and magazine employees know they still have a role to play in making reader contributions as accessible and representative of the brand as they always have. This of course has meant workload implications: it shouldn't be assumed that user-generated content means magazine workers need do nothing more than post content online. But as an NUJ commission on user-generated content has argued:

> The challenge for journalists is to stay one step ahead of their employers. By pre-empting the changes and developments in the industry, journalists will be able to help shape their roles in the way that best suits them ... This is an opportunity to seize the moment and change things for the better. (NUJ Commission on Multi-Media Working, 2007)

What else has the web changed?

Few in the industry would deny that the internet is key to the future of magazines (see Chapter 8), but in order to fully comprehend contemporary practice in the industry one has to appreciate what Jim Douglas, editorial director of Future Publishing, calls the 'big cultural change' that magazine companies have been engaged in over the past decade as they finally begin to work out ways to operate effectively and profitably in a 24-hour media world.

The magazine industry experimented with digital content in the mid-1990s and many magazine employees left their jobs on print publications believing the future lay online. However, with the dot.com crash of March 2000 they swiftly returned to print as they, and the industry, quickly realised they had no idea how to make money from the internet and panic set in.

'A lot of people got burned,' says Sarah Hart, former editor of *Mother and Baby* and *Pregnancy and Birth* (Hart, 2008).

Digital income is still very much a growth area. Giles Barrie (2008 Personal Communication) says: 'We have a turnover of about £15 million a year and only about £1/2 million of that is from the website, chiefly from job advertising and the sponsored webinars.

However, with ad spends beginning to migrate online and publishers working out ever more innovative ways of generating revenue, the picture appears more upbeat than it was a decade ago, at least for some. Says Jim Douglas (2008 Personal Communication): 'It's taken a long time but it [their digital business] has started to really work. Year on year growth for us is in digital. We have a good print business but where we're seeing serious growth is in our digital revenue'.

At *Future*, Douglas and his team have been experimenting with new ways of making money through online advertising, often making up new funding streams as they go along: 'One idea is, if someone's reading our review of a Fendi guitar on our music portal, they might then click to a retailer; then we can take a share of that *click through* or that subsequent sale – the idea being that we should get some benefit because they started their buying journey through us'.

Other financially lucrative arrangements with clients include *deep linking*, where a magazine website has a hyperlink pointing to a specific page or image on another website rather than just to that website's home page, or a tenancy agreement where retailers will be a magazine company's *shopping partner* – a recommended partner for buying goods talked about in the magazine. Reader promotions or *creative solutions*, the technical term for sponsored editorial (generally a feature in the style of a normal magazine feature but paid for by advertisers), are also increasingly prominent online agreements. 'As it ended up working in consumer magazines, creative solutions can work online too', Douglas says. 'Advertisers see a real premium in getting a good level of association, a bespoke editorial promotion with a particular online magazine. Rates for bog standard pop-up banner ads are coming under pressure because there are so many sites and advertisers can buy so many, so they are looking for ways to add value and we try to offer them a more coherent, targeted campaign. It's an exciting time being involved as all this is being worked out'.

The online revolution: implications for journalism

Editorial integrity and the march of advertising

However, while the emphasis on advertising and sponsored editorial grows increasingly strong in an online era some editors fear that editorial integrity and objectivity have never been under greater pressure. This may come as a surprise to various academic critics who often imply that magazine staffs are in league with their advertisers, engaged in a continual conspiracy by encouraging them to seek remedies to their problems through consumerism:

> Most women's magazines help to develop insecurities and anxieties in women by constantly repeated themes in features and advertising. While magazines are not always the initial cause of anxiety, they often encourage and exacerbate these feelings and suggest that increased consumption is the remedy. (McCracken, 1993: 138)

There is some truth in this of course. Sara Cremer, editorial director of customer publishers Redwood, argues that: 'There aren't many editors in the world who aren't very conscious of themselves as marketers ... All magazines are, in the end, a business and I think consumer editors have become more and more aware of that' (Burrell, 2008). Equally, the drive to develop magazines online has been just one part of a process of magazine brand development which has seen magazines branching out into their own radio stations (*Heat, Smash Hits, Kerrang!*), clothing lines (*Elle, Bliss*), CDs (*New Woman, Q, NME*), club nights (*Vice*), awards (*More* Fashion Awards, *Elle* Style Awards) ,and what Giles Barrie (2008) calls 'face to face': 'We do a lot of events where we meet the readers, such as shows, awards dinners, conferences and exhibitions. The hard part is finding the time to do them, but you've got to develop the brand and they're great for that'.

However, while inevitably conscious of market forces, most magazine employees have also traditionally been deeply concerned to maintain a healthy distance from their advertisers and marketing teams. Few editors (let's face it, *no* editors) could get away today with what Gloria Steinem, then editor of *Ms*, did when she banished advertising from her pages after constant pressure to provide a 'supportive editorial atmosphere or complimentary copy' for advertisers (Steinem, 1994: 131). But most will have at least had a go at defending their editorial integrity against the march of advertising. Morrish argues that: 'There is no more vexed issue than the relationship between the editor and the advertising department ... A certain distance is desirable if the independence and integrity of the editorial department is to be maintained' (2003: 103).

Today's editors fear that distance may no longer be possible however. O'Riordan argues:

> With circulation revenues falling, ads are becoming much more important and if you have your brand online, the only way to make money is through ad revenue so it's very difficult for magazines. We are becoming much more of a one stream industry. We used to think the power of the reader mattered more than anything but I'm concerned now that with ads becoming more important it will lead to more advertising led editorial. (2008 Personal Communication)

Sarah Hart echoes her concerns, highlighting the way sponsored editorial can work against what editorial teams have traditionally felt best serves their readers:

> Creative solutions – sponsored copy, columns, special sealed sections... – are tough to flatplan (the process of deciding which material goes on which page). You end up having to split up editorial to fit them in to the point where you can't flatplan in any way that's going to be pretty for your readers. (2008 Personal Communication)

As well as ruining the look and feel of the magazine, 'creative solutions' can also increase the workload on editorial staff, she argues:

> It is in the interests (of an editorial team) to work on the ideas to ensure that nothing is agreed on by the advertising team that will seem completely alien to your readers. Then, when the deal is agreed, [you have to] make sure the copy works for your reader *as well as* the client. There's a lot of compromise. And then you'll have certain advertisers [pulling out] at the last minute because other advertisers are in already so you have to be really on the ball. It can be difficult to get sympathy from your publishers too who often seem to feel that there is a long way to go before the readers will notice what's happening. (Hart, 2008)

The rise of creative solutions and advertising is just one way in which magazine editors feel increasingly under pressure to defend the integrity of their product. Another enemy, which predates the online era, has been what O'Riordan calls 'the crack addiction of *covermounts*', the marketing phenomenon of free gifts on magazines that has enveloped UK magazines since the mid-1990s. The 'covermount' began as a failsafe way of instigating a rapid sales hike for a particular issue, but has now become so ingrained that many publishers are afraid to 'go naked' i.e. let their magazine appear without a complementary gift. Editorial objections to the practice are on ethical grounds – things like bags, vests, and flipflops are produced in the developing world for around 50 cents or less per gift (Rowan, 2001) – and for strong editorial reasons:

> You're essentially buying readers so there's no reader loyalty – you just don't know if they're buying your magazine for the content or because of the gift. (Conklin, 2006 Personal Communication)

The practice may also discourage advertisers, who would question how much readers really engage with editorial – and consequently, with their advertising – when they have bought a magazine purely for its freebie (Nice, 2007a). According to O'Riordan, it represents a runaway train that everyone wants to get off but no one wants to be the first to jump:

> Covermounts eat into your profits and [at *Marie Claire*] we had to pay out more and more on them so it was a business strategy with diminishing returns. You put a bag on and readers just say, I've already got one this month because *Cosmo* has a bag. (2008 Personal Communication)

Yet there is some room for editorial optimism on this. Just before she left *Marie Claire* in 2008, O'Riordan saw glimmerings that her publishers had finally had enough of the practice.

> For the first time, we took the decision to scale them right back and I'm thrilled about that. The problem has been that everybody does them and if *Glamour* has something expensive and we've only got a bar of chocolate, it's not going to do us much good. We did well with a *Body Shop* body cream but we also did well with our big editorial promotion [i.e. with no gift but a 'special issue' approach]. Our 'Eco chic' issue showed, encouragingly, that innovation will still work in magazines – it flew off the shelves even though we took a risk [by covering it] with brown paper packaging – obviously, we could hardly package it in plastic, given the subject matter. It worked because for our readers it's the issue of their lifetime and it's our job to recognise that and reflect it. It really chimed with their lives. (O'Riordan, 2008)

Perhaps, in the end, editorial integrity has a future after all?

Staffing issues

The increased potency of creative solutions and advertising are just two indirect ways in which the internet has contributed to making life more exhausting for magazine employees. A more obvious impact has been the actual experience of setting up new websites in the first place. As Jim Douglas (2008 Personal Communication) argues:

> For a daily paper, (setting up) a web operation is easier logistically: they are already used to the rhythm of daily publishing. But on a magazine, we've been all about producing 164 pages once a month so the challenge (has been) working out how to still make good magazines *and* have a credible web presence. Should you be updating content every five minutes or only when something big happens? Should you update based on user behaviour, i.e. only first thing in the morning and at lunch time because you know that's when people usually look online? We don't want staff sitting around waiting for news to happen either. So, it's been a matter of getting to grips with a different way of publishing. (Douglas, 2008)

The online revolution has also meant some interesting 'restructuring' of staff. *Future* has some people working on the web only, some on print only, and some doing both. (Douglas says 'those are the ones who need to be quite schizophrenic'.) He is upbeat about the process of 're-calibrating teams' and re-educating magazine journalists with new skills, particularly in online news writing and learning to be *'search engine friendly'* (using *'keywords'* to ensure that your stories appear first on the big search engines like Google and Yahoo). However, it has been a challenge financially:

You can't afford to double your resources so you have to work out how to benefit from the content already being created by your magazines – for example, reviews work well in both media. You would think the size of our web team was much bigger considering the volume and content we provide, but you have to cut your cloth. (Douglas, 2008)

For some however, that 'cutting your cloth' process rings alarm bells. The NUJ Commission on Multi-Media Working (2007), which looked at multi-media development across *all* media, found that few companies matched the expansion of their online operations with recruiting extra staff. In their survey, 37 per cent of respondents said that journalists covering all media now worked longer hours and 75 per cent believed online integration had led to increased workloads for some or all staff across all sectors of the union. In some cases internet work had been introduced voluntarily, with staff being asked whether they *wished* for online training. But in most cases compulsory online working had been imposed with little or no negotiation with the union (NUJ, 2007).

Another recent study of British journalism over the past 20 years by the Cardiff University School of Journalism found that while the number of editorial staff in the national press had actually increased slightly during recent decades, journalists were producing three times as much copy as they had done 20 years previously, largely because they were required to produce more versions of stories for multimedia platforms (Lewis et al., 2008, in Hujanen et al., 2008: 96). As with all too many academic explorations of the media, the study omitted to include magazines. However, few magazine employees would dispute its findings. Says one former editor:

In some companies, print journalists have been effectively asked to do another job on top of their current job and that can be hard to manage. It's sold to people as 'we need to grow the brand and it will mean extra skills for you' and a lot of people don't have a problem with that. But at the same time, cost is the big issue – they want to launch these websites but to do it in a way that isn't going to hurt them financially. On one magazine I got my team working across platform, yet still lost head count. I heard a presentation from a newspaper editor about how he'd created 'hubs' and got all his writers and subs working across media and it was really inspiring – but then I spoke to some people who worked there who said it was horrible! That's journalism, though, isn't it? The school of hard knocks. Journalists are notorious for putting up with stuff because we love what we do.

Some journalists, particularly those with news training, would however argue that the online revolution has been extremely positive for them. Sharon Wright, an NCTJ-trained former national newspaper and magazine journalist, added online journalism to her skills set during a stint as senior content editor on Disney's parenting website ukfamily.co.uk. She argues that discovering how 'easily transferable' her journalistic skills were to the internet proved to be an uplifting experience:

> Sometimes I (joked) that I 'used to be a journalist' but actually what (I did there wasn't) so far removed. I still (wrote). I still (commissioned) stories. I still (edited). It's different in that with print, once it's written, it's there forever, whereas with the web you can just go online and change it. But that's no bad thing, especially because, with online, there's nothing between you and the page so there are no subs or editors to spot your mistakes! (Wright, 2008 Personal Communication)

Sharon acknowledges that she found some of the technology difficult at first: 'I used to sit there wondering what on earth people were talking about. All those sophisticated systems with *click maps* which tell you *where* people are clicking on your page and testing your pages' *stickiness*' (the proportion of visitors who enter a site at a particular page and then go on to visit more pages in the site). However, she also adds:

> Now I think it's really exciting to be part of the transition generation, the last group of journalists who've had to learn this new form of communication just as it's taking off. And I don't feel threatened by the technology either. In the end, a story is a story is a story – it's just another way of people communicating with each other – and it's still journalists who know best how to do that. (Wright, 2008 Personal Communication)

Other issues facing magazine practice in the 21st century

Declining standards?

The internet revolution, of course, has not been the only issue facing magazines over the past decade. Some commentators see the profession of journalism as under threat not just from user-generated content and the march of advertising, with its resultant pressure on staff and integrity, but also from a more general decline in journalistic standards per se. Few of the plethora of academic studies of 'tabloidisation', (e.g. Sampson, 1996; Franklin, 1997; Langer, 1998; Sparks and Tulloch, 2000; Allan, 2004; Davies, 2008; etc.), discussing the perceived dumbing down of the media have considered magazines (Bird, 1992, being one of a few notable exceptions; see also Nice, 2007b) (see Chapter 7). But Davies' (2008) ideas, based on the Cardiff study by Lewis et al., about journalists' increased dependence on 'ready made' news rather than their own investigations, rings true for magazines as well. *Cosmopolitan*, for example, was recently censured by the actress Scarlett Johansson after it ran quotes from her, bought from a features agency, about her new husband, which she argued she could not possibly have said since the alleged interview had taken place before she was actually married (Akbar, 2008). Says Sarah Hart (2008 Personal Communication):

'Everyone is using the same global media resources and reporting the same news', a view reflected by the Cardiff/Lewis et al. study which found that 60 per cent of press articles came either from PR material or from wire services, while only 12 per cent of stories showed evidence that their principal facts had been checked (Davies, 2008: 53).

No such survey of the sources of magazine content has ever been undertaken but, if it were, the influence of PR-driven material would be a major factor, as has always been so in a medium that relies heavily on product placement. Magazines' greatest problems with PR however have taken on a new complexion in recent years – with the rise of celebrity journalism.

The rise of celebrity journalism

Celebrity weeklies, which began their rise in the late 80s and early 90s with the launches of *Hello* and *OK!*, really began to ignite in the last decade with the sudden circulation explosion of *Now* and *Heat*, followed by *Closer* (which also includes real life) and a plethora of copycat titles such as *New! Reveal* and *Star*. The academic literature thus far has explored whether an obsession with celebrity represents a 'populist democracy' or a 'cultural decline' (Evans and Hesmondhalgh, 2005: 14–15). For magazine journalists though, an obsession with celebrity culture has meant working in an increasingly crowded market, where magazines are forced to fight over access to the same celebrities and ultimately cede long-held journalistic standards in the process.

'During my time on pop magazines and in the gossip mags it's shocked me the degree of control that PRs have,' says assistant editor of gossip weekly *New*, Jonathan Bown. 'They insist on copy approval, picture approval and constant retouching so you can guarantee that [all your work is] going to be ripped apart at the eleventh hour. Even the celebrities you imagine are desperate for column inches are chancing their arm. Only this week I sent a journalist to do an interview. The person they were speaking to hadn't had particularly good press in the past so this was a very positive piece. But, on press day, we had three hours of PRs 'uming and ahing', until [the piece] finally came back no better than a press release. It's sanitising everything and goes against every journalistic instinct but it's increasingly being seen as the norm and they think they can get away with it. You have PRs sitting in on interviews and a list of things you can't ask which are always the things you want to ask and you have to try to be tenacious and work around it but it's getting harder and harder. They will go through the rules and regulations and in the end everything is off limits except what they want to plug'. (Bown, 2008 Personal Communication)

Bown believes journalists need to fight back, as Piers Morgan did as *Mirror* editor in November 2001 when he banned copy approval in a bid to destroy the power of stars' PRs. However, increased commercial pressures now make this stance increasingly unviable: '[It's always about] do they need you more than you need them?' Bown concedes. 'But in a really competitive market you need to do everything to maintain your position'. Often the only journalistic solution is to be 'really creative with the copy and the way you sell it on the cover. It's a tightrope between what was said in the interview and trying to make the copy as interesting as possible'.

But even this can lead honourable journalists into difficulties. Bown recalls interviewing (a major US celebrity) in New York for *Smash Hits* and finding her so 'inexperienced' that her PR ended up putting words in her mouth rather than leave him with literally nothing to write about: 'I [wanted] to get her to say that she fancied a British male pop star [for a headline] so I asked her: "Who would you like to be locked in a British recording studio with?" She said "Madonna." I actually had to tell her that she wasn't British. Eventually her PR saved her and said "Craig David." It was sad, but she just had nothing to say'.

Disguising the truth about celebrities, to save face for them, and retain often mutually beneficial relationships between star and publication, has, some journalists concede, become a way of life on many magazines. As one writer recalls:

> I interviewed a well known [British] celebrity mum. After weeks of trying to pin her down, even though her 'people' came to us with the idea, I finally got ten minutes with her. The questions, which had to be (agreed) beforehand, were incredibly anodyne but even so she seemed to find them impossible to answer. You've got to wonder when a mum can't think of a single thing that she sings with her kids in the car. Did I put that in though? Of course not.

Magazine journalists who rely on celebrities to sell magazines are becoming increasingly afraid to print the 'truth' about them for fear of offending their 'stars'. While editing *Bliss* this author was faced with a similar dilemma when the *Westlife* pop star Bryan McFadden, a huge idol to readers, expressed a rather sexist attitude to his then pregnant girlfriend Kerry Katona when he made revealing remarks about how she would obviously be giving up 'work' (as a singer in the band *Atomic Kitten*) but he wouldn't be changing any aspect of his life whatsoever. Despite concerns that printing his true feelings uncensored would alienate our readers, who idolised him, as well as the two 'stars' who regularly appeared in *Bliss*, we decided to run his comments, feeling we should allow our readers the courtesy of hearing his true thoughts and judging for themselves. The pair's subsequent bitter divorce perhaps bore out our decision – and neither of them ever complained, or even put up the familiar cry of celebrities who later think better of their own ignorance, that they had been 'misquoted'.

'I would like to think (what we read about celebrities is) 50 per cent true,' says one celebrity journalist. 'To say it's all lies would be an unfair generalisation. Remember Madonna's divorce from Guy Ritchie? For months they were saying nothing was wrong – it's very easy for celebrities to say it's all lies and blame media intrusion. But, strangely enough, it turned out to be right'.

Fifty per cent truth is hardly impressive journalism but the reasons for such a conservative estimate are all too clear to hard pressed magazine journalists who, like the newspaper journalists (or 'churnalists') in Davies book, are 'no longer out gathering news but reduced instead to passive processors of whatever material comes their way, churning out stories, whether real event or PR artifice, important or trivial, true or false' (Davies, 2008: 59).

Bown agrees: 'There's a lot of recycling and not enough new information: you assume readers haven't read everything but in the same five days of course everyone has access to the same stories and pictures. There's a lot of putting stuff together, from all the tabloids and particularly from the web, which has changed things a lot. No sooner have I finished writing a piece, by the time it's back to me, I've got another four things to put in which have just come through from Perez Hilton (the US celebrity gossip website) or wherever'.

Increasing reliance on freelance contributors

The other main issue facing magazines has been falling circulations, particularly in certain, increasingly crowded markets such as the women's monthlies (see Chapter 8). Says Peter Genower (2008 Personal Communication): 'The biggest issue of recent years has been falling circulations, with the women's monthlies, in particular, desperately trying to reinvent themselves'.

One result of this desperation, which is felt particularly acutely by publishers, has been to reduce core staff and employ more freelance contributors who don't get holidays, pensions, or other benefits and thus are a cheaper way to provide content. Project this trend and one possible scenario is a largely casualised workforce, along the lines of the film industry's. David Hepworth has taken this idea and proposed a very different model for employment practices – where publishers contract independent production companies to provide the content for their 'vehicles'. A partial realisation of this has already been put into action by BBC Magazines, who have outsourced the listings content of *Radio Times* to the *Press Association*.

While individual arrangements may have their benefits, as a general trend, an over reliance on freelancers can put magazine staffers under even greater pressure. Just as user-generated content creates its own workload, so freelancers working across numerous publications can often struggle to provide copy in the 'house style' and careful briefings are essential if hard pressed magazine employees aren't going to to end up redoing most of the work themselves. Says Giles Barrie: 'We don't tend to use freelancers as our area is so specialised. They're fine with consumer mags but in B2B (business to business magazines) you have to be a bit more steeped in your industry day to day. There are just a handful of good freelancers in our area and even for them it's hard to be on the pulse with the good ideas' (Barrie, 2008 Personal Communication).

Giles Barrie, however, is in the fortunate position of having 23 editorial staff so his few freelancers' strategy is unusual. Although weeklies often tend to retain fairly large numbers of people (*Grazia*, for example, employs 32 journalists), many other consumer and B2B magazines are following the pattern of the specialist titles and reducing their core staff down to six people or fewer and employing more freelance contributors. Indeed, the development of computer programmes such as *In Design* have literally meant that anyone can produce a magazine from their dining room, as Sarah Todd actually did from 1998–2005 when she edited *Yorkshire Life*.

> Looking back, even I baulk when I realise I used to let them put my home address on the opening page. What about security? But it was a very deliberate ploy to let everyone know I lived in Yorkshire and to create this image of me in my dining room, with the dog. It was very different to working on a national magazine: I didn't have anyone between me and the public so I wasn't shielded to just get on with my job of producing the magazine. The ad people always wanted me to meet clients and even at weekends, readers would be phoning up asking me for tips. It became a way of life and I was only able to take six weeks off when both my children were born. I eventually quit just after my son's first birthday. It had just become too much. (Todd, 2008 Personal Communication)

Todd, who now freelances for the *Yorkshire Post*, *Country Life* and the *Daily Telegraph*, among others, got around her lack of staff (she had just one designer, working from Lancashire) in the way of all magazines with tiny teams – she relied on freelancers, enterprisingly turning them into local 'celebrities' at the same time:

> I had a budget to commission freelancers and photographers and we badged them as our 'experts': the *Yorkshire Life* food and wine editor, the gardening editor, the fashion editor and so on. They became greatly in demand locally and were quite a loyal band who seemed happy to work for us because of the prestige, which was just as well as I wasn't able to pay them until publication and even then the fees weren't high.

This increased reliance on freelancers by many magazine companies has been a boon for some. For Michelle Rawlings (2008 Personal Communication), who freelances from South Yorkshire, one of the major changes of the past ten years has been the extra work generated by an ever-growing crop of competing magazines in some of the weekly markets. 'There are a lot more magazines so they have to pay more to make themselves more attractive to freelancers. And some of them aren't as picky as they used to be and will take stories I wouldn't have been able to sell before because there are so many more of them with spaces to fill'.

But other freelancers talk of 'stagnating rates' (Toner, 2009 Personal Communication) or 'being asked to do twice as much work for the same money'. Eleni Kyriacou (2008 Personal Communication), a former editor who has freelanced for a decade, says the very fact that magazines have been going through a more difficult time with falling circulations and advertising rates has made life tougher than ever for freelancers: 'Because most magazines don't have such big teams, freelancers are having to work much harder. Sometimes what we're being asked for is verging on the ridiculous'. And while working from home has its benefits – chiefly its flexibility, particularly with child care responsibilities – many freelancers do feel vulnerable, knowing they are liable to be dropped by a magazine at any moment and not certain of when exactly they will get paid.

'I think for a lot of women especially it's a lifestyle choice,' says Sarah Hart. 'It can be quite lucrative but you don't get any benefits and the worst thing is when the features editor who's been commissioning you regularly leaves to go freelance too. Suddenly, without warning, your work dries up'. She adds that some of the payment practices towards freelancers are 'a bit difficult'. 'I worked for one company where you didn't get paid until publication [which is a problem particularly if they sit on the story for months at a time]. Budgeting becomes really difficult because companies are thinking about cash flow, not about freelancers paying their mortgages' (Hart, 2008 Personal Communication).

John Toner the NUJ's freelance representative, says the union is often called upon to help its 8000 freelance members chase companies for money.

Freelancers don't get the respect they deserve. Companies see them as dispensable and are quite happy to phone them at short notice, get them to do the work, but then pay no thought to when they will be paid. One example sums it up. A member received an email from a well meaning staff member to tell her the shifts she had been booked in for had been cancelled. 'Never mind', it said, 'you can just put your feet up and watch some daytime TV'. There was just no understanding that she needed to earn a living and that had just been snatched away from her. (2008 Personal Communication)

Toner says freelancers need to be careful of working for start-up companies, who may well commission them to do a lot of work but then may also go bust: 'A lot of people think setting up a magazine is easy but being a good journalist doesn't make you good at business. I spoke to one member recently who was owed £6,000' (2009).

The NUJ has also noticed a worrying trend 'sweeping through' magazine companies where freelancers are asked to sign contracts which will give away their intellectual property rights, meaning that if the company sells on a freelancer's work, they will lose the right to receive any money for it: 'It's vital that freelancers read these contracts, respond to them and try to negotiate. If you ignore them, and continue working for them, then effectively you are agreeing to the terms' (Toner, 2009).

This may be more alarming than many freelancers realise. One magazine company recently had to be dissuaded by the NUJ from including a personal indemnity clause in its contracts, meaning that if anyone tried to sue over a story, the freelancer themselves would now be liable. As Toner says: 'You could lose your house'.

Toner also stresses that there are of course good employers, while North London-based freelancer Moira Holden says the freedom freelancing provides is worth almost any price:

> There's the lovely feeling that my future doesn't rely on whether or not my boss rates me. I can't get fired. Journalism is like politics and showbiz – you can go out of favour overnight. So, being able to rely on your own talents and ability is great, especially if you have a few irons in the fire and are versatile enough to be able to write for magazines, newspapers, and websites. (2008 Personal Communication)

But that aside, Helen Gent a Bedfordshire-based freelancer since 1994, says it's important for journalists not to expect a lot of thanks:

> It takes five seconds to email back and say they have received your copy and maybe ten seconds to say they liked it but that hardly ever happens. Then, out of the blue, when you're working on lots of other deadlines, they'll suddenly contact you and ask for lots more material that they never asked for initially and because you want to keep them sweet, you generally feel you have no choice but to do it. Sometimes you feel, I've been a journalist for 20 years, does my name not have any respect attached to it? Don't I get any Brownie points for being at this so long and for getting my copy in on time? (2008 Personal Communication)

It is worth asking here about how this new landscape will affect the magazine journalists of the future? For a start it is creating dilemmas for those who are training these erstwhile journalists. Should journalism tutors prepare their students for the media landscape as it really is – or for a halcyon image of how it ought to be?

According to Peter Cole director of journalism at the University of Sheffield, the situation requires a mixture of both:

> We must be setting the standards, even if the real world makes it hard for (our students) to achieve them. As with all education, it's aspirational. It's setting big goals, even if ultimately they may be out of reach. But at the same time, we should be shouting out our concerns about the way things are going. Ideally, not in a nostalgic, fogeyish way but in a way that embraces the fact that journalism is changing and that we understand those changes but are still not bashful about saying that some standards, like truth, fairness and accuracy, are there for all time. (2008 Personal Communication)

Similarly, Moira Holden (2008 Personal Communication) says the key to succeeding in an increasingly tough profession is 'a good, basic training in journalism': 'I learned how to cover council meetings, magistrates' courts, crown court, and how to "doorstep". Those skills and experience transfer to any medium of journalism'.

'Any medium' is of course the key to today's training methods with 'convergence' now the buzzword as magazine course leaders at colleges and universities switch their focus away from print exclusivity and endeavour instead to prepare their students for careers in multimedia environments.

The same thing is happening to training within the industry. Margaret Coffey who co-runs ETC, an editorial training consultancy based in Haslemere which provides training courses for most of the leading magazine companies, has found the demand for online skills within the profession has escalated hugely, particularly in the past two years:

> We're constantly called upon to help with the integration between the print side of a magazine business and its online content. Magazines have finally said: 'Oh God, it's really happened. Let's get a website again'. They're realising that they have to have a brand and have got to integrate: they just can't pretend it isn't happening any more. So, we're getting requests for training along the lines of: *How to make your website work* and *How to make your team comfortable thinking across platform*. We still teach how to write news but it's now about how to adapt to a changing environment of shorter attention spans and smaller word counts. The web is the new obsession. (2008 Personal Communication)

But the new focus on preparing magazine trainees and employees across platforms is just one part of a major change in journalism training that has been going on over the past decade in periodical publishing.

About ten years ago, when this author was editing *Bliss* magazine (2000–2001), work experience students tended to be 15 year olds, one of whom, on one particularly memorable occasion, announced: 'I'm sorry, I don't know how to make a cup of tea'. But now work experience is done by highly trained journalism students who can do as much, if not more, than junior staff.

This change was reflected in a 2002 survey by the Journalism Training Forum which found that 98 per cent of all journalists had a degree or postgraduate degree level qualification and nearly half had also taken a postgraduate qualification, usually in journalism, from universities such as Cardiff and City (Wilby, 2008). Of course, there remain many examples of magazine journalists, particularly those over 35, who trained on the job or who got there via nepotism (a common accusation made against the magazine industry in particular), but anecdotal evidence also backs up the view that entry level magazine journalists are increasingly graduates from expensive training courses. Says Will Cooper:

> When I first started, people said 'oh, you don't need qualifications, just enthusiasm and a bit of relevant experience'. But the last three people who were hired at my company (at entry level) had all done journalism qualifications. There's definitely a move away from people just showing an interest (in journalism) to people who come in actually

knowing what they're doing. More and more journalists of my generation have done accredited courses and more and more companies are recognising the need for trained staff. I think in trade magazines in particular, NCTJ qualifications are invaluable. (2008 Personal Communication)

There are two major accreditation bodies, the PTC (Periodicals Training Council) and the NCTJ (National Council for the Training of Journalists). The PTC currently has 13 accredited magazine courses while the NCTJ, which has historically focused more on newspaper training, has five. Both bodies have very different approaches to training – the NCTJ is highly pre-scriptive and requires students to take its own examinations, while the PTC is much more outcome-oriented and relies on its training partners to assess learning. Both hold regular and stringent accreditation visits to ensure indus-try standards are being adhered to and basic requirements include practical, hands-on experience writing news and features, subbing skills, magazine creation, business awareness and media law. Even shorthand, which histori-cally has been rarely seen in magazines offices, is making a comeback.

'Accreditation is increasingly important,' says Loraine Davies (2008 Personal Communication), director of the PTC. 'Universities need it for marketing and for employ-ers it's essential; a guarantee of what you are going to get. Our priority is to promote the value of it to employers and make clear what they will get taking someone from an accredited course, as there is still quite a bit of ignorance as to what accreditation actu-ally means. I heard of one student going for an interview and the editor was NCTJ trained but did not realise they had done an "accredited" course. So it's still about educating people and building stronger partnerships between employers and universities'.

The media's traditional reluctance to value higher education journalism courses has been much documented, having been borne out of a suspicion among many practising journalists that journalism courses were all 'media studies' courses, where not particularly bright students learned, from lectur-ers who had never been in a newsroom, how to disparage the media rather than how to write for them. This view, as unfair on most media studies courses as it is on most students studying journalism (and their tutors), is thankfully becoming increasingly outmoded. Indeed, when Nick Davies sug-gested at the 2008 AJE (Association of Journalism Educators) conference in Sheffield that the as then unwritten 13th chapter of his book *Flat Earth News* was to be about journalism courses taught by staff with no journal-ism experience he was all but laughed out of the room. Things have moved on (if it were ever the case) and the employers who are waking up to this fact and realising that journalism graduates who arrive with experience and training are rather more profitable prospects that someone's niece who has hung around the fashion cupboard for six months and will 'probably do' are already beginning to see the benefits.

Loraine Davies insists that 'industry training is essential from cradle to grave. And you can't stop once you get into the industry. The best people are those who take the trouble to continue their training throughout their careers'. However, despite the many reputable courses for people already working in the industry, including those offered by the PPA (Periodicals Publishers Association) industry training remains piecemeal, under-funded, and 'the first thing to be cut from budgets', according to editorial consultant, Peter Genower, a former editor of *Chat*, *What's on TV* and *TV Times*. This means recruits who are professionally trained from the outset on accredited university courses become even more valuable.

But the current undergraduate and postgraduate training system is not without its difficulties. The arrival of former practitioners into the academy has not always been smooth with ex-journalists often finding that, until they begin publishing in academic journals, they are less appreciated than they might have hoped, considering the large incomes they generate from students keen to gain from their professional expertise. High teaching loads also militate against the time they have available to develop as academic researchers, so in universities in particular, where research publications are all, the career development for 'hackademics' is often limited, leaving many feeling 'bruised by their experiences with more elitist academic colleagues, as well as confused by the sociologese in which some scholars theorise' (Errigo and Franklin, 2004: 47).

The different approaches adopted by the two accrediting bodies have been another issue which has complicated matters, but calls for the NCTJ and PTC to merge have generally been resisted not least because, as Loraine Davies (2008 Personal Communication) says, their basic requirements are always going to differ to some extent:

> There are some core things that remain fundamental for a journalist if you're working in newspapers or magazines and, with all of us having to write online, do video casting and so on, there's an argument for converged journalism training. But for magazines, appreciation of who your reader is is core, which is not true for national newspapers, although it might be more true for regionals. And for us, the feature writing craft is essential, which again is less true for national newspapers. So, while it's easy to say that we should all be converged, we have to be careful that we don't lose the things that differentiate the sectors. (Davies, 2008)

That said, a new Joint Journalism Training Council forum (JJTC), designed to help journalism training in the 'converged multi-media world', was announced in November 2008 after the Society of Editors brought the PTC and NCTJ together with the BCTJ (the Broadcast Journalism Training Council) to produce what NCTJ chief executive Joanne Butcher called 'a coordinated and joint approach to achieving the high journalism standards we are all committed to' (Townend, 2008). So while differences remain, all accrediting groups seem to be moving forward together on convergence.

Less easy to solve are issues of diversity, in a system which now supports only the students who can afford circa £5,000 for a postgraduate course, or increasingly ludicrous undergraduate fees over three years of what will soon be up to £27,000 following recent Government legistlation. The (2002) Journalism Training Forum survey found that more than two-thirds of new entrants to journalism came from 'professional' homes, with fewer than 10 per cent hailing from any kind of working-class background and only 3 per cent from semi-skilled or unskilled occupations: 96 per cent of the journalists surveyed were white (Wilby, 2008). Another survey by the Sutton Trust in 2006 (*The Educational Backgrounds of Leading Journalists*), and also cited by Wilby, found that of the country's 100 leading journalists – national newspaper and broadcast editors, columnists, and news presenters – more than half had been to fee-paying schools and 45 per cent to Oxford or Cambridge. Many in the magazine industry are concerned that, as Loraine Davies (2008 Personal Communication) says, 'diversity is clearly not at the top of the list'. 'You look at students on courses and see that it's not just about race but also about class. And what does it mean for the industry if the only people [working in it are] white middle-class girls?'.

Jonathan Bown (2008), a graduate of De Montfort University's journalism course, argues that geography reinforces the problem. Although there are regional magazine companies, the majority of the magazine media is focused on London and the South East:

> It really bothers me that you need to live in London or within the M25 (to get a job in magazines) which means you get a preponderance of people from privileged backgrounds, ... A passionate, articulate young journalist from Leeds can't necessarily get a job in London because they can't afford to live there and wages are so low ... As a result, you see a lot of laziness in journalism, people who are there simply because they're the only ones with the (financial) means to stick it out. (Bown, 2008)

Lindsay Nicolson, Editorial Director of The National Magazine Company, has also been outspoken on this issue, campaigning against the widespread practice of making aspiring journalists serve their time doing unpaid work experience. This, she says, has contributed to the 'Serena Syndrome', whereby magazines end up being staffed by middle-class people with names like Serena and Rupert because they are the only people who can afford to work for nothing. 'The industry is hideously white, to coin a phrase, and that is reflected in the magazines we produce', she says. 'If you landed from Mars and the first thing you saw was a magazine you would think everyone was white, attractive, and under 40' (Cozens, 2006).

The PTC issued guidelines against unpaid work placements in 2004 in line with the government's minimum wage legislation, insisting that an unpaid placement must be 'likely to last no more than two weeks up to a maximum of four weeks'. Interns (generally taken on for 12 weeks) and students who had recently graduated 'must be paid' at least the statutory minimum wage (PPA online, 2009). The PTC will investigate any infringement of the guidelines, although Loraine Davies (2008 Personal Communication) has dealt with only two incidents of placements lasting too long 'which were immediately rectified as soon as we made the company aware of the rules'. However anecdotal evidence collected from our students suggests that the practice is more widespread. One Sheffield MA Magazine 2008 graduate was asked to work six months for free after a successful internship. Another was offered a 'one day a week' job, with an option to work for free on the other days. Both students declined the offers, wondering how they were expected to live on thin air.

Says Victoria Marston, another 2008 Sheffield graduate now working at *Horse and Hound:* 'I've been really surprised by how supportive the working environment is – it's not *The Devil Wears Prada* at all'. However, she also adds: 'It surprised me how quickly you can slip into taking the "workies" for granted once you have a staff job. It's something I try really hard not to do' (Marston, 2008). Industry, take note?

Conclusion

More academic study of real experiences of magazine journalists working in the field is needed if authentic conclusions are to be drawn about magazine media practices. Hitherto, only Ben Crewe's (2003) study of the men's market demonstrates a comprehensive attempt to actually speak to a variety of senior magazine journalists and explore their backgrounds and motivations, while the two most oft-cited media academic traditions, after Althusser, that magazine employees are either exploited media workers unaware of their role in propping up the status quo or 'cunning publishing entrepreneurs' consciously engaged in a drive to dupe readers into rampant commercialism (Gough-Yates, 2003: 9), are simplistic at best and can't possibly be validated without more detailed research into the personnel staffing magazine newsrooms. This must change, and hopefully will, particularly as more journalists enter academia, bringing with them the access and background knowledge that have restricted much of the (limited) research into magazine *production* so far (see Chapter 6).

That is not to say that academic study of magazines to date has been without merit, not least in its ability to highlight some of the dichotomies and contradictions which those working in the industry day to day may not even have considered; exhaustion, commercial pressures, and trying to do several jobs at once all have a tendency to restrict reflexivity somewhat.

Clearly though, from any perspective, the magazine industry, when under scrutiny, is far from perfect. Journalistic integrity, job security, diversity, and perhaps even the health and sanity of journalists, have arguably never been under greater threat. And yet a (2007) study by Hanna and Sanders found that the number of journalism students in British universities had risen fivefold between 1994/5 and 2004/5, from 415 to 2035 (p. 406), suggesting that the next generation of journalists are even less daunted by low pay (by comparison to many graduate careers), even lower levels of appreciation, and a society that loves nothing more than to blame them for most of its ills than their predecessors.

No such student should go into the industry unaware of the contradictions within it or they will find they are gravely disappointed. One University of Sheffield student journalist remembers an internship where: 'I was devastated when they asked me to write the horoscopes!' Another student journalist found her first job on a leading monthly positively eye opening:

> There was a safety issue with a product but in a features' meeting it was decided that we couldn't report it because the company was one of our biggest advertisers. It really shocked me because my sister (used that product). You kind of have to navigate your own way through it and work out what your priorities are: do you want to get promoted or not?

Such incidents aside however, the 25 journalists interviewed for this chapter all spoke for over an hour because, a few gripes notwithstanding, most were convinced their job was the only thing they could possibly ever want to do, perhaps even more so thanks to the many exciting changes and challenges brought by the new online environment. Says PTC director Loraine Davies who hails from industry rather than journalism:

> I think this is the best sector I have ever worked in. Of course it's competitive but I've never worked in such a supportive and encouraging environment. There really aren't that many divas, OK, but only one or two! (2008 Personal Communication)

And interestingly, it was the person who had been in the industry the longest who was the most upbeat of all. After a magazine career of over 40 years, Peter Genower, argued that magazine journalism has never been better:

> 'It's easy to say everything's got worse but that's actually the opposite of what I've seen. When I look at magazines I worked for in the sixties and seventies I blanch with shame at the ponderous writing, unimaginative photography, and the unexciting look of the pages, one or two notable exceptions aside. We were selling lots more copies then but the truth is we just weren't as good. Now we've sharpened up our connection with our readers, we've employed far better design techniques, and the web has taught us how to really write material in small, punchy sections that are easier to navigate and absorb than anything before. I see so much more to celebrate than to dislike and I don't think magazines have evolved even close to as far as they can'. He smiled, then added: 'So, who knows how much better they will be in another 40 years? I, for one, can't wait!' (Genower, 2008 Personal Communication).

6

THE INTERNATIONAL PERSPECTIVE

In 1962 Marshall McLuhan wrote, ' ... electro-magnetic discoveries have recreated the simultaneous "field" in all human affairs so that the human family now exists under the conditions of a "global village"' (McLuhan and Zingrone, 1995: 126). Although he was writing in the age of television and radio, around the time when Telstar – the first satellite capable of relaying television signals – was launched, this insight can be seen as a prediction of every subsequent development in electronic communication, from mobile phones to the internet, from online bulletin boards to iPad apps.

The phrase 'global village' itself also neatly encapsulates the complex concept of globalisation, by which we mean the ways that national or regional economies and cultures have become intertwined or interdependent through the development of international matrices of trade, transport, and communication. Although globalisation can refer to any number of strands (political, technological, social, cultural), the most salient aspect when considering magazines within a global context is economic – general trade, flows of capital, inward investment, and the formation of joint ventures or subsidiary companies within particular territories.

Chapter 2 highlighted the increasing importance of international syndication and licensing to the political economy of magazine publishing – that is to say, the political economy of magazines in western, developed economies. The most frequently cited example of a 'global' magazine (and certainly the case study most subject to academic analysis) is *Cosmopolitan*, a title that was applied to a succession of periodicals in various genres before settling down in 1965 as a magazine aimed at young, single women; it was edited by Helen Gurley Brown and published by Hearst Magazines, the periodical arm of William Randolph Heart's media empire. It is hard to imagine a more quintessentially American product – rampantly individualistic content created within an unyielding capitalist (and nationalistic) organisation. And yet, to repeat the statistics from the magazine's media kit yet again, *Cosmopolitan* has 58 international editions, is published in 34 languages, and is distributed in 100 countries. Naturally it is available in the rapidly developing economies of the so-called BRIC bloc of countries – Brazil, Russia, India and China – and even though its brand values may be relatively consistent across all its editions, *Cosmopolitan* (or any other title) cannot get away with merely reproducing identical material from the home publication without at least some nod to the local audience (see van Leeuwen and Machin, 2005). Nevertheless, licensing can create a homogeneity on the newsstands that on the one hand may provide comfort for the globetrotting magazine reader but on the other can be disconcerting at best and at worst may be distorting, or even destroying, the national, regional, or local magazine economy.

Earlier in this book I essayed a General Theory of Magazines and although it was intended to describe developed, or mature, magazine markets, the principles underlying it can still hold true in a global context. However, application of the theory needs to be tempered by taking into account the general and specific factors of growth or development that affect the magazine industry.

The eight general conditions are:

1 *Educational reforms increasing literacy*
   There can be no large-scale print media industries without a reading public.
2 *An increased professional and middle class*
   Both Habermas (1989) and Ohmann (1996) are clear about the link between an expanding middle and professional class, the quality and tone of the public sphere, and the demand for cultural and economic capital that magazines often supply.
3 *Increased leisure/conspicuous consumption*
   As with literacy, without the time to read, there can be no mass reading and without the growth of a cult of consumption (Veblen, 1994) the consumer culture within which magazines flourish will not develop.
4 *Mass production of commodities*
   Commodities must be produced in large numbers and with a degree of choice between similar products for consumption to reach the tipping point between purchasing by necessity and purchasing for pleasure.
5 *Concentration of population in towns and cities*
   The agglomeration of potential consumers into geographically compact clusters makes distribution and retail more efficient and practicable.
6 *Efficient national distribution (transport, wholesale, and retail)*
   Without reliable and cost effective infrastructures in transport (road, rail, air), wholesaling (getting goods from factory to market) and retailing (shops, kiosks, hawkers) there is literally no way to stimulate mass consumption.
7 *The development of MARKETING and ADVERTISING*
   Having the means to create a distinction between essentially similar goods and brands and the skills and ability to stimulate consumer desire for those goods and brands goes hand in hand with the development of mass consumption and the need for media platforms in which to express those skills; it also brings with it the need for reliable metrics of sale and readership.

8   *Technological improvements (printing, paper making, digital, phone networks)*
    The development of mass print culture depended on technical improvements to print-
    ing presses and, crucially, paper manufacturing; this continues with the develop-
    ment, extended availability, and reduction in cost of more recent media platforms
    and substrates.

There are two further conditions that are generally applicable to all industry
sectors but which must be specifically aligned to the needs of a particular
industry, in this case magazine publishing:

9   *A well trained workforce*
    This refers to both editorial content providers and advertising sales people.
10 *Skilled management*
    Without skilled managers who understand the particular marketplace within which
    they are operating, the systems and procedures needed for efficient control, and the
    particular requirements demanded of the workforce, the magazine industry will not
    develop fully.

The interplay of the factors above is complex and non-linear, which is to say
it is not possible to infer direct or specific connections between the state of
cultural, social, or economic development and the development of the
magazine industry. Nevertheless, there appear to be a number of evolution-
ary stages that are common across magazine industries worldwide: in other
words, globalised points of progress. Among the most frequently encoun-
tered of these points are:

1   a demand for reading material of good quality as the population receives more education;
2   the provision of infrastructure;
3   the predominance of news magazines in the times of political uncertainty that gener-
    ally precede the acceptance of democratic political structures and/or a market-
    oriented economy;
4   the growth of general interest titles followed by the growth of specialised or niche titles.

Several of these points are referred to in a company profile of Editoria Abril,
which describes itself as the 'undisputed leader in the Brazilian magazine
market' (Duffin and Nacer, 2010: 4), and of its founder Victor Civita that
appeared on the FIPP website in February 2010:

- Brazilians had low reading habits and Victor Civita saw this as an opportunity to
  launch more magazines. 'Make a good magazine and everything else comes along',
  he used to tell journalists that worked for him.
- The local printing plants didn't have the necessary capacity to print, so Civita built his
  own, Abril Distribuidora.
- Created and launched by Roberto Civita in 1968 in a tough military government
  period (1964–1985), the [news] magazine [*Veja*] confronted political censorship and
  the pressures of successive governments.

- Abril itself is a powerful brand. Under the name 'Abril Coleções', the current series of multi-volume books repeat the sales phenomenon experienced in the 1960s and 1970s, when ordinary people began to have access to high quality publications such as the Bible, encyclopaedias, literary classics and cookery books. (FIPP, 2010)

What none of the above does, though, is resolve the chicken-and-egg question of whether developing political-economies are inevitably and ineluctably influenced by western/developed standards. The electricity that powered McLuhan's global village definitely flowed from the USA, just as the juice that has traditionally powered consumer magazine growth – advertising – flows to the globalised brands, as this summary of the situation in Latin America indicates:

> However most of the advertising is found in international women's magazines as opposed to domestic ones. There are noticeable exceptions, such as Claudia in Brazil and Vanidades in Mexico, but local editions of Cosmopolitan, Elle, Marie Claire and Harper's Bazaar still demand the larger share of this type of advertising expenditure. Further growth of pan-regional titles and international imports, particularly from the US, is likely. (FIPP, 2003)

It is significant that a list of the top ten advertisers in Brazilian consumer magazines is headed by the US-based giant corporation Unilever and that a further five of the names are overseas companies (Duffin and Nacer, 2010: 83).

Case studies

The sub-sections that follow comprise brief statistical and discursive overviews of magazine publishing in the four BRIC countries, drawing on data published by the FIPP in *World Magazine Trends 09/10* – the FIPP, by its very nature as an organisation that represents magazines worldwide, is by far the most reliable and comprehensive source of material in this field. India will be given more exposure than the others for reasons that will be explained below.

Brazil

- Auditing body: IVC (Instituto Verificador de Circulação)
- Consumer titles: 3,833 (2007); 3,915 (2008)
- B2B titles: 1898 (2007)
- Retail/subscription ratio: 59/41 (2009)
- Magazine advertising revenue in $US: 1,002m
- Advertising/copy sales ratio: 41/59 (2007)
- Significant growth in titles aimed at: children/pre-teen; teenage girls; women.

The magazine publishing scene in Brazil is dominated by national companies, with only Editora Reader's Digest and Panini Brasil bearing the names of

American- and Italian-based businesses. Of the ten magazine sectors listed in *World Magazine Trends 09/10*, six are headed by Editora Abril's titles and one each by Editora Globo, Editora Caras, Panini Brasil and Editora Reader's Digest.

Advertising revenue, circulation, and the number of titles published have been on upward trends in the last decade, although the projected figures for 2009 and 2010 show a slight dip.

Brazil is a country with a low median age (28.6) and the growth in titles aimed at children and teenagers is a phenomenon that would be worth tracking as it might form an illuminating comparison with the history of teenage titles in the UK.

Russia

- Auditing body: GIPP (Guild of Press Publishers)
- Consumer titles: 20,433 (2008)
- B2B titles: n/a
- Retail/subscription ratio: 71/29**
- Magazine advertising revenue in $US: 2,316m*
- Advertising/copy sales ratio: n/a
- Significant growth in titles aimed at: parents, cooks, business.

* This is for all print publications; no separate figure for magazines
** Data from Tagiev (2006)

International joint ventures or subsidiary companies feature large in Russia's magazine publishing scene – Axel Springer, Burda, Gruner + Jahr (Germany), Condé Nast, Reader's Digest (USA), Sanoma (Netherlands), Hachette Filipacchi (France), and Egmont (Denmark) are all active players.

The business itself appears to be still finding its feet – there are no readily available data for magazine circulation generally and none of the titles listed by *World Magazine Trends 09/10* had an audited circulation figure. The GIPP states that part of its remit is 'developing and introducing civilized market practices, professional standards, and business ethics' (bit.ly/GIPP-mags). The FIPP also draws on data from TNS Russia (part of TNS Gallup Media), which collaborated with Edipresse-Konliga to conduct a National Readership Survey among adults in Moscow, St Petersburg, and the rest of Russia. (See bit.ly/TNSRussia for more details.)

In 2006 Ruslan Tagiev, the media research director for TNS Gallup Media, wrote a summary of the Russian situation for FIPP. Among other points he noted:

... achieving effective distribution outside major cities is difficult, and postal delivery in many areas is unreliable. Russia has its specific single copy distribution system left over from the old Soviet era and this is considered one of the biggest obstacles to growth in the industry. Publishers sell the magazines in bulk to the distributors, who then sell them at kiosks or on the street for whatever price they can get. They do not report back to the publishers on net sales. To enter the retail market and ensure sales, publishers are obliged to transfer the proprietorship for 100 per cent of their title's circulation to the contracting party, according to law. But the publishers do not get the profit the distributors make. Publishers are trying to fight this in different ways. Some print the recommended price on the cover, so that readers do not overpay, some try to negotiate with their distributors, and some with the local authorities. (Tagiev, 2006)

He also notes that 'magazine advertising is far larger than advertising for newspapers. In 2005, US$290 million was spent on newspaper advertising, but an impressive US$580 million was spent in magazines (a growth of 23 per cent year-on-year)'. Current data suggest that magazine sales and advertising revenue have been hard hit by the recession of 2009 but readerships remain relatively stable. The most popular titles overall are in the TV guide and women's sectors.

Transformations in the women's magazine market in Russia – not least the changes caused by moving from a directed economy to a free market – have been studied by Sian Stephenson (2007). In a similar vein, the Aleksanteri Institute of the University of Helsinki has undertaken a major research project into success factors in the Russian magazine market. (More details can be found at http://bit.ly/Aleks-Russ.)

The 2008 report by the Federal Agency for the Press and Mass Communications, *Russian Periodical Press Market: Situation, Trends and Prospects*, can be downloaded from GIPP's home page at http://www.gipp.ru/english/.

India

- Auditing body: Indian Readership Survey (IRS)
- Consumer titles: 73,000*
- B2B titles: n/a
- Retail/subscription ratio: n/a
- Magazine advertising revenue: 11bn INR**
- Advertising/copy sales ratio: n/a
- Significant growth in titles aimed at: niche markets and B2B.
* Total number of magazines
** Ernst & Young 2010, not converted to US$

If China has surprisingly few magazines for the size and variety of its population (see further in chapter), India has an astonishing 73,000 titles. This figure was arrived at by international auditors Ernst & Young in a report compiled for the Association of Indian Magazines (AIM) and presented at that organisation's 2010 Annual Congress (the methodology and survey techniques are not revealed). The report, *The Indian Magazine Segment: Navigating New Growth Avenues*, is a key element in the AIM's mission to fully represent, promote, and consolidate the magazine publishing industry in India and as AIM President Pradeep Gupta notes, there has been no previous document that has comprehensively tracked the magazine industry itself. Indeed, the otherwise comprehensive *Magazine World Trends 09/10* has no data whatsoever for India, although previous editions of the annual have.

As might be expected from such a massive number of titles, the existing market is highly fragmented but at the same time it is ultra-competitive in certain sectors. There are nine languages represented in the survey results, with Hindi emerging as by far the most important: 24,908 (34 per cent) of the titles found are Hindi, with English a distant second (9,692 or 13 per cent). The other languages are, in order of market share: Marathi, Bengali, Tamil, Gujarati, Kannada, Telegu, and Malyalam.

Ernst & Young report that 2,943 magazines were launched in 2009, despite an economic slowdown; in 2008 the number was 3,286. Of these new titles, 40 per cent were Hindi and 15 per cent English. Despite this apparent healthy expansion, the report states:

> The reach of the magazine sector in India is still largely insufficient – more than 300 million literate individuals do not read any publications. (Ernst & Young, 2010: 2)

The market itself is still largely at the stage of evolution that sees news magazines and general interest titles dominating.

However, one of the major problems with the Indian market, from a business perspective, is the lack of reliable metrics: 86 per cent of the companies surveyed were not satisfied with the current measurement metric used by clients and agencies, the Indian Readership Survey (IRS). Among the concerns was the perception that the IRS was more suited to newspapers than magazines as it does not:

> effectively represent the purchasing power of magazine readers ... does not consider other qualitative factors such as the targeted, focused audiences provided by magazines (as against the diverse audiences provided by newspapers who have to cater to a larger mass of readers), the longer shelf life of magazines, and the increased opportunity-to-see (OTS) that magazines have against newspapers. (p. 20)

Metrics is not the only or even the most significant drag on growth in the industry; distribution is seen as an even larger problem:

> More than two-thirds of the respondents believed that the distribution network was ... the most significant issue being faced by the magazine segment ... Most believed that using the government postal service was not a reliable means of distribution, and using private and local courier services was expensive, and could only be used by magazines with very

high cover prices. In addition, they mentioned that the number of kiosks was very limited, and was being further reduced, in certain cases, by city beautification programs, out-of-home tenders, etc. Hence, the certainty of sale would always remain an issue. (p. 19)

One other significant negative factor is the relatively small size of work-force with magazine skills. Whether considering editorial, advertising or management, 'the poaching of personnel is rampant in the magazine segment' (p. 20), which argues the need for specifically focused education and training.

Nevertheless, overseas companies have not been slow to take advantage of economic policies that have freed up the media marketplace, resulting in licensing agreements, joint ventures, and wholly owned subsidiaries. Hearst Magazines, Condé Nast, Dennis Publishing, Bauer Media, Groupe Marie Claire, Haymarket, and BBC Worldwide are just some of the publishers that have brought their global brands to the Indian market – and not just English language versions, either:

Autocar launched a Gujarati version to target the affluent population in Gujarat. Hearst Magazines is also planning to launch the Hindi edition of Cosmopolitan, an up-market fashion magazine, to reach out to a wider audience. World Wide Media [BBC Worldwide's joint venture with the Times of India group] also intends to launch the Hindi version of leading magazine titles such as Top Gear, Hello and Grazia. (p. 13)

There are, of course, strategic business reasons for this. Although English language magazines currently account for the majority share of advertising revenue, advertisers are beginning to focus on regional consumers (outside the big cities) in the higher and middle income groups, whose consumption of media products including magazines is on the increase. Not all publishers are equally sanguine about the prospects for growth; Nick Brett, who occupies a similar position at Worldwide Media in Mumbai as he does at BBC Worldwide in London, sees all the signs as set fair for success, whereas N Ram, editor-in-chief of *The Hindu* newspaper group, which includes the news magazine *Frontline* and the sports magazine *Sportstar*, remains to be convinced, not least because specialised niche titles are likely to remain unaffordable to the majority of people for the foreseeable future.

And it is from niche titles (travel, motoring, interiors) that further growth in the traditional magazine market is expected to come. The B2B sector has also been earmarked, as a result of continued economic growth and the narrowing focus of specialised business communities. However, this is the 'standard' model for a maturing magazine market and it is possible that Ernst & Young have based their predictions on well-established western patterns of development: the Indian market may turn out to be entirely different.

Perhaps most significant are the predictions concerning non-print opportunities and alternative revenue streams such as events and digital delivery.

These are 'expected to account for 20%–50% of total revenues within the next three years' (p. 2), especially in the B2B sector. And, just as in the more mature markets of the west.

> The magazine segment may not yet have successful strategies and business plans in place to profitably monetize the digital space, but it will soon have to address this concern, because global trends are increasingly moving in that direction. The media consumption habits and preferences of consumers are visibly evolving, and this will only be spurred on by the government's 3G and broadband policy. Some other revenue sources that magazine companies will soon need to consider include internet paid publishing and the development of content for the omnipresent mobile phone medium. There is an opportunity here that needs to be harnessed. (Ernst & Young, 2010: 16)

With over 600 million mobile phone owners in India already, and 20 million new subscribers joining them every month (Wade, 2010), that opportunity is massive and, as predicted for China below, the businesses that eventually harness it may well come from outside the traditional media organisations.

China

- Auditing body: CPA (China Periodicals Association) + GAPP (General Administration of Press and Publication)
- Consumer titles: 9,851* (2009)
- B2B titles: 3,000**
- Retail/subscription ratio: n/a
- Magazine advertising revenue in $US: 3,102m (2008)
- Advertising/copy sales ratio: n/a
- Significant growth in titles aimed at: luxury markets

* All magazines; data from GAPP
** Approximate figure from Zhang (2008)

Trying to analyse the magazine market in China is a complicated business. It is not that there is no information available, but that the data are not straightforward and so their interpretation must be highly nuanced. As with almost all of the Chinese economy, magazine publishing is a controlled industry that comes under the aegis of the General Administration of Press and Publication (GAPP).

In order to publish a magazine legally, a publishing licence (*kanhao*) is required and only GAPP can issue these; this is why the official number of magazines in China was stuck at 9,468 until 2007 and then increased to 9,549 in 2008 and 9,851 in 2009. This is a remarkably small number of titles for a population of 1.3 billion people – especially in a country that has enjoyed unprecedented economic growth and which has many regions and regional languages. Even though some magazines do enjoy very large print runs, – *Duzhe*, for example, the Chinese equivalent of *Reader's Digest* is

China's most popular magazine and has a circulation of over 5 million – the per capita consumption remains very low.

Henry He Hailin, of Chinese publishers Family Periodical Group, has suggested that one reason for the lack of growth has been the inability of many magazines to make money:

> ... many of these titles are not making profits from circulation or advertising revenues. It is widely believed that only one third of Chinese magazine publishers make money from their products, and that the other two thirds either break even or make a loss. (Hailin, 2009)

As a result, many magazines are dependent on government subsidies at a time when government economic strategy is aimed at reforming this system and phasing out such subsidies. Furthermore, according to a report by Jiang Xueqing in *China Daily*, only around 1,000 titles are actually available in retail outlets, with the rest being 'research periodicals, academic journals and brochures produced by government departments' (Xueqing, 2010).

However, Chinese publishers are reluctant to relinquish their *kanhao* as this official permission to publish is a valuable asset in itself – particularly where globalised magazine brands are concerned. Overseas publishers are not permitted direct ownership in China but can form joint ventures with, or license their titles to, Chinese publishers – who clearly must be in possession of a *kanhao*. Feng and Frith (2008) examined this in relation to women's magazines but perhaps the most frequently cited example concerns *Rolling Stone*. This venerable rock magazine formed an alliance with the publishers of *Music World*, so that issue 240 of the Chinese magazine became the debut issue of *Rolling Stone China*. However, only that first issue was ever published as the authorities clamped down on the American title for reasons that are said to range from the choice of a slightly subversive cover star to the excessive prominence of the *Rolling Stone* logo (Yuan, 2009).

If the situation surrounding consumer magazines is confusing, that of B2B titles is even more so. On the one hand Zhang claims a long and distinguished history for trade titles in China, a history that was interrupted after 1949 when:

> Those former B2B magazines became business guide publications carrying the content of the respective industrial policies, industrial business trends and industrial exchanges of developmental experiences. The ministries and commissions under the State Council were usually organizers and publishers of these B2B publications. (2008: 55)

When the Chinese economy began to open up in the late 1970s, 'B2B magazines rose again with the development of the new market economy' ,but perhaps tellingly the publication Zhang cites as a pioneer of the new movement is *Computer World*, a title brought to China by IDG (the International Data Group) of the USA and published as a joint venture.

On the other hand, the publisher of trade title *Batteries + Energy Storage Technology* (BEST), which in October 2010 launched a Mandarin version, appears to have a rather different take on the scene. In the press release announcing the launch, Gerry Woolf was quoted as saying: 'Chinese trade magazines have hardly been invented. What passes for them are little better than catalogues and business-to-business communication is something the West can do well in China. Our western advertisers are very excited by the move' (accessed at bit.ly/Woolf-Best).

Older and more experienced China hands, however, may have broader and deeper perspectives to offer. When Paul Woodward left Hong Kong after 25 years in publishing he wrote a detailed but succinct summary of his experiences for *InPublishing*. Looking forwards as well as back, he observed:

> Consumer magazines remain strong in the markets of Asia too although the B2B magazines sector has never been large or healthy and looks unlikely ever to develop in any significant way in terms of print. Companies such as Global Sources (Nasdaq: GSOL) now report half of their revenues coming from online, 30% from events and just 20% from print titles.

And this gives us some indication of where we might look for the competitors of the future:

> they probably won't emerge from among the traditional media companies. I believe that the most interesting media businesses will emerge from the internet in Asia to establish exciting new businesses in events, marketing services and, who knows, even possibly print. Top of my list for this is the Alibaba Group, best known for its Alibaba.com B2B website, now listed in Hong Kong and a hugely profitable, fast-growing business. The group also controls Taobao, the eBay busting B2C site, Alipay, a payment service and Yahoo! China … Alibaba's user base is over 30 million strong and growing fast. With a live database that powerful, they have the capacity to launch almost any media product they can imagine. (Woodward, 2010)

7

THEORISING THE FIELD

Several important aspects of magazine-related theory have already been addressed in Chapter 1 (History) and Chapter 2 (Political Economy). The subject also featured in the introduction of *Mapping the Magazine* (2008), an edited collection of papers from the conferences of the same name held at Cardiff University. Some of the material that follows is expanded from those previous sketches – but the magazine form is so flexible and lends itself to so many different forms of analysis and theorisation, that the study of them is 'inevitably interdisciplinary' (Pykett, 1990: 4). It is also important to look at contemporary parallels and consider how much they, and the debates surrounding them, have really changed. Would those who have debated the content of, say, women's magazines, over almost 30 years (McRobbie, 1978; Ferguson, 1983; Frazer, 1987; Winship, 1987; Ballaster et al., 1991; McCracken, 1993; Hermes, 1995) not have drawn similar conclusions while studying the *Ladies Mercury* and the *Ladies Magazine* (1749) as they have when examining more contemporary titles like *Cosmopolitan*, *New Woman* and *Woman's Own*?

Similarly, the ubiquitous debates about sex in teenage magazines appear to have their origins not in the birth of the teenage glossy in 1995, nor even in the controversial 1970s' *Jackie* – described by McRobbie as forcing readers into a 'false sisterhood' which imprisoned them in a world where all that mattered was finding a man, losing weight, looking one's best and learning to cook (1978: 3). In fact, as Beetham observes, arguments about the reading matter of 'sexually ignorant young girls' and concerns about the use of sex as a 'sensationalist' tactic to boost sales were rife in the 1890s (1996: 115–130), illustrating once again the necessity for a historical frame of reference in the study of magazines.

Magazines' possibly unique ability to contain contradiction, 'as femininity itself is contradictory' (Ballaster et al., 1991: 7), has also been explored, while McRobbie revised her earlier stance and addressed a new question: if the current women's magazines aren't 'good enough' what sort of women's magazines do feminists want to see, bearing in mind that they would need to be something that readers would actually want to buy. (McRobbie, 1999).

On the teen side, the perspective of 'concern' (Hermes, 1995: 1) has perhaps unsurprisingly been even more acute, particularly in the area of body and body image. The fear expressed in Evans et al. that teenage magazines propound 'an underlying value that the road to happiness is attracting males for a successful, heterosexual life by way of physical beautification' (1991: 110) has been oft repeated (e.g.Tiggeman et al., 2005; Lin and Reid, 2008) but here too there are cross-currents of alternative readings, with McRobbie pointing out 'the overall message to girls to be assertive, confident and supportive of each other'and 'to insist on being treated as equals by men and boyfriends, and on being able to say no when they want to' (1999: 55), while others (Buckingham, 1993; Currie, 1999; Duke, 2000) have implied that teenage readers may be far more capable of rejecting magazine messages than previous scholarship has asserted. In fact it is teenagers themselves who have had the last word on this matter, rejecting formerly popular titles like *Just 17* and *Smash Hits* so completely that they ceased publication (see Appendix 1).

Some work has also been conducted on magazines for men, more accurately, in the sub-category identified as LadMags, which are seen as a 'significant site' (Gauntlett, 2008: 154) for discourses about male masculinity and identity.This work considers the impact on modern male masculinities of one-dimensional texts that override feminism, treat women as sex objects, and reinforce gender polarities. (e.g. Jackson et al., 2001; Benwell, 2003; Crewe, 2003).

Margaret Beetham's attempt to provide a theorised definition of the periodical, which she calls 'the characteristic modern form of print' (1990: 19), certainly touches on a number of important facets of the form, but she focuses particularly on the relationship to time, the actual periodicity.This is relevant to regularly issued print magazines but, as we have seen earlier, periodicity is no longer a defining characteristic of the magazine in its modern embodiment. Her conclusion however, 'We need ... to develop a theory of the periodical as a genre', remains pertinent, especially in the particular genre of magazines.

One of the key aspects of magazines is their potential to assist the transformation of subcultural phenomena or emergent socio-cultural formations into mainstream culture. This has been commented on by scholars from such different backgrounds as Hebdige (1979; marginal youth subcultures moving to centre stage), Habermas (1989; the emergence of the bourgeois public sphere), Ohmann (1996; the formation of the Professional Managerial Class) and Moeran (2006; fashion magazine narratives help shape identity), and their conclusions lead to the proposition that the magazine is an important space for the formation, playing out, and resolution of such a transformative struggle.

Richard Altick, the scholar of literacy, found a similar sentiment in a book published by Thomas Constable in 1873:

'The lower orders,' a correspondent wrote to Archibald Constable in 1825, 'at present are somewhat in the same situation in which the higher and middling ranks were at the time when Mr. Addison and the other authors of the Spectator, etc., took them in hand, and contributed so much to their improvement by dealing out to them constant doses of religious, moral, philosophical, critical, literary sentiment and information, and may be said to have formed the minds of the better orders for successive generations'. (1957: 331–332)

Magazines also feature largely in what Habermas calls 'representative publicness' (1989: 9), a concept elaborated by Richard Ohmann (1996) who makes the claim that some magazines of the late nineteenth and early twentieth centuries, titles such as *Munsey's*, were not simply aimed at the emergent middle class, or the Professional and Managerial Class (PMC) as Ohmann characterises them, but that they actually assisted that class to emerge both as a social formation and as a set of consumers. In this view, then, magazines may both chart small or emergent social formations and contribute to their promotion from 'emergent' to 'mainstream'.

This seems to reinforce the earlier citation from Conboy, who perceives magazines to be 'heralds of social and cultural change' (2004: 163), and to lend more weight to Valerie Korinek's belief that as magazines generally have a longer lifespan than 'television programmes, movies, music, and other examples of popular culture', they therefore offer a window of opportunity covering perhaps decades to analyse and observe the changing 'concerns of their readers and the communities they serve' (2000: 3). Putting this concept into a specific time frame, Walter Houghton, editor of the 1966 edition of the *Wellesley Index to Victorian Periodicals*, noted:

> ... there are some aspects of Victorian culture, minor ones, no doubt, but parts of the total picture which simply do not exist in published books, or if they do, are entirely hidden because there is no subject index to Victorian ideas and attitudes ... Also, because reviews and magazines reflect the current situation, they are indispensable for the study of opinion at a given moment or in a short span of years. (1966: xv)

As has already been noted elsewhere, academic work focusing specifically on current magazine journalism is relatively sparse, considering the ubiquity and popularity of the genre, and disproportionately focused on women's titles. However, Victorian periodicals have also received significant critical attention and in this context Pykett (1990) elaborates the potential to draw the study of magazines into broader theoretical traditions and methodologies that range from political theory to sociology and cultural studies.

Questions concerning the impact of the mass media on audiences (from the Frankfurt School's perspective to Fiske) lend themselves to analysis through magazines, as does the underpinning of much feminist criticism in discourse analysis (especially Foucault), structuralism (especially Althusser), semiotics (Barthes, Williams), and social theory (Gramsci). The relevance of culturalist perspectives such as Hall's encoding/decoding model with its emphasis on the possibility of 'alternative readings' of texts is also obvious.

However, in order to facilitate an initial taxonomy of magazine theory, we can categorise approaches under the headings of social, cultural, psychological, economic, and business factors.

Socio-cultural conditions: many magazines for the few

The technological advances that permitted the physical production of magazines to expand so enormously in the Victorian period were noted in Chapter 1, but whatever the technical possibilities there can be no sustainable expansion of output, no increase in consumption, without a corresponding demand from consumers – in this case, readers. And expansion there was:

> The upsurge in consumer magazine publishing ... came in the second half of the [19th] century. The popular family journals *Titbits* and *Answers* were selling 900,000 copies per week in the 1880s and 1890s, while the number of women's magazine titles grew from four in 1846 to fifty by 1900. (Nevett, in Vann and Van Arsdel, 1994: 223)

It is possible to identify many arguments and theories concerning the increase in demand for magazines, and specialised magazines in particular. Some of the headings under which these can be analysed are identity, psychology, society, economy, publisher theory and culture.

Identity

Although both Valerie Korinek ('One of the reasons that *Chatelaine*, along with many cultural products addressed largely to women, has, until recently, been ignored by scholars is the disdain accorded to commercial women's magazines'; 2000: 9) and Joke Hermes ('The field of research concerned with women's media, and in particular with women's magazines, confirms at a glance that it is a marginal area that is neglected by mainstream academic research'; 1995: 149) have complained that the study of women's magazines has been overlooked or marginalised, the already stated fact is that there is a far larger body of work devoted to the examination and interpretation of women's magazines than any other magazine sector. In many ways the story of magazine studies is also the story of women's magazines. The pioneering works in the canon – Friedan's *The Feminine Mystique* (1963), Cynthia White's *Women's Magazines 1693–1968* (1970), Marjorie Ferguson's *Forever Feminine* (1983), and Janice Winship's *Inside Women's Magazines* (1987) – all examine aspects of the same subject and have inspired many of the more recent studies.

Ballaster et al. provide a useful precedent by sub-categorising these works into 'two "dominant" analyses of women's magazines' (1991: 2), which may be characterised as: i) the baleful influence and ii) the bringer of pleasure. However, there are grounds for establishing a third category into which some recent studies would fit – namely positive resistance. This is, of course, an extremely crude taxonomy because the works themselves, especially if they are surveying the territory, frequently have leaky boundaries.

The baleful influence

Betty Friedan's *Feminine Mystique* (1963) is usually credited with founding this sub-category and maintains a steady influence as 'the starting point for all researchers of women's magazines' (Korinek, 2000: 10). Friedan's argument was that women's magazines peddled a false image of a woman's role in the world, the family, and the house and thereby lowered women's expectations of their lives, kept them in thrall to patriarchy and consumerism, and inculcated the 'problem that has no name' for which Friedan coined that famous phrase (1963: 19).

As later critics have pointed out, however, Friedan focused on the fiction published in women's magazines rather than the overall editorial and this, together with her reliance on a 'dominant ideology' approach (Ballaster et al., 1991: 21), has rendered her conclusions problematic.

Friedan's book was, in any case, not mainly about women's magazines. A more comprehensive approach was taken by Cynthia White, who set out her objectives for *Women's Magazines 1693–1968* very clearly. Her concern was to

> ascertain what is actually being communicated to women, week by week, both as an initial step in estimating the nature and extent of the influence of the women's press, and to provide a basis for an evaluation of the medium in sociological terms ... Correct interpretation ... depends upon the ability of the researcher to supply an historical perspective in the field of publishing for women. (1970: 17)

The result is a classic of magazine studies encompassing social trends, demographics, commercial and technological developments, and content analysis. White undertook it as a sociological project and her conclusions fall firmly within the baleful influence category:

> The vast majority of women's periodicals are by tradition trend-followers rather than trend-setters. The status quo is their frame of reference and the image of women they convey is a conventional one ... This has meant that no significant modifications in the frame work for women's periodicals could take place without having been preceded by corresponding changes in the social condition of women. (p. 279)

White's work is widely acknowledged as a milestone but perhaps because its theoretical underpinnings subscribe to a dominant ideology, the book has been called on as a 'valuable historical study' (Ferguson, 1983: 194) and 'a detailed publishing history' (Ballaster et al., 1991: vii) by other researchers.

Marjorie Ferguson moves the argument along with the help of Emile Durkheim's theories on religion; although she still ascribes a highly normative role to women's magazines, which, she argues, 'comprise a social institution which serves to foster and maintain a cult of femininity' (1983: 184). She also allows that they 'set out to foster a woman's sense of her own worth' and 'preach the ideal of a woman's power of self-determination' (p. 185). This is still a dominant ideology model but it does allow the consumer some agency to change herself and – unlike White – Ferguson's content analyses lead her to conclude that magazines are 'sometimes leading, sometimes lagging behind, the attitudes and actions of their followers' (p. 186). However, Ferguson concludes that despite the conflict between the positions of defined norms and self-help, the resolution is that the message continues to be that 'within the cult of femininity ... Woman remains the cult object ... and Man remains the goal ...' (p. 190).

Ferguson's study has another interesting aspect which is sometimes overlooked; as a former journalist she had been privy to the internal workings of magazines as commercial and editorial entities and she includes not only her own awareness but she also interviews editors for their opinions and explanations of what they do (and what they try to achieve). Although this additional input permits a contrast with the academic point of view, there is still a major voice missing from *Forever Feminine* – the reader's.

Perhaps because of that missing voice there has so far been little to indicate why, if women's magazines are such normative, baleful influences, women would read them. The simple answer, identified instantly and unambiguously by Ballaster et al., is that they give readers pleasure.

Bringers of pleasure

Bringing pleasure is not, naturally, without its problems, especially where academic analysis is concerned. *Women's Worlds* (Ballaster et al., 1991) is predicated on the fact that magazines are highly problematic constructs, offering conflicting versions of femininity, excluding or making deviant anyone who does not fall within the editorial idea of the reader ('self-evidently middle-class, white and heterosexual' p. 9). The authors are familiar with the tropes of editorial rhetoric – the emphasis on differentiation, the focus on lifestyle and the personal – but consistently dismiss them as effects of the economic system:

> The differentiation of the female reader is then bound up with the exigencies of capitalist markets; collective character is determined by what we (are able to) buy. (p.11)

On the other hand, the authors readily admit that 'consumption is, undeniably, pleasurable ... we cannot afford simply to reject it as cultural brainwashing' (p. 15).

Their project, like Ferguson's, is to establish that women's magazines assist in the construction of femininity, or gender identity/difference, but rather than taking the religious theories of Durkheim as their starting point they adopt the tools of discourse and ideology. Their position is that women's magazines are addressing 'women' as a class and that concepts of differentiation are functions of capitalist consumerism, but at the same time they are able to note that human subjectivity is split and fragmentary and that

> This formulation of subjectivity as radically split resonates with both feminist experience and theory: women are addressed as sensible mothers of three by one magazine, single pursuers of the ultimate sexual fix by another, as feminists by a third. (p. 25)

Precisely so – but they have already identified the answer to this problem by also noting that publishers differentiate between types of reader (or different lifestyles) because while there may be only one meta-class of women, there are many different groups of women within that class. It is hard to understand the need to wrestle with this non-conundrum and they answer it again on page 77: 'Publishing ... depended on identifying or creating markets in order to make profit, as it still does'.

There are also points where the authors appear to claim that the only kind of magazines produced are women's magazines. Commenting on the heterogeneity of the magazine as a factor in the success of the form, they note:

> It does not demand to be read from front to back, nor in any particular order, and its fragmentary nature is admirably suited to women's habitual experience in modern society of the impossibility of concentrated attention (distracted by calls on their time from men, children, to conflicting demands of work and home). (p. 30)

Although there may be specific factors cited here which affect women more than men, it is nevertheless true that very similar comments could be applied to magazines targeted mainly at men. The magazine is a successful textual form because of its miscellaneous nature; successful magazines achieve that success by addressing the interests of a specific group of readers. However, not all magazines which succeed in those terms necessarily succeed in commercial terms.

Another example:

> The history of the development of the women's magazine as a commodity is also the history of the construction of the woman as a consumer, and it is the peculiar and specific relation of these two factors that gives the women's magazine its distinct and separate place within the economic and ideological determinants of the publishing industry. (p. 47)

Substitute any social or consumer group you like for 'woman' and the statement remains true.

Nevertheless, although it is possible to take issue with some of their specific observations, what Ballaster et al. do very successfully is to position the magazine as a site of serious study thanks to their sweeping and rigorous overview of the theories of text and culture which have been and might be used to analyse the form.

Although *Women's Worlds* does subscribe in large part to the baleful influence school, it goes beyond a dominant ideology to allow the reader a degree of agency and this is reflected in the use, and reproduction, of interviews with several groups of readers to try to discover how they actually use or interact with various magazines. The book's historical analysis is prefaced with:

> The pleasures which women's magazines offer their readers are not simply liberating nor simply repressive but themselves participate in and contribute to this constant making and remaking of cultural definitions. (p. 36)

and the authors' conclusion is that

> Throughout their history, women's magazines have offered their readers a privileged space, or world, within which to construct and explore the female self. (p. 176)

But this must be balanced against the judgment from an academic height that 'it is not our view that the constructions of femininity we find in magazines are harmless and innocuous' (p. 131) or the musing of 'should we be seeking to do away with the form altogether, rather than writing a book about it, sensitive to its pleasures?' (p. 173).

Positive resistance

Joke Hermes takes issue with this *de haut en bas* attitude in *Reading Women's Magazines*, her 1995 study of the actual ways in which women read, use, and value the publications aimed at them. On the very first page of the book she declares:

> Almost all of these studies show *concern* rather than *respect* for those who read women's magazines [italics in original] ... The worry and concern in older feminist media criticism lead to a highly unequal relationship between the feminist author and 'ordinary women' ... Feminists using modernity discourse speak on behalf of others who are, implicitly, thought to be unable to see for themselves how bad such media texts as women's magazines are. They need to be enlightened; they need good feminist texts in order to be saved from their false consciousnesses and to live a life free of false depictions as mediated by women's magazines, of where a woman might find happiness. (p. 1)

For her own part she starts with the 'appreciation that readers are producers of meaning rather than the cultural dupes of the media institutions' (p. 5) and this leads, via her interviews with readers, to conclude that

> Women's magazines of all kinds address what readers perceive as sensitive areas that they have less control over than they would like to have. Thus, like other media, women's magazines are used indirectly in identity building and maintenance, which is an important part of attaching generalized, evaluative significance to texts. (p. 27)

This makes it sound as though the magazines have a peripheral role in their readers' lives – and one of the things which Hermes found both surprising and (initially) disappointing was that her interviewees had so little to say about their reading matter. But on reflection she finds this to be entirely appropriate. Magazines aimed at women, unlike those aimed at girls, 'do not create audiences that develop strong narrative interests or cult followings' (p. 14) and this leads on to another important insight. The texts of popular culture should be taken seriously but that does not mean they should be treated in the same way as high culture, for

> there are dire consequences to such an approach: general, everyday media use is identified with attentive and meaningful reading of specific texts, and that is precisely what it is not.

> Media use is not always meaningful. From time to time it is virtually meaningless or at least a secondary activity. (p.15)

Hermes then interprets her findings using the concept of the 'interpretive repertoire', which allows her to categorise the everyday uses of reading. Among those repertoires are Practical Knowledge, Emotional Learning, Melodrama, and Moral Duty, but one of the most important – if not *the* most important – is Relaxation: the magazine is easy to pick up and just as easy to put down; it fulfils the same function as a cup of tea.

Richard Altick can be called on again to find a historical parallel here, for he observes that William and Robert Chambers, Edinburgh publishers, started the successful *Chambers's Edinburgh Journal* (1832), followed in 1833 by an extensive series of books aimed at the common reader:

> All these publications were devised on the shrewd theory that most readers disliked reading too long upon a single subject; therefore they resembled magazines more than books, offering potpourris of science, geography, history, literature, fireside amusements, and other material with popular appeal. (1957: 280)

Or again:

> Great as was the increase in book production between 1800 and 1900, the expansion of the periodical industry was greater still. This was only natural, for of all forms of reading matter, periodicals – including newspapers – are best adapted to the needs of a mass audience. They appeal to millions of men and women who consider the reading of a whole book too formidable a task even to be attempted. They can be read straight

through in an hour or two, or picked up for a few minutes at a time; for on the whole they do not require sustained attention, having been dedicated from their earliest days to the principle of variety. (p. 318)

Comparing magazines (or popular books) to a cup of tea might seem to give them an insignificant role but there are many publishers who would be glad to have their traditional wisdom underwritten in this way and many academics who would agree. If the magazine is a source of relaxation, something to be turned to in one's own time and space, it most certainly can be taken and trusted as a 'friend' (Beetham, 1996: 81: 'I ... feel as if we were friends.', quoting a correspondent to the *Englishwoman's Domestic Magazine* in 1874; Korinek, 2000: 71; Consterdine, 2002: 6).

Like Hermes, Valerie Korinek sees readers as agents rather than simply receivers. Her study is of a single magazine for Canadian women (*Chatelaine*) but her access to the surviving editorial staff and to the archives of reader and corporate correspondence gives *Roughing it in the Suburbs* (2000) an unparalleled depth. Using this material in conjunction with cultural theories from Foucault and Fiske she is able to claim that

Ultimately, *Chatelaine* readers were active readers, and their interaction with the variety of material published in the magazine provides a full portrait not only of the content of *Chatelaine* in the fifties and sixties but of the way in which the readership community negotiated these messages. (p. 21)

Korinek spends some time focusing on the production of the magazine. Unlike many other feminist studies, she does not assume that media producers have one agenda, or uniform goals about the product; her research – with the people who produced the magazine – shows it to be a site that is, in fact, 'highly contested' (p. 31). In this context she also notes that: 'Magazines occupy an intriguing place within the mass media. Like newspapers, they are a print medium, but in composition they are equal parts print and illustration, editorial copy and advertising material' (p. 73).

And on the subject of the magazine as a 'friend', Korinek discovers evidence that magazines can foster actual social interaction. After quoting a reader's letter praising *Chatelaine* as an aid to conversational topics, she notes:

Her [a reader's] analysis of magazines as a common currency among women, or as a stimulus to conversations, was often repeated. Magazines served a social function and were not merely solitary pleasures. (p. 77)

This idea is reinforced when Korinek focuses on *Chatelaine* in the 1960s as a focal point of the Canadian feminist movement, which 'had an unofficial leader in Doris Anderson' (p. 309), the editor. Korinek cites some editorial examples to demonstrate the magazine's progressive stance, about which she states: 'For a mass-market women's magazine, they are astonishing' (p. 313). That said, she moves on to show that the editor was often frustrated at the lack of impact which such material had among many of the readers (p. 314), raising the perennial question about the media – do they lead or do they follow public opinion?

Korinek does not essay a direct answer to this question, but does, thanks to extensive quotes from correspondence in response to various articles, point to a different possibility – the fostering of debate. If *Chatelaine* did not directly lead opinion it could certainly get readers to react; sometimes this was expressed as a knee-jerk negativity, but there were plenty of readers who seemed glad to have something to think about and who were grateful for the information to help them form opinions. Repeated in enough individual cases over enough years, this could very easily influence the national debate. On the other hand, Korinek concludes that one of the reasons *Chatelaine* changed from a 'closet feminist' publication to a glossy fashion magazine was that circulation fell as readers tired of activism and demanded a return to a more entertaining tone.

Nevertheless, this is an important point – it seems entirely feasible to claim that magazines can exert an influence on the social agenda. Taken in conjunction with Hermes' findings that magazines seemed to have little direct importance, that they were adjuncts to everyday experience and thus not privileged sources, it helps to explain the understated significance of magazines as agents of social and cultural change: the individual effect may be weak but the cumulative effect of those individuals when combined may help to shape trends in everyday life.

Psychology

In his detailed (1997) study of the popular magazine, David Reed draws on Festinger's theory of cognitive dissonance to explain the boom in specialist titles. Festinger proposes that the individual will go to great lengths to avoid contradiction, or dissonance, with either the self or others, and will prefer its opposite or consonance. This leads to the hypotheses that:

1 The existence of dissonance, being psychologically uncomfortable, will motivate the person to try to reduce the dissonance and achieve consonance.
2 When dissonance is present, in addition to trying to reduce it, the person will actively avoid situations and information which would likely increase the dissonance. (Festinger, 1962: 3)

Reed uses these proposals and their subsequent refinements to suggest that Festinger's work 'exposes the psychological roots that nourish the fragmentation of the magazine trade into its special interest sectors, the cynosures that pad the mental cell. Women's magazines for women. Financial reports for financiers' (1997: 10–11).

Up to a point, perhaps. Financiers want financial reports not just because they help promote consonance but also because they provide the necessary information to allow them to work effectively. Women want women's magazines for all sorts of reasons, information and entertainment being among these (see above). But any individual is more than just a single thing; the financier might read a financial magazine for work and a gardening magazine for leisure; a female financier might also choose to read a woman's magazine at home.

As Joke Hermes found when she was researching women's magazines:

> Commercial market research would lead you to believe that each category [of Hermes' informants] reads a particular kind of magazine, but they do not. Home-makers do not necessarily read domestic weeklies, and high-powered executives do not exclusively read expensive glossies ... Rather, readers read unpredictable and changing combinations of magazines. (1995: 144)

According to Festinger's theory, people will actively seek information that might reduce dissonance and actively avoid information which might increase it (1962: 22); further, they will be highly selective about this and turn to sources expected to 'add new elements which would increase consonance but ... avoid sources which would increase dissonance' (p. 30). This could certainly be used to build a theory as to why people look for magazines (as sources of information) which cover particular topics, and why they might buy one magazine rather than another (because the editorial tone is more or less dissonant), but it does not explain the creation of those magazines in the first place.

Some of the other work which Festinger draws on might well be useful to a study of how it is that people develop strong relationships with magazines, or how the opinions expressed in magazines affect readers' own opinions. For example, he cites Osgood and Tannenbaum's findings that in circumstances where a person's well regarded source of information supports positively (or negatively) an opinion which that person regards negatively (or positively) there is 'a marked tendency in that person to change either the evaluation of the opinion involved or the evaluation of the source in a direction which would reduce the dissonance' (Festinger, 1962: 8).

Thus a magazine reader encountering a piece of writing which ran contrary to her or his own beliefs or opinions might either have a change of mind about the topic being written about or might conclude that the magazine was no longer worth reading and look around for a different one. This gives us a plausible factor to help explain why there is often a proliferation of titles within a specialist sector, but it is not the only reason. Taken to extremes, the avoidance of dissonance would see every individual wanting to read a personalised periodical (the 'daily me' proposed by Nicholas Negroponte in *Being Digital*, 1995). The dictates of commerce make this a highly unlikely scenario (although the dictates of personal communication technology have made it a reality).

The theory of dissonance cannot, in and of itself, account for the provenance of specialist periodicals. Festinger states that dissonance may arise from a number of sources (1962: 14) and that the empirical measurement of consonance and dissonance presents serious difficulties. He also encourages the reader to remember that 'two cognitive elements may be dissonant for a person living in one culture and not for a person living in another, or for a person with one set of experiences and not for a person with another' (p. 15). Culture and experience, then, play an important part here.

There is, however, another point which may be even more germane. In an example that concerns a person's decision to attend or not attend a lecture on 'The Advantages of Automobiles with Very High Horsepower Engines' (p. 123), Festinger acknowledges that 'acquiring such information, particularly if it is connected with some interest or hobby, seems to function as a satisfaction in itself for many people. Active curiosity and the sheer pleasure of acquiring information for its own sake cannot be ignored in any discussion of voluntary seeking out of new information' (p. 124). Consonance and dissonance may have nothing whatsoever to do with it.

Society

There is also a social side to Festinger's argument. To avoid dissonance a person will tend to consort with others who are like-minded and avoid those who hold contrary opinions, leading to the conclusion that processes of 'social communication and social influence are ... inextricably interwoven with processes of creation and reduction of dissonance' (1962: 177). Again, this may help to account for the formation of 'communities' around particular magazines but it does not explain the initial existence of those magazines.

David Abrahamson also argues for a social reason to explain the rise of the specialist magazine. He uses a theory propounded by Jean-Louis Servan-Schreiber to the effect that, 'A general increase in social tolerance may have allowed the greater assertion of freedoms and tastes. This ... produced new, smaller social groupings which smaller, more specialized magazines could effectively address' (Abrahamson, 1996b: 25; see also Servan-Schreiber, 1987).

Abrahamson is referring to the 1950s and 60s, but as with printing and production processes, similar arguments can be applied to Victorian times. Notions of the construction of society had been changing since the decline of feudalism; first mercantilism and then industrialisation brought in their wakes a range of new social consciousnesses. Periodical literature not only appealed to those new sectors, it also helped to define them. In an overview of research in this area, Jon Klancher observes: 'The new work has been showing diverse reading audiences that were as much constructed by their texts as they were defined by social structure and historical change' before concluding: 'The English periodicals arose to construct, differentiate and develop reading audiences large and small, publics that did not simply already exist passively waiting for something to read' (Klancher, in Coyle et al., 1990: 876, 886).

Klancher refers not only to periodicals in the Poolean tradition, high-minded literary and political titles like the *Quarterly Review* and *Blackwood's*, but also to those catering for a radical working-class readership. He pays particular tribute to Katherine Shevelow's (1989) study of the *Athenian Mercury* and that publication's effect on the 'separation of male and female reading' (Klancher, in Coyle et al., 1990: 884). He has little time, however, for the notion that the commercial market was itself an important force for social change among readers – or at least that it is a notion that should be given critical respectability. 'Celebrating the "democracy of print" without a concept of ideology finally means ratifying commodity fetishism as the unspoken historical mode of the "reading habit"' (p. 880), he writes, before commenting on the intellectual integrity of the 'conservative or backward-looking' efforts of Queenie Leavis, rather in the manner of a union official bemoaning the uncertainty of a political landscape that did not have a Margaret Thatcher figure to militate against.

No study of periodicals in the Victorian period can afford to overlook market forces as at least one element in the force of social change, if only because of the fact that those publications which did not succeed commercially were not around long to effect the consciousness of even the smallest number of readers. Curran makes the point that market-led advertising revenue replaced formal state controls on the press like the stamp duty and advertising tax. When the tax was halved in 1833 the result was an increase in London advertising of 35 per cent and 27 per cent in the provinces (Curran et al., 1977: 216). A complete repeal of the tax in 1853 'transformed the economic structure of popular publishing ... Advertisers acquired a de facto licensing authority since, without their support, newspaper ceased to be economically viable' (p. 217).

This growth in advertising and marketing as a profession (or at the very least as an increasingly well defined area of business) also had an effect, and according to Curran et al. it was one that skewed the development of periodical publishing in a particular direction. Thus, one of the largest advertising agencies of its time categorised every newspaper in the country according to its political allegiance and this in turn led to a situation in which the 'working-class media were consistently discriminated against on the grounds that their audiences did not constitute valuable markets to reach' (1977: 218).

A number of periodicals and annuals dealing solely with advertising were established, among them *Mitchell's*, *Sell's*, *May's*, *Deacon's*, the *Newspaper Gazette and Guide to Advertisers*, the *Advertiser's Guide to the Newspaper Press of the United Kingdom*, *Successful Advertising* (1879) and *The Advertiser's ABC* (1886). At the end of the century William Stead Jnr published an influential how-to-do-it book, *The Art of Advertising: Its Theory and Practice Fully Described*, which revealed some of the secrets of this emerging profession.

And just as journalism tried to prove itself as a profession, so did advertising. The establishment of working practices and hierarchies specific to particular jobs was widespread during the Victorian era, and this was itself reflected in the magazines and periodicals of the time. Vann and Van Arsdel found that a common theme in their book of studies was 'the sense of an emergent professionalism throughout the nineteenth century in nearly all walks of life', whether it be authorship, science, law, the military, architecture, advertising, medicine or engineering (1978: 5). The overall result was that:

> the section of the press which did prosper and expand consisted of publications which conformed to the requirements of advertisers – professional, trade and technical journals providing a valuable segmentation of the market ... The rapid growth of advertising created the market opportunities for the launch of these categories of publication; it subsidized their costs, financed their development, and created their profits. Its impact can be observed in the phenomenal growth of magazines in the Victorian era (many of them trade, technical, professional and 'class' publications)... (Curran et al., 1977: 221)

John S. North sees, amongst other things, a social function to the diversification permitted (or encouraged) by this new business model:

> periodicals, whether religious, political, class, business, professional, scholarly or popular, were a primary source of entertainment, instruction, information, news, and one of the most notable means of social bonding. (1997: 10)

Given the above, it seems impossible to discuss the contributions of periodicals to the formation of class structures, audiences, and readerships without considering the role of the market in determining the very existence of those periodicals. In this instance the possibilities of human growth and development 'on the scale normally attributed to Woolworth's' cannot be overlooked. (Klancher, in Coyle et al., 1990: 880). Furthermore, there may even be a circular or self-supporting argument here; if the market shaped, or helped to shape, social and cultural groupings, could it be that those social and cultural groupings would then be used to reinforce – or resist – the market?

Economy

In *Get Me A Murder A Day!* Kevin Williams sees another side of the importance of specialist magazines: they were a key element in the growth of mass communications, mass advertising, and mass consumption.

> [T]he history of mass communication is about the development of media which serve the interests of particular groups or classes in our society – the emergence of women's magazines or the Black press or the working-class press of the last century ... The balance between treating members of the audiences as citizens, who must be provided with the information and education necessary for them to play a full and constructive role in the political and social process, and as consumers, who need to be entertained and encouraged to participate in the consumption of products which are made available through mass advertising, is central to tracing the growth of the mass media. (1998: 11)

According to some researchers, the burgeoning magazine industry may also have had an important economic effect on the more mainstream 'press' (and here, as is so often the case, the magazine researcher must complete the irritating task of translating 'press' into its actual meaning of 'newspapers'), at least as far as changing the expectations – and purchasing habits – of consumers.

Dr Jeremy Black observes that in the late eighteenth-century, newspapers had ceased to concentrate largely on political matters and had broadened their range of content to include

> social habits and fashions. Literary, particularly theatrical, news had become a regular feature; and sporting news, largely absent in the first half of the century, was regularly carried by the 1780s, with such news of horse racing, boxing, cock fighting and cricket. (1992: 14)

This he attributes to an increase in monthly magazines earlier in the century that had 'habituated the public to seeing a greater variety of material in print'.

Work by Dawn Currie on current magazines for adolescent girls in the United States draws similar conclusions to those of Williams about the commercial imperative that permeates modern periodical publishing, and she also relates it to concepts that could be considered in the light of the foregoing discussion of dissonance. Noting that 'magazines are constructed to capture a large readership among a specific audience', Currie states:

In practice, the construction of successful advertising 'campaigns' ... is facilitated by social research which helps to ensure that meanings provided by the texts will be received in specific ways by their intended audience. For example, *Mizz* carried out extensive market research before being launched and retains a group of 500 regular readers who test out and comment on magazine material every month ... This practice reminds us that shared meanings are necessary to sustain magazine circulation ... (1999: 102)

It might seem a major leap from the late Victorian period, when commercial models were still in development, to late capitalist production when models have been successfully defined and then studied in detail by academics who apply non-commercial concepts such as feminist semiotics, but these studies have opened up many useful avenues of exploration for all types and conditions of magazines, bringing with them both concepts and insights that can be applied retrospectively. The 'shared meanings' referred to by Currie would seem to be an eminently Festingerian concept and are clearly important to the creation of communities around magazines, but on her way to this statement she has already apophthegmatised an important concept that is situated on the border between commercial and cultural considerations. Writing of magazines aimed at Black women she concludes that, 'racial difference, like sexual difference, is transformed by commercial interests into a speciality consumer group' (p. 38). Once advertising had been introduced into the commercial mix of publishing, which it certainly had been by the end of the nineteenth century, the concept at the heart of this statement seems inevitable and ineluctable.

Publisher theory

Though dismissed rather sniffily by Ballaster et al. as 'peculiarly symptomatic of the perspectives and attitudes of the producers of women's magazines. Its authors affect a consistently triumphalist tone in celebration of the entrepreneurial and creative business of periodical journalism and publication ...', *The Business of Women's Magazines* by Joan Barrell and Brian Braithwaite (1988 [1979]) does exactly what the title would lead you to believe. Furthermore it seems extremely useful to have those 'perspectives and attitudes' made clear; to criticise publishing professionals for writing within the context in which they have forged a career is akin to criticising cats for not being dogs.

The Business is a fairly swift romp through the history of women's magazines (with a gracious nod to Cynthia White) combined with insider background about how the industry actually works. It also contains some honest appraisals of business practice. Writing of the trick of 'folding' a failing title into a thriving one, the authors comment: 'It is usually a confidence trick on the reader who seldom recognises anything of her old magazine in the new title she has been exhorted to buy' (p. 28).

They do not hold back from castigating the industry (with hindsight) for not moving with the times, either. Writing of the 1950s they say:

> It is hard to understand ... just why the publishers ... were so ploddingly slow to hack away at the old fashioned, dated and ponderous titles and editorial styles in their attempts to stimulate the market with exciting new ideas ... failing to recruit the exciting talents who should have been attracted to all sides of the industry. (pp. 29–30)

These examples demonstrate it is not an entirely blinkered, pro-industry book. The closest it comes to what might normally be considered theory is in the chapter that considers launching a new magazine, and the pithiest paragraph there contains the following:

> Lesson one in launching, or endeavouring to create a new magazine, is not to confuse need with condition. A condition is simply a state of being – a circumstantial existence – which in itself does not necessarily constitute a magazine audience of sufficient numbers or buying power to interest an advertiser. A need is a readership which actually wants something from a magazine – such readers being a market. (p. 95)

This is as far as Barrell and Braithwaite are prepared to go, but what they say here surely opens up the possibility of lines of theoretical enquiry into what constitutes 'need' and what constitutes 'condition'.

Their book also provides a certain amount of material with which to mount an 'anti-dominant-ideology' argument, inasmuch as it recounts tales of various launches that proved expensive flops, thus demonstrating that mass advertising, expensive promotion, and wide availability do not necessarily secure success if the product is not what consumers want. To take a couple of examples from opposite ends of the glamour scale, consider *Fashion* in the 1960s and *In-store* in the 1980s.

Fashion was a would-be challenger to *Vogue* published by a branch of IPC, but it never attracted sufficient numbers of readers even though 'Fleetway put a lot of power behind the launch, and were prepared to get heavily involved in the necessary and expensive merchandising and promotion operations that advertisers need in this market' (p. 48). The title lasted for a year thanks to the publisher's 'massive misjudgement of the number of readers who could have been lured away from the existing titles' (p. 49).

IPC made another major misjudgement with *In-store*. Launched in the spring of 1985 with a then record-breaking promotional budget of £1.3m, this was, essentially, a shopping catalogue in the guise of a magazine. It failed to attract either readers or advertisers in the projected numbers and was folded into *Ideal Home* after 18 issues. (Strangely enough, this idea resurfaced more recently, as MediaGuardian reported on 13 September 2004: 'Posh publisher Condé Nast has formed an unlikely alliance with Littlewoods to produce what is called a magalogue – a cross between a catalogue and a magazine': see media.guardian.co.uk/mediaguardian/story/0,7558,1302959,00.html [accessed 24/9/04]).

On the other hand, *Slimming* magazine was launched with a budget of £2,000 by Tom and Audrey Eyton from a room in their house. In 10 years they had built a circulation of 350,000 per issue and a network of slimming clubs, as well as owning a health hydro, and finally sold out for £3.8m. This magazine was clearly addressing a widespread socio-cultural need; in fact it perhaps illustrates precisely what Barrell and Braithwaite mean by need and condition. Being overweight is a condition; wanting to be slimmer is a need. A magazine aimed at overweight people per se would almost certainly fail, whereas one aimed at overweight people who wanted to feel better about themselves not only succeeded in itself, it also established a whole new market sector (p. 55).

Another aspect that Barrell and Braithwaite highlight, even if inadvertently, is the importance of timing a launch. They recount the tale of *Faces*:

> an attempt to emulate the highly successful *People* published in the USA by Time-Life. But America can support a huge number of famous personalities and *Faces* was launched positively as a women's magazine. This per se meant that sports stars were not of interest and the weekly pages would have to be fed, like a voracious monster, by the faces and stories of television stars, royalty and the dwindling band of the truly international jet-set. This was a narrow front on which to base 52 issues each year and *Faces* was never up to it ... *Faces* died after 13 issues. (p. 67)

Yet this seems to describe almost exactly *Hello!*, *OK!*, *Now!*, *Heat*, and any number of high-circulation celebrity magazines. The difference is that these were launched some 20 years after *Faces* and the culture had changed in the interim. Indeed one of the major changes was to those very sports stars previously considered beyond the pale; it is surely not necessary here to list the many sports men and women and their spouses without whom many magazines and newspapers of the 1990s and 2000s would have been bereft.

One of the keys identified by Barrell and Braithwaite is the editor and this applies in two different contexts. On the one hand, advertising sales staff will find that 'the best selling aid is often the editor. She is the very heartbeat of the magazine – she is the one to relay the real sales message ...' (p. 121), while on the other hand, for those who consume the magazine:

> The editor's image is firmly implanted with the magazine, creating the ideal one-to-one ambience which all editors seek. The good editor, and her staff and contributors, must

identify their readers, recognise their needs, never talk down to them and stay one jump ahead of them with new ideas. Equally, they must never go too far ahead of the reader so that she is alienated by the changes which race ahead of her own life-style. (p. 140)

The authors do not theorise this further but, like needs and conditions, this is another area that seems ripe for research.

Brian Braithwaite revisited some of this material on his own in 1995 when *Women's Magazines: The First 300 Years* was published. His stated intention was 'to record the history of the women's magazines, the comings and goings of titles over the years' and this he does, putting fact into a narrative while once again acknowledging his debt to Cynthia White. Many familiar names (magazines, proprietors, editors, advertisers) do recur but some less commonly cited ones also crop up, sometimes giving rise to the kind of interesting question that could be pursued further. For example, Braithwaite refers to the launch of *The Matron* in 1906. This magazine was 'designed for the older woman, not the senior female figure in a hospital', but it was also an 'antidote to all the publishing activity for young women'. Publishing magazines for older women is still a rarity because, according to this former industry insider, 'publishers believe that a woman of sixty, say, will buy a magazine to reflect her interests (house, garden, fashion, etc) rather than her age' (1995: 23). This is one of those assumptions that seems to be true empirically, but there are all sorts of issues of culture and gender implicit within it.

Ballaster et al. might also want to consider something else Braithwaite notes:

The turn of the century must have been an encouraging and stimulating time for magazine publishers. Women were emerging as a political and social force – they were getting jobs, travelling, motoring, cycling, joining clubs for their hobbies and becoming avid readers of magazines. (p. 23)

And they might find it interesting to look into his assertion about the market research undertaken before the UK launch of *Cosmopolitan* in 1972: 'Class and educational level were much less determinants of readership than being unmarried' (p. 99). There is much more to investigate there than the debate about tight-lacing which seems to figure so large in many academic studies of Victorian and Edwardian women's magazines.

Furthermore, Braithwaite unearths some superb extracts from the magazines he studies. The *Queen*, commenting on radio broadcasting in the 1920s, is a wonderful corrective for anyone who thinks the debate about 'dumbing down' is anything new. (p. 37).

One final pointer to further investigation, especially in light of the oft-proclaimed enjoyment (often guilty and/or furtive) of consuming women's magazines:

She set out to be fun – a new idea in magazines for women. It had one simple ambition, to entertain, and was a unique mix of punning headlines, peculiar photographs, jokes, personalities and chumminess, which found an immediate market. (p. 67)

Another key work in this area is Guy Consterdine's *How Magazine Advertising Works IV* (2002), produced for the Periodical Publishers Association. It does exactly what the title suggests, examining and analysing a number of surveys into why companies advertise in magazines and how readers are affected by and will respond to those advertisements. It is perhaps the quintessential 'publisher theory' document in that it is intended almost solely as a means of encouraging companies and agencies to include magazines in their advertising schedules, yet it covers ground that is of great interest to researchers coming at this from a different angle. The concept of readers' relationships with magazines and the formation of communities around them is gone into in some depth, and one of the reasons why magazines are said to be such a good medium is that readers 'trust' them and therefore trust the adverts. Clearly this should not be taken at face value, yet there is a good set of empirical data to examine.

'Publisher theory' is certainly not the same as academic theory, but far from being dismissed it would appear to be a seam that should be mined avidly for insights that might not occur elsewhere.

Cultural

Curran et al. believe that the post-stamp duty, post-advertising tax, market-oriented press had a distinctly homogenising effect. It 'helped to divide and fragment the working class movement' and it was also a powerful source of social cohesion. The values and perspectives that it mediated were at total variance with those mediated by early radical newspapers. A construction of reality as a system of exploitation gave way to a new definition of society in which even the existence of class conflict was denied ... (Curran et al., 1987: 222).

Nevertheless, the market is rarely allowed to have things all its own way; no dominant culture will be. Stuart Hall and others point out that a dominant culture is never homogeneous; it is layered, it reflects traces of the past and emergent elements, and subordinate cultures may exist within it (Clarke et al., *Subcultures, Cultures and Class*, in Hall and Jefferson, 1975: 12). In modern societies the most fundamental groups are the social classes and the major cultural groups are class cultures, but within them there may be sub-cultural groupings:

[Sub-cultures] must be focussed [sic] around certain activities, values, certain uses of material artefacts, territorial spaces etc. which significantly differentiate them from the wider culture ... Sub-cultures ... take place around the distinctive activities and 'focal concerns' of groups. (p. 14)

This is an area that has often been explored in relation to youth culture and sexuality, but the general principles behind it can usefully be deployed to examine the development of any specialist magazine and the issues that surround this type of publishing, notably the concept of 'community' which has been cherished within publisher theory. Specialist magazines, if they are to gain credibility with their intended reader group, must be aware of the values, artefacts, and spaces referred to above. The writers must employ at least aspects of any argot or jargon associated with the subculture and must also display a familiarity with subcultural practices.

This is not new. It has been going on since John Dunton published the *Ladies Mercury*, but it received a major boost during the Victorian period – and note the interesting use of the word 'sect' in the following:

> Yet another area in which there was a massive growth in the second half of this period was in the great range of specialist journals. They were the publications which served to keep the members of a sect or an economic interest or a profession in contact ... (Lucy Brown, 'The British Press 1800–1860', in Griffiths, 1992: 29)

There are two further effects from this. Firstly, some aspects of subcultural practice (perhaps especially material practice) may cross the boundary back into more mainstream culture. Carole Vance has noted that:

> Subcultures give rise not only to new ways of organising behaviour and identity but to new ways of symbolically resisting and engaging with the dominant order, some of which grow to have a profound impact beyond the small groups in which they are pioneered. ('Social Construction Theory and Sexuality', in Berger et al., 1995: 42)

And Dick Hebdige took one of the outstanding examples of how this can happen when he chronicled the punk phenomenon. Punk was a number of things – attitude, music, clothes – and while it may have begun in what might be called ultra-specialist periodicals (such as the fanzine *Sniffin' Glue*), it soon gained exposure in mainstream media such as newspapers, music magazines (*NME* went for it in a big way, launching the careers of Julie Burchill and Tony Parsons) and, famously, television – sinking the career of presenter Bill Grundy when he challenged the Sex Pistols to swear live on air and they took him at his word (also calling him a 'dirty bastard' for good measure). Hebdige wrote of the circular effect such media exposure can have in establishing, defining and confirming subcultural styles and practices:

> much of what finds itself encoded in subculture has already been subjected to a certain amount of prior handling by the media ... So a credible image of social

cohesion can only be maintained through the appropriation and redefinition of cultures of resistance (e.g. working-class youth cultures) in terms of that image ...
Subcultures are, at least in part, representations of these representations, and elements taken from the 'picture' of working-class life (and of the social whole in general) are bound to find some echo in the signifying practices of the various
subcultures. (1979: 85–86)

If this is the case, then specialised publications may both feed and feed off
the targeted subculture; they may help to build a community and also to
bring in what might be called 'fringers' who will dilute, or at least change,
that community.

But above and beyond even this, according to Marshall McLuhan's oft-
expressed beliefs (see *Understanding Media* or *Counterblast*, for example), the arrival of print as one of the technologies which are 'direct
extensions, either of the human body or of our senses' (McLuhan, 1969:
38) increased 'specialism and alienation' (McLuhan and Zingrone, 1995:
150) and thus, according to this theory, increased the likelihood of both
the development of subcultures and the magazines that would serve
their interests.

Conclusion

There can be no pretence that this survey of theory associated with the
study of magazines is exhaustive. Recognised omissions include the literature of fan culture, some of which is contiguous with and applicable to
magazines (see for example Kate Egan's paper 'The Video Nasty's Journey
Through Fear and The Dark Side: The Role of the British Horror Magazine
in the Construction of a Subculture', presented at *Mapping the Magazine*: I,
June 2003) and literature connected with visual analysis, obviously an
important aspect of this highly visual medium.

However, there are grounds for arguing that the overview is both ade-
quate and indicative. One of the indications, and perhaps the most important, is that there is not and cannot be a unified approach to the research
and study of this media form. Magazines are polymorphous and polysemic
cultural artefacts, incapable of analysis through a single strand of theory or
a single method of deconstruction. They are at once readerly and writerly
(to borrow the terms Roland Barthes coined in *S/Z* in 1974) – produced
with one intention but received who knows how. They affect the form of
Gemeinschaft but they are actually *Gesellschaft* (to use Tonnies' terminol-
ogy); published in the ostensible service of a community, while selling that
community's purchasing power to commercial interests.

Magazines may be indicators or purveyors of conservative social and identity formations; bringers of joy; sources of personal and social repertoire; important elements in the expansion of the mass media; reference points for subcultural practices. In short, they are microcosms of the mass communication process that may help to shed light on much larger social processes and would undoubtedly repay their study through the lenses of numerous theoretical traditions and methodologies.

8

FUTURE DIRECTIONS

Magazine journalism, despite huge technological change and a recent economic downturn, will not die; it will simply return in a different form, or so most industry professionals currently believe. Peter Cole, director of journalism at the University of Sheffield, spoke for most of the 30 editors interviewed for this chapter when he argued that while 'nobody has *completely* incontestable answers as to how to function truly effectively in a multimedia environment', magazine journalists have less reason than most to panic about the future:

> It's not as though this is the first time the media have faced huge technological change from stopping hot metal and going to Wapping, back through the invention of television, radio, to the Gutenberg press. When you're around and this is happening, it's the biggest thing but [the internet] is just an invention after all. We forget how much is still published and bought in the *traditional* media. And history tells us that every time there is a new technology, people always say it's the end of the previous media, yet it never has been. No new publishing platform has ever killed another – and, in my view, it never will. We're simply far too adaptable and that's true of magazine journalists, perhaps more than any other print media, because they have always been so much braver creatively and have already made such great strides towards bringing the internet and the print media together. (Cole, 2009 Personal Communication)

Cole's testimony is particularly interesting, coming from a former *newspaper* editor (editor, *Sunday Correspondent*; deputy editor, the *Guardian*), because he argues that magazines have distinct advantages over newspapers where declining circulations and advertising revenues have been more marked. Temple puts newspapers at 'a critical crossroads, facing the most serious challenge to [their] future existence since the *Daily Courant* rolled off the presses in 1702' (2006: 206). According to Franklin, this is debatable: although the future for newspapers can look 'bleak, if not dire', 'adapting to increased competition, often driven by new technology, is historically … what newspapers have always done' (2008: 3). But a 'slow and consistent slide in British newspaper sales' is inarguable, while magazine sector development has been 'brighter' in recent years, with traditionally 'higher average profit margins than in the newspaper industry' (Hujanen et al., 2008: 30).

'Magazines have a great advantage', says Cole (2009). 'They have always been more speculative and flexible and are used to an "invent, then kill" cycle, launching quickly in response to a particular Zeitgeist, but not being afraid to fold when something doesn't work and try something new. They are also more used to thinking in terms of brand development and this is the age we are entering – an age of premium brands, where print has to offer something unique to keep readers on board. Magazines are used to that approach – understanding their audiences and targeting them with laser-like precision – which gives them a big head start'.

However, days after presiding over the closure of her magazine, *Page Six* – the supplement that was given away with the Sunday *New York Post* – editor in chief Margi Conklin was rather less optimistic:

[In the US magazine media] there's no money coming in from circulation and the economy has killed off the flow of money from advertising so there are just no revenue streams, which means there soon won't be any money to pay anyone to do their jobs. It really is that bad: the only ads that seem to be circulating right now are for Dunkin' Donuts, McDonalds and Hooters. Even *Condé Nast* has closed a magazine – *Domino* – and when that happens, you know something is very wrong. (2009 Personal Communication)

Conklin, who has worked in the USA since 2006 after a ten year career in British women's monthlies and weeklies, believes the UK magazine industry needs to keep a close eye on the US magazine market and heed the warnings:

Magazine journalists need to wake up and realise that the business side of things is about to seriously affect them. After all, whatever magazine journalists like to think, this *is* a business. It's not art. (2009 Personal Communication)

Kristin Nieto, deputy style director of US celebrity fashion weekly *Life and Style*, agrees:

It's crazy to see what's happening in the industry over here. Many of my co-workers and I have been saying for years that we think the industry is dying and now the recession is really speeding that up even more. It feels like each week another major publication folds or we hear of dramatic layoffs at a magazine. It's certainly like nothing I've ever witnessed in my lifetime. People are being given pay cuts and downgrading their paper quality. Luckily, at *Life and Style*, our editor in chief has increased the magazine's sales, so that raises our feeling of security slightly. But many magazines are trying to operate differently in an effort to survive, sometimes having editors do their own photo research and cutting the photo staff, things like that. We're all taking things day by day, really, just waiting for it to be our turn on the unemployment line. (2009 Personal Communication)

If the picture is as bleak as these US journalists predict, UK magazine journalists face an undeniably difficult future, in the short term at the very least. As well as redundancies, magazine closures, and challenging advertising and circulation revenues, they are still in the process of adapting to the 'new media' and the rise of 'free' media generally. For example, the 2007 launch of *Shortlist*, the free men's weekly magazine distributed every Thursday at key commuter points in London, Brighton, Birmingham, Leeds, Manchester, Liverpool, Newcastle, Glasgow, Edinburgh and Aberdeen, has been a success, further reinforcing in readers, some editors believe, that paying for our media may well become a quaint custom of the past:

> People are becoming accustomed to free media, either getting it online or handed out free on the train. If you can get features, fashion and news for free, why spend £4 on a magazine? It's becoming really difficult. (O'Riordan, 2008 Personal Communication)

The collapse of certain magazine markets has further reinforced predictions of doom. Says Periodical Training Council director Loraine Davies (2008 Personal Communication): 'Some people say the death of *Eve* [Haymarket's monthly title which closed in August 2008] was the death knell to women's glossies', while Sharon Wright, former content editor of ukfamily.co.uk, is concerned that the collapse of the teen market may indicate a disturbing long-term trend that could signal the collapse of magazine reading altogether:

> There's a feeling that we are entering the 'end generation', the last generation of readers who automatically read magazines for pleasure. It's all very well taking that well worn argument that cinema wasn't killed by TV but at the end of the day if teenagers don't start reading magazines now, when will they? Indeed, will they ever? (2008 Personal Communication)

With the picture in the magazine industry changing almost daily, it can be difficult to assess exactly how the future for magazine journalists will finally pan out. Other changes, mentioned in Chapter 5, such as the rise of graduate training and experiments with different ways of working, will also have an impact on the industry which can be hard to predict, as has the rise of the supermarkets, piling distribution difficulties onto already hard-pressed magazine editors and making publishers increasingly reluctant to launch new products. However, this chapter will seek to explore these key issues currently facing the world of magazines in more depth and consider the industry's likelihood of overcoming them. It will also explore magazine academics' engagement with the issues and consider how their perspectives are likely to adapt to the changes ahead. So much has happened to alter the face of magazine journalism over the past decade – what will be the future for magazines ten years from now?

The magazine industry: dead or alive?

The UK magazine industry in the twenty-first century is a £26.7bn sector comprising about 8,326 magazines in the three principal sectors: consumer, business to business, and customer (PPA online, 2008). Despite the economic difficulties that began to take hold at the end of 2008, the overall number of magazines being sold in the UK in that period rose year on year by 3.7 per cent to a total net average of 81,227,572, according to the July–December 2008 ABC figures (Brook, 2009). Magazines in the TV market are still holding their own, despite small dips in circulation, with H Bauer's *TV Choice*, IPC's *What's On TV*, and BBC Magazines' *Radio Times* all still selling over a million copies a week. At the same time while weekly women's titles such as *OK!* took a big hit – it was down 25.6 per cent year on year – and *Grazia* (down 5.5 per cent year on year) has been slowing down after strong periods of growth, *Closer* was still relatively stable, *Bella* and *Hello* were up (16.9 and 7.1 per cent respectively), and even the high street shopping magazine *Look* was still showing year on year growth (2.6 per cent), despite fears for such an overtly retail-based title in the current economic climate (Luft, 2008). Overall, the women's lifestyle and fashion sectors have increased their circulations during the last ABC period by 7.4 per cent, with both *Red* and *Vanity Fair* recording record circulations (ibid) and *Glamour* and *Vogue* remaining steady. Although the 'teen' sector (e.g. *Sugar, Bliss)* is in terminal decline, the children's market demonstrates another healthy trend, with new titles like *Bratz* and *In the Night Garden* doing well: according to Toni Round, managing director of youth and children's magazines at the BBC, 'This market is relatively resilient from the internet and has not been decimated by new technology, as the teen market has' (de Castella, 2008).

Other positives can be seen in what's become magazine publishing's fastest growing sector, customer publishing, which saw 16 per cent growth in the latest ABCs (Sheahan, 2009). *Skymag*, BSkyB's publication, is the highest circulation magazine in the UK (at 7.2 million) and is the most widely read magazine in the UK, followed by *Tesco Magazine* (Cedar Communications, 5.9 million readers) and *Asda Magazine* (Publicis Blueprint, 5.1 million readers) (PPA online, 2009). Customer magazines are becoming an increasingly popular 'vehicle for brand management in the media' (Dyson, 2007), having 'moved from being above-the-line advertising's poor relation to becoming a central cog in the marketing mix' (Crawley-Boevey, 2009). They now account for 12 of the top 20 magazines in circulation and more than a quarter (29) of the top 100 (Sheahan, 2009). Customer publishing, which used to be 'pretty shonky, unsubtle corporate propaganda in the guise of a magazine', according to Christian Cull, director of communications at Sky (Crawley-Boevey, 2009), is now arguably overcoming this by increasingly luring high quality journalists into the fold, such as Sara Cremer, former editor of *New Woman* and *Eve*, and now editorial director at customer specialists Redwood Publishing. Cremer argues that 'some of the best creative work is coming out of customer publishing agencies' and says the sector is no longer regarded within magazine circles as 'being slightly second-best' (Burrell, 2008).

Meanwhile, Julia Hutchison, chief operating officer of the APA (Association of Publishing Agencies), believes the recent economic downturn has actually 'exacerbated' the success of customer magazines because many brands are now acknowledging magazines to be one of the best methods of engaging with their customers:

> The medium is so effective because it allows for consumers to receive a physical embodiment of a brand in times when they are receiving less and less for their money. (Sheahan, 2009)

Hutchison is not the only executive determined to see the recession as a potential positive for at least some magazines. News and current affairs titles have also shown growth – particularly *The Week*, *Prospect*, and *The New Statesman* (PPA online, 2009), a trend which some will applaud as a positive sign for the future of journalism since these are magazines known for their 'journalistic emphasis' on investigation, background, analysis, and international and domestic commentary (McNair, 2003: 18). The current circulation uplift surrounding business/personal finance magazines might also be attributed to readers' current economic concerns, with *Moneyweek* up 16.6 per cent (year on year), the *Economist* up 3.1 per cent (year on year), and the *Spectator* up 2 per cent to a record sale of 77,146 (Brook, 2009).

Specialist consumer titles like *Xbox World 360* and *Computing Nintendo* are also holding their own, while BBC Magazines' *Easy Cook* is up 20.4 per cent year-on-year, *Golf World* 19.2 per cent, *Runner's World* 6.6 per cent, and gadget magazine *Stuff* 7.9 per cent. Indeed, many in the industry believe that the future of the magazine industry may well lie in specialist, or 'hobbies', magazines. Says Jim Douglas, editorial director of specialist specialists Future Publishing:

> In times of economic hardship, our magazines are the last thing people stop buying. It's that one luxury that everyone can still just about afford. (2008 Personal Communication)

His creative director, Robin Abbott, adds:

> The guy who reads *Motorcycle News* does it because everyone in his life is telling him he was wrong to spend £800 on that new exhaust. But for just £3.90 a month, there will always be someone to tell him, 'actually, you did the right thing there, mate'. And that's why specialist magazines will always have a place in the market. (2008 Personal Communication)

The editor of business to business title *Property Week*, Giles Barrie, has also found reasons to be cheerful in the economic climate because regular tales of companies going under actually provide opportunities for great copy:

> It's been absolutely riveting writing up the flatplan every week, because there's always a great story. The Bank of Scotland, HBOS, Lehman Brothers, were all heavily involved in property which has been great for circulation. We've even had a record ABC on the back of it. (2008 Personal Communication)

However, for every positive trend, magazines are always liable to have a high 'death rate' (Hujanen et al., 2008: 17). David Hepworth, editorial director of Development Hell which publishes *The Word*, believes that magazines are 'in ruder health that they should be' in a recession but still observes:

> Whenever I ask magazine editors about business at the moment, the nearest I get to an optimistic response is the guarded 'holding our own' or the slightly more artful 'actually, surprisingly well'. Deep in their eyes you can glimpse the fear. (Hepworth, 2008)

For many editors, fear is a way of life. When she was editing *Marie Claire*, Marie O'Riordan saw its sales fall overall during her seven year editorship from just over 400,000 to 316,765. This, of course, doesn't tell the whole story. With the ABC figures coming out every six months O'Riordan regularly experienced sales uplifts during that time and, in those moments, editors can appear invincible. However, they also know that they are only as good as their last sales figure and that unless their publishers hold firm, one bad sale, such as *Marie Claire*'s Colleen McCloughlin cover in 2006, can make them feel vulnerable. O'Riordan says:

> It doesn't help if you have a long way to fall, which we did. Then there's the fact that magazines have a natural life cycle – how long will it be 'your time'? And if you do have a successful brand difference, which for us was focusing on real women, then everyone will want to launch into your market and take a piece of that pie. So, first reality TV came in, things like *Wife Swap*, which was about dissecting a marriage, clear *Marie Claire* territory. Then came magazines like *Easy Living* and *Red* which meant more rivals in the 30-something sector. Then *Grazia* joined the fashion market, but by doing it weekly they could be more reactive. And then *In Style* took celebrities! We were attacked on all sides as big brands always are. (O'Riordan, 2008 Personal Communication)

Her subsequent resignation, though partly caused by personal factors – 'the death of both of my parents in a year caused me to reassess the way my life was going' – was also prompted by a realisation. When her publisher suggested that it was time for yet another 'relaunch', the industry term for when a magazine endeavours to reposition itself in the marketplace with a revamped editorial and design, she finally came to the conclusion that even the most enthusiastic editor has only so much to give:

> With a magazine like *Marie Claire*, it's about constant reinvention to keep pace with your changing readers and it's exhausting. I'd reinvented *Marie Claire* five times in eight years and when the publisher told me to do it again I just thought, 'you're kidding me'. It gets to everyone, that burnout, and I had finally reached the point where I knew I simply didn't have the energy to do it all again. (2008 Personal Communication)

Despite individual editors opting for time out, the industry ploughs on. But it is becoming increasingly hard going with even the most optimistic promoters of the sector acknowledging worrying signs for the future in the current economic climate – indeed, PTC director Loraine Davies says the industry faces 'the hardest 24 months in publishing yet':

> There's real pressure on editors with the rise of free magazines, websites, and the growth of customer publishing because consumers want more and more for nothing. There's a real urgency to understand how to engage with web users and advertisers are being increasingly conservative: now it's about page spending in terms of weeks so it's harder to plan ahead. (2008 Personal Communication)

If Peter Cole is right that magazines have in the past managed to launch themselves out of trouble by simply bringing out a new product, another worrying trend, particularly for smaller publishers, is the increased difficulty of launching new titles on the newsstand. Says Martyn Moore, then editor of Bauer *Automative*, now editor of *Fleet News*:

> Supermarkets are calling the shots, holding publishers to ransom and struggling with our distribution model which is forcing us to seek alternative routes to readers. (2008 Personal Communication)

This growing power of the supermarkets over magazines has been much written about in the past decade. With the decline of many newsagents, publishers are increasingly becoming hostages to the supermarkets who will stock only around 1,500 titles, leaving thousands of others denied access to the most prominent shelf space in the land.

> Supermarkets will ask only one thing – is the space taken up by this title making us enough profit? – which is bad news for many and leaves all publishers vulnerable. (Greenslade, 2006)

At one point, publishers accused one supermarket chain of acting like a 'schoolyard bully' after the company demanded two pages of editorial or advertising space each month in titles chosen by them, a move which industry insiders called 'tantamount to blackmail'. The supermarket's request, showed, they said, 'a complete failure to comprehend the costs of producing a magazine' (Cassidy,

2008). On that occasion the supermarket backed down, but the suggestion in the article that 'publishers are unable to publicly retaliate over the demands because of fears of delisting' (ibid) demonstrates a carefully negotiated power struggle which many editors believe is liable to implode at any moment.

Publishers meanwhile are trying to get around these difficulties. Says Loraine Davies:

> To get on newsstand will cost millions today. So, you get launches like *Shortlist*, which has done very well because it misses out the newsstand altogether. Or, you'll see a lot of publishers looking to launch supplements like *Property Global* which add value to the original brand [*Property Week*] rather than introducing a brand new product into an uncertain market. (2008 Personal Communication)

However, many traditionally reliable markets do seem uncommonly uncertain. Editorial consultant Peter Genower predicts a tough time ahead for B2B magazines as print products for example:

> Their content is migrating to the web. Their ad model stacks up online so you'll see them launching new web products but I think it will be a long time before we see another B2B launch in print. (2008 Personal Communication)

The editor of *Property Week*, Giles Barrie, believes B2B titles still have a strong print future:

> Advertisers are always going to want what we offer – the opportunity to get in front of a specialised, premium focused audience. At *Property Week*, we have 100,000 readers who are precisely the 100,000 people our advertisers want to reach. (2009 Personal Communication)

However, he also sees 'everyone making redundancies' and 'some of the smaller [B2B] magazines' increasingly under threat, particularly 'controlled circulation magazines' which are sent out free to industry and have traditionally relied purely on advertising revenues (particularly job ads) to survive:

> These days you need display *and* recruitment advertising *and* subscriptions *and* big events in order to keep going and even then it's not going to be easy. (ibid)

Recent developments in the B2B sector appear to back this up. B2B publisher Centaur, which publishes *Marketing Week* and *New Media Age* and has already cut staff numbers by 15 per cent, recently reported a fall in half year tax profits of 86 per cent, with plans for further cuts, changes to magazine formats, and reduced paginations. Emap, another B2B publisher (e.g. *Retail Week, Nursing Times*), recently announced plans to cut all its magazines to A4 size to save on production costs, while at Reed Business Information, home of *Travel Weekly*, the construction business magazine *Contract Journal*, and the chemical business magazine *ICIS*, journalists recently balloted for strike action to 'defend journalistic standards' after 35 jobs were cut (Amos, 2009).

As for consumer magazines, according to Barrie (2009 Personal Communication), 'it can be even more difficult, not least because there are so many of them'. *The National Magazine Company*, a subsidiary of the US magazine giant Hearst which owns *Cosmopolitan, Esquire* and *Good Housekeeping*, recently announced plans to make about 15 per cent of its staff redundant following a 6.8 per cent decline in total circulation in the latest ABCs and what it called 'unprecedented economic challenges to the business'. Ominously for magazine producers, it also promised to make further savings by cutting 'operating expenses' with chief executive Duncan Edwards talking about 'the worst conditions that we have faced in my 20 years at NatMags' (McNally, 2009).

So the overall 3.7 per cent rise in magazine circulation, cited earlier as an example of an industry determined to remain buoyant against a choppy tide, could equally be put down to the growth of customer and/or free magazines which doesn't necessarily bode well for the overall health of the industry. The once thriving men's weeklies (e.g. *Nuts, Zoo, Maxim*, and *Loaded)* and celebrity weeklies (*Heat, Closer*) were the big success stories of the 1990s, but even they have seen sales begin to fall with the men's market in particular experiencing 'heavy losses'. *Maxim* was down 4.1 per cent year on year, *Nuts* 13.3 per cent, and *Zoo* 18.7 per cent (Brook, 2009). High-end titles like *Tatler, Country Life*, and *Horse and Hound* were also hit, along with the *home interest* sector where 19 out of 24 titles lost sales. Worst of all is the picture in the teen market. The erstwhile market leader *Sugar* now exists only online while its long time rival *Bliss*, which sold 300,000 copies in 2000, is now selling a mere 85,985 (ABC report, December 2008), a crushing 29.8 per cent down year on year. The two other main titles, *Shout* and *Mizz*, were also down, *Shout* by 5.4 per cent to 81,904 and *Mizz* by 18 per cent to 58,302.

Some commentators believe that it is this teen market fall which may be the most significant of all for the future of magazines, if it is indicative of an overall trend in which the internet is slowly beginning to kill off magazines or, perhaps more worryingly still, if it suggests a teenage readership that have simply stopped reading, leaving no one at all to buy any kind of print media in the decades to come.

Can print survive the internet? A case study of the teen market

The teen market has been in long-term decline since the early 1990s: long gone are the days when *Just Seventeen* (1983–2004) sold half a million copies a fortnight and 'raked in advertising money like there was no tomorrow' (Holmes, 2007). In the past decade however that decline has accelerated at an alarming rate, with titles like *Sneak, Elle Girl, J17, 19, B, Big, Cosmo Girl, Live and Kicking, Looks*, and even the iconic *Smash Hits* all finding their way to magazine heaven in rapid succession, and two of the biggest

UK magazine companies, IPC Media and Emap (now Bauer Media), offloading their once thriving titles *Mizz* and *Bliss* to Panini UK Ltd. Says David Hepworth (2006): 'Teenagers don't read magazines any more' and the teen market is 'going south at speed'...

The internet has been specifically blamed for the market's demise. An Ofcom report found that 15 to 24 year olds were reading fewer magazines and turning their attention away from traditional media towards the internet where social networking sites such as MySpace and Bebo were now doing the job traditionally performed by teenage lifestyle magazines (Ofcom, 2006), while the pop music-based magazines have suffered from the competition for 'bedroom time' coming from the internet and mobile phones. According to former *Smash Hits* editor Mark Frith, the pop magazine died because 'Today's teens want faster, deeper information about music and can now satisfy their hunger by accessing information on a whole range of new platforms including TV, the internet, mobile and so on' (Milmo, 2006).

As with all media, the net cannot be the only culprit for sales decline. Writing about newspapers, former *Guardian* editor Peter Preston stated: 'The Net may be delivering the *coup de grace*, but it's not truly to blame for what's gone wrong over decades. Human living patterns, changing, moving on, have done that' (2008: 643). His argument could equally be applied to teenage magazines. Other suggested reasons for the teen market's collapse, along with claims of a demographic decline in the number of teenagers, include a rise in what's known in marketing circles as the KGOY phenomenon, 'Kids Getting Older Younger' – which many commentators believe has led teenagers away from media traditionally designed for them towards magazines aimed at older markets, such as *Heat*, *Glamour*, *Cosmopolitan* and *Closer* (girls), and *Nuts* and *Zoo* (boys). As David Hepworth argues:

> All the products teenagers favour have one thing in common. They're not aimed at teenagers.. Add to that the increasing claims on teenage pocket money and attention from mobile phones, MP3 players and 24/7 music television and it's not hard to see why attention-deficient teenagers might have migrated away from the teen genre. (Hepworth, 2007)

On the other hand, however, some magazine companies have seen the internet revolution as an opportunity – a way to meet their audiences in different ways. *TV Hits* magazine (Essential Publishing) is now an exclusively online product, while *Sugar* owners Hachette presented the decline of Sugar as an opportunity to exploit the *Sugar* brand online and via mobile phones (Andrews, 2006). Similarly, *Nuts* have launched *Nuts TV* and Dennis Publishing's digital-only young men's product *Monkey*, which is emailed to subscribers for free, has been seen as a successful e-business model with an eABC of 283,541 copies a week and a recent brand extension of a free mobile TV channel, sent direct to readers' mobiles and sponsored by Twentieth Century Fox (Billings, 2008). On the back of *Monkey*'s success, Dennis have launched two further digital only titles, *iMotor* and *Gizmo*, but finding the right balance – and market model – for a digital product is still an embryonic process. After *Cosmo Girl* folded in July 2007, The National Magazine Company launched a digital product for girls and young women, *Jellyfish*, designed to be 'the best of the web every week'. It seemed a great idea – cheap to launch, environmentally friendly, and easier to distribute to readers. However, it failed to last beyond its 20-week trial period, with Natmags unable to 'see a sustainable business model emerging' (*Press Gazette*, 2007). This is a common experience. Editorial director of *Future*, Jim Douglas, whose company has seen its greatest profit margins in digital in the past year (see Chapter 5), also acknowledges that 'the web revenue issue' is far from solved:

> It's tempting to invest everything online to be the best but you have to [be careful]. Some companies are funding the web out of their mag profits but we are putting our profits back into print too – we'll probably launch four print titles [this] year. We have quite a few web products not generating profit yet: they're a year away from making a positive contribution. We need to give them time to grow and make sure we are getting the balance right. (Douglas, 2008 Personal Communication)

'Time to grow' is not a luxury that most teen publishers have however. When *Cosmo Girl* closed, Natmags' managing director Jessica Burley predicted the end of the teen market in its current form:

> Perhaps having something so overtly targeted at teens isn't as relevant now as it was five or six years ago. With huge regret, we have had to concede that the marketplace in that format, targeting girls, or girls who wish to be adults, is just not sustainable on an ongoing business basis. (*Press Gazette*, 2007)

But have teenagers stopped reading magazines entirely as Burley believes, have they simply 'switched markets' – or have they stopped reading print media altogether? According to the Ofcom report, among the young, 'the internet has appeared to reduce especially the consumption of print media' (2006: 43) and recent research shows they certainly aren't reading newspapers, or, if they are, they are doing so in ever declining numbers (Raeymaeckers, 2002, 2004; Panagiotarea and Dimitrakopoulou, 2007). In Belgium, for example, fears about newspaper consumption among young readers have become so severe that the Flemish government has launched a 'Newspapers in Education' project which has been specifically designed to promote newspaper reading in schools (Raeymaeckers et al., 2007).

One reading of this trend is that the 'end generation' (Wright, 2008 Personal Communication), the last generation of readers to regularly buy newspapers and magazines, is already upon us. Or perhaps this has already passed? If so, the consequences for democracy are obvious. Equally, however, it could be that children have never particularly enjoyed reading the 'news' in the print media, particularly if that news refers to political or economic material (Raeymaeckers, 2002), and that they will simply come to newspapers when they are ready for them. One US study, for example, found that for election coverage, children overwhelmingly preferred to access their news information from television and radio rather than from print media, even if their families subscribed to a newspaper (Simon and Merrill, 1997). In addition, magazines are not generally bought by younger readers for their political news anyway, rather for their lifestyle advice, celebrity gossip, or special interest topics. Therefore the potential 'end generation' threat may not apply to magazines anyway, even if it does indeed apply to newspapers, which is still arguable – Nicky Cox, editor of the children's newspaper *First News*, which has an ABC of 38,183 and is available in 'a quarter of schools', certainly believes that news can be 'popular' with children if it is presented in the right format (Newall et al., 2009). Indeed, if teenagers are not reading magazines yet, or at the very least not reading the magazines designed for them, where is the evidence to suggest that they won't engage with the medium at some point? Says Peter Cole:

> I've no idea why people get so hung up on whether the print media are getting younger readerships. I don't even see a problem if the *Daily Telegraph* has an average readership age of 51. So what? We're an aging population. So, young readers may not want to read the *Telegraph* now but that doesn't mean they won't want to when they reach the requisite age. And once they are that age, the chances are they'll live another 20 or 30 years and will still be *Telegraph* readers for all that time, so where's the difficulty? (2009 Personal Communication)

This point ties in with some preliminary research findings from a pilot project being conducted in Sheffield schools which looks into the future of newspapers and magazines in an internet age (Holmes and Nice, unpublished paper, 2009), According to 'Edward', 15:

> We don't really buy newspapers at the moment but they shouldn't change them to try and make them more youthful: that would be stupid. They should just keep them as they are. Because, when the time comes and we are ready to read them, we'll want them to be the way they are now.
>
> Speaking about magazines, 'Lucy' added: 'I like to buy *Vogue* but I can't really afford to buy it religiously. I buy a lot of the fashion mags but don't really mind which ones. The celeb mags are good too, especially *Heat*. I sometimes look at *Closer* too 'cause my mum buys it'. (2009 Personal Communication)

Of 30 Year 10 and Year 11 pupils (male and female) interviewed so far, all were magazine readers, though less interested in newspapers. However, they were unlikely to be aligned to a particular magazine and were almost entirely disinterested in the magazines aimed at them: only one teenage girl named *Sugar* as her magazine of choice. All the other (21) girls said they typically read magazines which have generally been defined for an older audience such as *Heat, Now, Closer* and *Inside Soap*. The boys tended to read 'special interest' titles such as *Four Four Two* or *National Geographic*.

These findings are only at a very early stage but certainly warrant further investigation as, if correct, they suggest that teenagers do still read – they just read *more varied* media than they used to, their loyalty to lifestyle magazines in a covermount generation is more disparate – if almost non-existent – and they spend a lot of time (a minimum of an hour a day) on the internet, 'particularly social networking sites'.

In many ways then, digital changes aside, the difficulties facing teen publishers are no different to the difficulties magazine producers have always faced: what is the best and most effective way to reach your readers and speak to them in a language they can understand? In a study contrasting the perceptions of internet producers and their teen audiences with a website designed to increase young readers' civic engagement, Livingstone (2007) found that 'reaching the "average" young person is clearly difficult … because the communicative relationship between producer and user is inadequate. Despite the best intentions (of producers), and despite the many invitations to "have your say" … young people (did) not believe that their emails, discussions or contributions to websites (were) being listened to'. Her solution – 'the more the text offers a collaborative, open approach to the reader, the more effective is the communication' – sounds like a solution a teenage magazine editor would come up with (speaking as a former one myself), but knowing what to do and actually pulling it off are very different things.

In a 2007 study of teenage magazine editors, nine teenage magazine editors past and present all agreed with then *Sugar* editor Annabel Brog that there would always be a future for teen magazines because:

> Today's teenager might be a new species … media savvy, style-obsessed, sophisticate, the trainee adult – but she still has the same insecurities she's always had about boys, spots and fitting in (Brog, 2005).

In light of *Sugar*'s 2011 closure and current teen sales figures, however, that view is today clearly stretching credibility and the confidence teen editors displayed then in their ability to speak to readers in 'a language they can understand' and be a 'big sister' (Nice, 2007b) now appears to have been misplaced. Indeed, perhaps the truest challenge for magazine editors working in younger markets today lies not in the threat to their publications from outside, uncontrolled sources (the internet, demography, changes to the music market) but in a basic failure to communicate with a readership that has changed too quickly for them to keep pace. *Sugar* publisher Judith Secombe said that teenagers use the internet for different activities to those offered by magazines (playing games, sending emails, and visiting social networking sites) so teen magazines should, in theory, have been able to 'complement online activity' rather than be destroyed by it. But, the teen brands are now hanging by a thread, undone by what Secombe called the teen publisher's 'biggest challenge' – the ability to engage the audience and represent value for money (Preston, 2007). The lesson there for magazine journalists across all markets seems to be that if they are to resist the march of online, they must arm themselves with the one weapon they have always relied upon but have perhaps not fully worked out how to employ in a digital age. Says former *Sugar* editor (1999–2000) Sarah Pyper:

> The hardest challenge as a teen editor was finding the right 'voice' to speak to your readers. Perhaps, what teenage magazine editors and writers have lost more than anything in a multi media environment is the simple ability to do just that. (Pyper, 2009 Personal Communication)

Magazines' academic perspectives: the future

Studying the issues facing the teen market provides a useful microcosm that applies not just to the rest of the magazine industry but also to the academic study of magazines which also faces an interesting and unpredictable future. While the magazine industry has been wrestling with whether the teen magazine form can even survive, academia has been predominantly concerned with teenage magazines' impact on readers, with scholars generally approaching the medium from gender and identity perspectives, expressing concern for young girls (apart from Ticknell et al., 2003, they rarely seem so bothered about young boys) who are being subjected to normative, potentially demeaning messages about body image (Grogan, 1999; Wykes and Gunter, 2005), stereotypical gender representations (McRobbie, 1978; Evans et al., 1991; McCracken, 1993; Duffy and Gotcher, 1996), unrelenting heterosexuality, and alarmingly intoxicating commerciality. Put another way:

> In the rites of passage to femininity through teen-mags, men become the prize of looks but only certain kinds of looks achieve men. If you do not conform you can buy many products – clothes, make up, cosmetics, services – to change yourself by adornment so long as the underlying structure of your body is the 'acceptable and desirable' size and shape to fit these. If not, the covert message may well be – change your body. (Wykes and Gunter, 2005: 93)

This 'concern' perspective has been revisited by postmodernists such as Frazer (1987), Buckingham (1993), Currie (1999), and Duke (2000), who suggest that teenage readers aren't necessarily 'cultural dupes' worthy of pity (Hermes, 1995), but rather like researchers themselves do actually have the ability to reject magazine messages, particularly if they deem them irrelevant to their own lives (Duke, 2000: 367–387). This view is also problematic: as Gauntlett argues, just because readers are able to criticize a text this 'does not mean they would never be influenced by its content' (2008: 191), but it is interesting to see McRobbie, once so scathing about *Jackie* magazine, which, she argued, forced readers into a 'false sisterhood' where all that mattered was finding a man, losing weight, looking one's best and learning to cook (McRobbie, 1978: 3), arguing more recently that, by encouraging girls to be assertive, confident and supportive of each other, young women's magazines may actually be quite feminist (McRobbie, 1999: 55) and that it is far too simplistic to talk of 'evil' writers and 'victim' readers (Gauntlett, 2008: 219).

McRobbie's work on the young women's market in the late 1990s is rare however in that, unlike most research work on magazines, it actually coincides with industry opinions about itself: in a 2007 study of teenage magazine editors, all claimed, commercial considerations notwithstanding, that they were about 'empowering' and 'educating' young women and 'taking our responsibility to our readers seriously' rather than attempting to fool them (Nice, 2007b). Had they been aware of it (and of course most magazine professionals generally have a nice place for filing academic 'critiques' of their media if they come across them at all, also known as the bin), they would certainly have been appreciative of McRobbie's attempt to consider who magazine producers actually are – was it too much of a stretch of the imagination, she asked, to consider that the generally well educated women who work in magazines might actually have womens' interests at heart, a rare and important step towards humanising magazine producers which, for most magazine theorists, had hitherto seemed a step too far.

The paucity of academic study into magazine practice/production has been referred to already in this book (Chapters 5 and 7) but it warrants further mention here as just one example of the 'neglect' of magazines (Holmes, 2007; Johnson, 2007) by those who study journalism as an academic subject. 'Nobody cares about magazines', one journalism academic told this author last year which, considering that 77.4 per cent of adults and 82 per cent of women read a consumer or special interest magazine (PPA online, 2008), seems rather odd. The remark wasn't meant unkindly however. It was a simple statement of fact.

A number of reasons for the tendency of journalism academics to 'underestimate and overlook' magazines (Holmes, 2007: 511) have been suggested. Holmes acknowledges that the vast number of magazine titles (over 8,000 in the UK alone compared to just ten national newspapers and 1,300 regionals), the many varied formats in which magazines present themselves (from consumer to business-to-business to contract to local to specialist to literary), and the greater complexity of magazines by comparison to newspapers (being 'highly diverse in subject matter' and placing 'more emphasis … on presentation') make them 'less easy to study' and 'read' than newspapers (ibid).

A less generous view might consider that a certain kind of sexism is to blame in some cases – although some academic study of men's magazines has been undertaken (e.g. Jackson et al., 2001; Benwell, 2003; Crewe, 2003) much of the best known magazine study has focused on the women's media and generally from the feminist perspective. It may also be a case of good old-fashioned academic snobbery – magazines have often been compared unfavourably to newspapers as being somehow a lower form of journalism (Nice, 2007a) just as feature writers are often disparaged by some in the industry as being 'lower' journalists than hard news writers.

'It may be because a lot of women work on features and in magazines', says Yvonne Illsley (2008), freelancer writer and former features editor of the *Daily Express* and *Take a Break*. 'But however much the news journalists pillory the feature writers, when it comes to the really big stories, like 9/11, then the features desk is the busiest in the building because it has the best writers, the people who can really make a story come to life' (Personal Communication).

Sammye Johnson also unearthed academic snobbery or perhaps simple disinterest not only towards magazine research as a whole but also towards researchers approaching the medium from a 'practice' perspective:

Research about the demographics, attitudes, beliefs and professional practices of magazines professionals have been neglected (2007: 525).

She argues also that what she calls the magazine 'research conundrum' has resulted from magazines not being located within one cultural, social, geographic, or financial area and from magazine scholars coming from such a wide variety of backgrounds including journalism, communication, advertising, history, English, sociology, psychology, gender, women's studies, art, marketing, and literature. As a result, she argues, many of them are left baffled as to what research methodologies are most appropriate and liable to get them published – no easy task considering that there aren't even any magazine journalism journals apart from *American Periodicals* and the *Journal of Magazine and New Media Research*, neither of which are 'exclusively devoted to magazines' (pp. 524–525).

Trying to get published in other journalism journals can be even more of a minefield. *Journalism Studies*' wonderful (2007) special issue on magazines, a balanced mix of practitioner and theoretical approaches, was so rare an example of what magazine journalism scholarship might be as to almost render it a collector's item: indeed, for many magazine researchers, not much has changed since Korinek (2000: 12) called them a 'small and relatively isolated community of scholars' a decade ago. In *Journalism Studies*, Johnson wrote that many papers which would have interested the magazine *industry* were all too often rejected by academic journals for having 'no theoretical hypothesis' or an inadequate literature review: 'Being too professional or applied can be the kiss of death' (2007: 527).

Equally, Johnson acknowledges that the magazine industry itself could do more to help bring the worlds of academia and industry together by being less proprietary about their own research and less suspicious of magazine theorists when they come to them for help and information, but clearly there is at present a great gulf between what the magazine industry wants to know and what academia wants to write about the industry. An article entitled: *Can teenage magazines survive after all?* or *What will replace teenage magazines as the most powerful text for young readers?* for example would, from an industry perspective, be a must read; however, no academic has ever tackled writing this. And therein lies the problem.

Looking to the future, can there ever be a coming together of the two sides; a world where it really would be viable to persuade the editors of academic journals to value 'essays grounded in primary and secondary research (though lacking in hypotheses)' (Johnson, 2007: 527)? Will it ever be possible for scholars to routinely visit magazine offices, interview magazine journalists about their craft, and come to understand that magazine journalists are not always 'the other', in the sense of being the unknown capitalist enemy, but are rather perhaps just as likely to be victims of the system, or as critical of it, as the researchers themselves?

A first step might be for both sides (and indeed there is a clear polarity) to begin to focus on the issues they have in common. Key industry issues such as staffing, circulation battles, and the rampage of the supermarkets are barely covered in academic journals and unlikely to be so in the near future, but there is a growing body of academic work looking at issues such as teen internet usage and the growth of new audiences which ought to be mutually illuminating. Another move in the right direction would be for a collaboration over issues that matter both to academics and the industry such as journalistic standards. Much as journalists tend not to welcome any scrutiny of their practices, particularly from those they tend to regard as being 'ignorant' of 'journalistic realities' (Greenberg, 2007), it takes little effort to prompt most of them into a rant about media standards, as, for example, with Jonathan Bown's views about the celebritisation of the media (Chapter 5) or Sarah Hart and Marie O'Riordan on the anti-editorial advances of advertorials and covermounts. Interestingly, there is academic literature around these issues. Evans and Hesmondhalgh (2005), for example, have explored the rise of the celebrity media. Of course their approach tends to be more semiotic than standards based, as they ask what certain celebrity representations mean for readers and for democracy, rather than what effect they will have on magazine journalism quality and outputs. But would it be too much of a switch to include both, as Dyson did when she explored the impact of the growth of customer magazines on editorial integrity and concluded that:

> The growing phenomenon of promotional material penetrating the space of editorial can be viewed as a form of privatisation of the symbolic domain of journalistic production (leading to an inevitable) blurring of boundaries between marketing, promotion and editorial. (2007: 635)

She adds:

> Those producing customer magazines do not have the qualms about the collapsing boundaries between promotion, marketing and journalism. With every surface of the magazine potentially a promotional opportunity, editorial space, previously 'sealed off' from advertising in all its various forms, including product placement, is now available to advertisers. (p. 638)

The gradual infiltration of magazine journalists into academia may also help accelerate a collaboration process: indeed, the authors of this book, both former magazine editors, faced none of the difficulties in gaining access to industry figures that Gough-Yates experienced during her (2003) study of magazine publishers' new approaches to readers in the 80s and 90s. Her exploration of editors' 'anxieties' as they sought to become 'cultural inter-mediaries' who could please both their advertisers and readers simultane-ously, rang true from a practitioner perspective (p. 154), but her acknowledgement that her focus was mainly on *formal* management prac-tices in magazines rather than on the individuals who actually produced them showed how far much magazine research by non-practitioners may still have to go:

> I have been unable to provide an account of the *informal* practices and activities of magazine practitioners and advertisers ... there is still much work to do in this area. (2003: 155–1566)

Similarly, Ben Crewe's illuminating (2003) study of the men's market, though also a valiant attempt to speak to editors, made clear that a lack of journalistic experience creates its own difficulties when attempting to obtain the 'production' perspective. Crewe felt he had to 'downplay' his academic credentials and found that editors tended to be resistant to analy-sis, both of themselves and the significance of their products (p. 206). He also acknowledged signs of his own vulnerability, as a non-journalist, to get-ting things wrong: 'Media insiders are ... most likely to identify factual inac-curacies in this book and [are] some of those most capable of challenging its arguments' (p. 207), and to being perhaps a little too easily 'seduced' by the glamour of the industry when 'paternal' executives praised him up and even offered him jobs and gifts.

> On more than one occasion, I felt that I was being offered a route into the profession ... I found such offers mildly, although only briefly, enticing [and] was left with a heightened sense of my own prospects. (p. 209)

After working in the magazine industry's seductive, hard sell culture for any length of time it would be rather harder to flatter a former magazine

journalist, so it is hoped that the publishers of academic journals may recognise the unique attributes former practitioners are capable of bringing
into the research field, in terms of contacts, background knowledge, and
interpretative powers: until they do so magazine production is likely to
remain the great unexplored realm of academic study. Ideally, academics
and former practitioners should pool interests and skills and work together
more: as much as an ignorance of basic magazine journalism principles,
attitudes, and tacit knowledge can be a handicap to researchers without
journalism backgrounds, it's equally the case that even when using tried
and tested academic methodologies former journalists (apart from the very
bitter ones!) can struggle to militate against an inevitable bias in favour of
former colleagues. They can also lack experience of appropriate methodologies and research approaches and would benefit hugely from guidance
from their more experienced colleagues. But someone has to make the first
move – or the next move – before another market, like the teen market,
dies with barely any useful analysis from either side as to how or why, or
whether it even matters at all.

Magazines: where will they be in ten years' time?

If there is any hope that the gulf between magazine practice and theory
really can be bridged, then there is surely hope for the magazine industry
itself in these difficult times. One thing the world of magazines certainly has
in its favour is its unrelenting optimism. Says Greenslade (2006): 'Magazines
have a confidence in both the present and the future that newspapers lack', a
confidence displayed, without exception, by all 30 of the journalists interviewed for this chapter. Freelancer Moira Holden argues that magazines are
just too lovable to put down:

> A magazine can fold up and fit into your handbag or can be held easily in your hand.
> How many people do you see standing at a bus stop or a train station flicking through
> a laptop to pass the time? And nobody's going to want to mug you for a women's
> magazine, are they? The free newspapers and magazines could be a serious rival, but
> I still believe there are plenty of readers who will always want to immerse themselves in
> a magazine to get away from the real world. (2008 Personal Communication)

Editorial consultant Peter Genower believes the recession simply means
that readers will want the feel-good factor their magazines can provide
more than ever:

> I see a really healthy future for the treat market in particular. In a recession, people
> just want to feel good and that's what glossy magazines have always been able to do.

You just can't beat them for bendability, flexibility, and their sheer familiarity which gives them three things the digital media simply can't replicate. It's still about being able to read them in the bath, the smell of them, the look of them, the whole feelgood thing: it will take several generations to get that out of our systems, maybe forever. If we look way, way into the future, perhaps there will be a means of connection we haven't even thought of yet. But even if it's not on paper, I think people will still want what magazines provide. (2008 Personal Communication)

And editorial director of Future Publishing Jim Douglas went so far as to predict a 'really healthy future' for magazines, or at the very least for those magazines in his own 'specialist' market:

Magazines prove again and again that they are very resilient. One of the reasons they have been around so long is that they are a uniquely powerful medium. It's an unsurpassable relationship. The trust and affection for your favourite brand and the credibility that magazines have still outstrips most other media and certainly the Net. (2008 Personal Communication)

So-called media experts have mused often, but generally unproductively, about what the magazine of tomorrow might look like. Will it be all about 'mobizines', where readers/users receive content direct to their mobile phones – and, in the ultimate reader relationship, send content right back? Will magazines become entirely digital, with a new generation of users reading magazines on their laptops that have pages that can turn digitally? Will we soon be walking around with all our magazines on our Kindles? Will we begin to relish the new magazine apps for our iPads currently being pioneered by Conde Nast and others rather than being slightly bewildered by them? Will magazines overcome the cost barrier that currently resists the march of electronic paper, first pioneered by *Esquire* magazine's special 75th anniversary issue, which showed images on its cover that could actually change before the reader's eyes? Will we see a worldwide takeover by e-zines, magazines produced in people's bedrooms that generally make no money but cement the citizen journalist as the magazine practitioner of tomorrow – and, if so, where does that leave highly qualified journalism graduates paying large sums of money for courses which might then lead them to only unpaid jobs?

Some of these high tech gadgets will no doubt have their place while some won't: for example, the technology for 'page turning' digital magazines is already widely available, though few readers appear to be responding to it so far. But graduates can be cheered by the knowledge that whatever changes come, they will be there from the start: technology represents not a handicap but a huge opportunity. It has already helped turn magazines into global brands: many already have global editions; e.g. *FHM* has 30 editions worldwide, *Marie Claire* 24 (IPC Media online, 2006). But a huge benefit of the Web has been the capacity it provides to develop what would previously have been a UK-only product into a global brand:

> Sometimes you can just put the brand online – as with *Total Film* and *T3* – but in other areas like cycling we've launched umbrella sites under our 'Radar' banner, so our music titles are represented in our *Music Radar*, our biking titles are under *Bike Radar*, and the same with games and technology and so on. The driver for that? We've got to look and feel global. We want to be a global leader and we know *Mountain Biking UK* won't translate as a brand online because all our websites need a big share of US visitors. So, they need to feel international, in order to sell ads to US clients. (Douglas, 2008 Personal Communication)

His recent troubles aside, newspaper baron Rupert Murdoch has also long seen technology as an opportunity. Indeed, he believes the media world is on the verge of a 'golden age' in terms of media and technological developments, which will give the journalists of tomorrow a new opportunity to halt circulation declines:

> I'm sure (newspapers will) still be available on paper, it won't happen that fast. But you'll be able to – for instance, I'm sure you can have a tablet beside your bed, and you subscribe to the paper, and it'll come there wirelessly, and you've gotta pick it up, and read every page of the paper, on an electronic or battery-driven tablet. That sort of thing will happen. You may choose to read the paper that way; or you may have a more old-fashioned idea about it, or you may have it read to you on a iPod-type thing, which you can stick into your car as you drive to work in the morning. (BBC online, 2006)

Either way, Murdoch doesn't see newspaper brands disappearing entirely, a confidence magazine practitioners share about print magazines. Sarah Hart argues that the so-called credit crunch will simply force magazine publishers and editors to be more specific in what they are trying to achieve:

> It's important not to get swept away by ideas that have no substance. I went to an editors' training day once and we were coming up with ideas for the new *My Space* and people were getting really excited but clearly it was going nowhere. If you say that though, you're a dinosaur. But companies need to be careful they don't forget what they are supposed to be doing. Internet income is nothing compared to print so you've got to be realistic before you start shoving everything online. Some magazines will make money online, some need to develop the Web to promote their brand, for some there's a combination, for some you need to ask, is the site just for your advertisers? And then there's the other Pandora's Box. Are the people using your website the same people who read your magazine? Sometimes they will be, sometimes they won't, and you have to adapt accordingly. Having a blanket strategy doesn't work, it's got to be specific (to your readers' wants and needs) which for editors and their staff basically means a lot of sleepless nights. (2008 Personal Communication)

It doesn't mean a jobless future however. She continues:

> It's down to the zoological basic thing of how humans work. We all absorb information in different ways and will go to different media depending on what we want. Print fulfils a particular way of getting a type of information and always will. It will get harder. Maybe now we'll see markets closing in a bit, the weaker titles fading out. But though we may have fewer titles, the good ones will keep going because they will still offer something people want. (Personal Communication)

Sarah Pyper, who has worked in the US celebrity market (*US Weekly, In Touch*) as well as on *Sugar, Grazia, Red*, and *Eve*, agrees that there will definitely be a falling away of some magazines and the industry will inevitably contract down to fewer, more relevant titles:

> Magazines won't die but we will see the end of the magazines that don't really serve a useful purpose. The big brands and those that can justify their cover price will keep going but the middle of the road magazines that aren't really 100 per cent sure who they are and what place they occupy in the market will go by the wayside. (2009 Personal Communication)

But even that, argues Giles Barrie, may be a good thing:

> We need only look to history to see that we have been here before. We are probably facing the toughest year ever seen in magazines but I wouldn't mind betting that 20 years ago, at the start of the last recession, people were saying the same thing. But the things that make magazines special, the look and feel of them, the in-depth coverage, the sense of spoiling yourself and being in the know, will always be addictive to readers. And as much as magazines are being battered now, they are in a better position than newspapers. They will get through this difficult patch because they always do. And the magazines that do survive will be better than ever. (2009 Personal Communication)

It would be easy to be critical, even cynical, in the face of such optimism and enthusiasm as day after day more magazines fold. But equally, it suggests that magazine journalism and the people who work within it are unlikely to go down without a fight. Even Margi Conklin (2009 Personal Communication), after closing her beloved *Page Six*, succumbed to optimism in the end: 'Yes, it's a crisis but out of crisis can come some of the best and most innovative work you've ever done'.

So the future will be, says Martyn Moore:

> Exciting. Diverse. Fragmented into niches. Celebrating quality, luxury, the experience, and a great place for 'branding' ads. And of course print magazines will survive. Why wouldn't they? In the same way as there is still a great future for radio despite telly; films despite DVDs; and bicycles despite (or maybe because of) cars: magazines will go on forever. (2008 Personal Communication)

APPENDIX 1

The following is a more detailed survey of magazine companies and particular titles selected for the impact they have had beyond their immediate field.

Key Magazine Publishers of the Late 20th Century

IPC

IPC, the UK's largest magazine publishing company, was formed in 1968 following the amalgamation of Associated-Iliffe Press, George Newnes and Odhams Press, the UK's three most important magazine publishing houses of the time. IPC Magazines Ltd was part of the International Publishing Corporation Ltd, which also owned the *Daily Mirror, People* and *Sun* newspapers. The Corporation was bought by Reed Group – which had its roots in paper manufacture – in 1970 and incorporated into Reed International.

In 1998 IPC Magazines was sold to venture capitalist outfit Cinven for £860m and in 2001 sold again to AOL Time Warner for £1.15bn. IPC now sits within Time Inc's portfolio of assets.

Although IPC has a reputation for playing safe and its magazines have to be mass circulation to justify their existence within such a large corporate body, the simple fact that it has maintained its position at the top of the tree for so long suggests that it is, collectively, smart enough to combine keeping up with trends with the ability to satisfy large and disparate groups of established readers.

EMAP (Bauer)

EMAP (now Bauer Media) was formed as a regional newspaper publisher (East Midlands Allied Press) in 1947, based in Peterborough. In 1953 it launched *Angling Times* as a tabloid news magazine, followed by *Garden News* and *Motor Cycle News* in 1956. Fishing, gardening and motorcycling provided the basis for a stable of successful consumer magazines but things really took off with the launch of *Smash Hits* (1978) and *Just Seventeen*. Corporately, Emap expanded into business publishing, exhibitions, distribution, radio and television channels. Overseas ventures included operations in France, licensing titles to foreign publishers and an ill fated, and ultimately fatal, excursion into the US market with the acquisition of Petersen Publishing for £1bn (1998) – offloaded for £366m three years later.

Business continued apparently as normal until 2008, when the company suddenly seemed to run out of steam. The consumer magazine and radio arms were sold to Heinrich Bauer Verlag KG for £714.3m and £422m respectively. The business publishing side was later sold to a joint company formed by Apax Venture Partners and the Guardian Media Group.

Haymarket

Founded in 1957 by Michael Heseltine and Clive Labovitch, the company started as Cornmarket Press, publishing *The Directory of Opportunities for Graduates*. Two years later the company attempted to resuscitate the proto-men's magazine *Man About Town*, with considerable critical but little financial success – in fact the magazine's printer Hazell Watson & Viney put up a financial stake, leading to the formation of Haymarket and allowing the company to buy *MIMS* (the bible of the pharmaceutical business) and *GP*, the trade paper for doctors. Labovitch left in 1966, taking Cornhill as his share, and Heseltine – who was elected as an MP in the same year – had to sell a large stake in Haymarket to the British Printing Company (later a part of Robert Maxwell's empire) in order to survive, although this allowed him to add more trade titles to his stable, including *Management Today*.

In 1968 the company bought *World's Press News*, the weaker of two trade papers serving the advertising industry, closed it down and from the wreckage launched *Campaign*. The new magazine was a brilliant mixture of style and substance with thoroughly researched journalism allied to superb photography and it rapidly dominated the market.

With stable finances Haymarket was in a position to expand into the perhaps more exciting field of consumer publishing, launching *What Car?* in 1973; brand extension into awards ceremonies followed in 1984 and exhibitions in 1990; there were also joint ventures in Spain, France and Italy. In 1998 the last piece of the jigsaw was put in place when Haymarket moved into Customer publishing by developing *Racing Line* for F1 competitor McLaren. Finally, the company has been at the forefront of developing digital media; these may be based on standalone Consumer titles (*stuff. tv*), aggregate B2B print properties (*brandrepublic.com*) or be entirely new entities such as *PistonHeads*.

Future

Future was founded by journalist Chris Anderson in 1985. From his garage he put together a single magazine, *Amstrad Action*, but what really distinguished it was the cover-mounted computer disk, thus giving purchasers both something to read and something to play with on their computers. This pattern was followed for many of Future's subsequent hobby titles. Future has had a somewhat chequered corporate history, including being sold to Pearson plc (1994) and re-acquisition by Anderson, Greg Ingham and Apax Venture Partners (1998) but by mid-2008 seemed to have settled down under CEO Stevie Spring. Its current portfolio includes official titles for *Xbox 360*, *PlayStation* and *Nintendo*, *Digital Camera*, *Total Film*, *Classic Rock* and *Guitarist*, along with associated websites and digital offshoots. Future has a very active overseas licensing division and a contract publishing division, Future Plus.

Chris Anderson now curates the TED (Technology, Entertainment, Design) conferences.

BBC Magazines

The BBC's first magazines were *Radio Times* (September 1923) and the *Listener* (1929-1991). In 1987 the BBC licensed Focus Magazines to produce a quarterly magazine to accompany the *Clothes Show* programme (it closed in 1997). When both the BBC and ITV were forced to provide advance listings to other outlets, the BBC sought to make up lost revenue by buying Redwood, a publisher of contract titles, and developing a range of magazines based on BBC brands like *Top Gear*, *Good Food* and *Gardeners' World*.

BBC Magazines parted company from Redwood in 1993, and since then has developed titles in many sectors, most of them based on programmes. Those that are not based on specific programmes, such as *All About Animals* in the pre-teen market, or *Top of the Pops*, where the magazine has outlived the programme, have to achieve a quality of 'connectivity' with BBC output and the corporation's values.

In 2004 BBC Magazines bought a small contract and consumer publisher based in Bristol. A number of smaller circulation titles (*BBC History*, *BBC Music*) were transferred to Bristol Magazines, which has launched titles based on the family history show *Who Do You Think You Are?* and the long running *CountryFile*.

BBC Magazines is the third largest publisher of consumer magazines in the UK, licenses many titles to overseas publishers, has a lively joint venture with the *Times of India*, is focused on making its brands platform neutral – and in 2010, as part of the BBC's strategic review, announced that it was seeking a commercial partner to take over its titles.

Dennis Publishing

Dennis Publishing was founded in 1973 by Felix Dennis with money earned from a biography of martial artist Bruce Lee that contained the last interview before he died. Early titles tended to be one-shots (single issues on a special subject, such as Kung Fu) and from these Dennis grew a personal fortune and a thriving publishing company that currently includes *Maxim* (at one time the most successful men's magazine in the USA and possibly the world), *Auto Express*, *Viz* and *The Week* among its brands. The latter title was a shrewd acquisition by Dennis, who has never been afraid of putting his money where he believed a profit could be made, and a concept that Dennis Publishing is rolling out globally. "There is no country in the world where the concept of *The Week* will not work," Dennis told Arif Durrani of *Media Week* (*Media Week*, 19/5/2009).

Dennis Publishing has also led the way into multimedia with the launch of *Monkey*, *iGizmo* and *iMotor* as digitally delivered magazines. Dennis Communications is the contract publishing arm.

Felix Dennis will always be tagged as one of the "Oz three" following his brief spell in jail alongside Richard Neville and Jim Anderson – punishment for being found guilty of publishing an obscene edition of the underground magazine. Doubtless he reflects on this often while contemplating the Caribbean from his luxurious villa on Mustique. He has several volumes of poetry to his name.

RBI (Reed Business Information)

RBI is acknowledged to be the world's largest business-to-business publisher and exhibition organiser. It publishes over 400 B2B magazines and their associated digital offshoots, supports 200 online communities and runs 500 associated events. It is divided into four sections, covering the UK, the US, the Netherlands and Exhibitions. Its 100-plus UK titles include *New Scientist*, *Farmers' Weekly*, *Personnel Today* and *Flight International*; among its US titles is *Variety*, the 'bible' of the entertainment industry.

RBI was formed after the British publisher Reed merged with Dutch publisher Elsevier to form Reed Elsevier. Reed started life in 1889 when Albert Reed bought a paper mill in Dartford, Kent, and five years later added another mill near Aylesford. The business soon specialised in newsprint, supplying *The Times* among others, and continued to expand into paper and paper-related fields, grew into a paper and board producing giant around the world, then acquired businesses that needed paper, such as newspapers and magazines. The Dutch side of the business goes back to 1880, when Jacobus George Robbers set up a publishing company in Rotterdam. He called it Elsevier after a noted family of 16th century booksellers and printers.

In 1970 the British company was renamed Reed International Limited and bought the IPC-Mirror Group. This brought the newspaper and significant magazine, periodical and book publishing and printing interests, including Odhams, George Newnes, National Trade Press, Pearsons, Collinridge, Amalgamated Press, Kellys, Thomas Skinner, Iliffe & Son, Hulton Press and Butterworths. Reed's publishing activities were separated into Mirror Group Newspapers and IPC in 1974 and the magazine side was organised into IPC Business Press Ltd and IPC Magazines Ltd.

Reed International and Elsevier merged in 1993, and shortly afterwards sold Reed Regional Newspapers in a £210 million management buyout – the papers were renamed Newsquest Media Group and later acquired by Gannett. The consumer magazine interests were finally disposed of in 1998 with a management buyout of IPC Magazines (see above). In 2002 the company changed its name to Reed Elsevier PLC.

The conglomerate has three operating divisions, Elsevier, Lexis-Nexis and RBI. In February 2008 Reed Elsevier decided that it no longer wanted to be in the advertising-dependent B2B magazine publishing business and put RBI up for sale at £1.25bn. At the time of writing (July 2010) it had not found a buyer.

Redwood

The three men who formed Redwood in November 1983 were, respectively, a former Fleet Street editor, a magazine company director and one of the pioneers of home computing. Christopher Ward (ex-*Daily Express*), Michael Potter (ex-Haymarket) and Chris Curry (founder of Acorn Computers) all believed there was a gap in the market for publishing magazines on behalf of other companies. Or rather, for publishing *good* magazines that their clients' customers would want to read.

The first Redwood-produced title was *E!*, sent to 230,000 American Express card holders. *E!* looked and felt like a quality magazine and contributors such as Kingsley Amis, Keith Waterhouse, Anthony Burgess, Jack Higgins, Max Hastings and Leslie Thomas helped to provide compelling content. Redwood confidently claim that the title 'earned its place in history as the first real customer magazine'. (Sara Cremer, personal communication)

Other landmark Redwood productions have included *The M&S Magazine* (qv), *Sky TV Guide* (qv) and the first iterations of BBC magazines – *Good Food* and *Top Gear* among them.

Key UK Titles of the Late 20th Century

Consumer Magazines

Angling Times (Emap: 1953–) was first published as a way of keeping the East Midland Allied Press printworks busy in downtime. Its appearance was much more like a newspaper than a magazine but it harnessed the enthusiasm and thirst for knowledge and information of a very broad, but specific, niche, fishing being the UK's largest participatory pastime. The profits from this specialist weekly laid the foundations for Emap to build one of the biggest periodical empires in the UK and a chain of radio stations ... before it all fell apart and was sold to Bauer.

Nova (IPC: 1965–1975) helped to define and document the swinging 60s for women and led to 'modern' women's magazines. The content caused some culture-shock for IPC's managers; speaking to Jeremy Leslie of magculture.com *Nova*'s art editor David Hillman explained:

> Our editorial director was also in charge of *Woman* and *Woman's Own*. They were full of knitting patterns, never upset anybody. Each magazine had editorial meetings every Wednesday, so he'd leave the *Woman* meeting where he'd be discussing which royal family story they were going to run, come upstairs to *Nova*, to find this months cover story was sexually transmitted diseases in woman's prisons. (http://magculture.com/blog/?p=587<accessed 2/7/10>)

But once *Nova* had beaten the path, Hillman continued, everyone else followed:

> We opened the door for every other fucking magazine in the UK. *Nova* talked about buggery, transvestites, gay this, gay that. The minute we did it even *Woman's Own* in its prim little way was able to approach the same subject. A taboo had been broken, we'd put our neck on the block. (loc cit)

Car (Natmags, ForceFour, FF, Murdoch, Emap/Bauer: 1960s–) took what had been a fairly dull technical/enthusiast genre and added literary writing, great photography and outstanding art editing. In doing so, it tripled sales and led to motoring magazines that offered entertainment, information and aesthetic pleasure, and thus to the international behemoth that is Top Gear. Former editor Mel Nichols remembers:

> I took its circulation from 33,000 to 90,000. I guess it was Wendy Harrop, the art director, and I who defined and refined the relationship between its journalism and its photography and graphics ... Apart from the more literary, experiential writing style we developed, *Car*'s approach to photography and design also profoundly affected many other motoring magazines, particularly in the UK and US but in Japan, Scandinavia and Germany too. (Mel Nichols, Personal Communication)

The Face (Wagadon, Emap: 1980–2004) captured a small but influential style-and-clubbing scene, aided by Neville Brody's trend-setting art design. Founding editor Nick Logan had achieved great commercial success for Emap with *Smash Hits* but *The Face* was where his heart lay. The magazine gained a second wind when Richard Benson took over as editor. *The Face* established a new sector that was also populated by *Blitz* and *i-D* and has caused much excitement over the years among academic commentators who discerned the identity formation of the 'new man' in its pages. Sadly for them, this aspect of gender role revision was wiped out by ...

Loaded (IPC: 1994–), the IPC launch that started the genre of lad mags, usually credited to James Brown but Mick Bunnage and Tim Southwell were important to the development of the new title. The magazine's strapline, 'For Men Who Should Know Better', implied a knowing and wilful reaction to the idea of the 'new man' but for all its descent into tawdriness, *Loaded* initially offered a breath of fresh air under James Brown's editorship; it was a magazine for men that was neither a hobby book nor a skin mag. Sadly, as the new sector became over-populated with would-be copycat publications quality and originality took a dive, leading its progenitor to disown it. At a PTC awards ceremony in 2000 Brown took to the stage to say:

> If I'd known when I started *Loaded* that the men's sector would descend into a conveyor belt of old soap stars in bikinis, I assure you I would not have done it ... Content-wise, I think the men's sector is stale, predictable and uninspiring. It is an embarrassment. The bigger companies that produce the magazines should be embarrassed with themselves because they have the finances to keep their titles stable and they haven't had the guts to do it. (Personal note of speech)

In October 2010 IPC sold *Loaded* to Vitality, a company best known for publishing the gay man's lifestyle title *Attitude*.

Smash Hits (Emap: 1979–2006) and *Just Seventeen* (Emap: 1983–2004) between them shook up, dominated and shaped the teen market that had previously been ruled by DC Thomson's *Jackie*. However, even these titles that influenced the way teenage girls spoke and that sold hundreds of thousands of copies at their peak proved unsustainable in face of socio-cultural change. Their readerships fell away, advertising revenue plunged and they closed within two years of each other.

When *Smash Hits* closed, former editor David Hepworth commented:

> Smash Hits began life as a pop music magazine. It wrote about anybody who got in the charts. Its early covers featured Donna Summer, Jimmy Pursey, Elton John and Plastic Bertrand. Founding editor Nick Logan's attitude was 'try anything and see what works' ... The problem in any media enterprise arises when you learn what works and then attempt to repeat it. This was no longer a pop magazine read by girls. It was a girls' magazine. Then it was a girls' magazine read by girls who liked the groups built for

girls. What had begun as a broad church turned into a narrow sect and then became less appealing even to that narrow sect until, like the 14-year-old Billie Piper with the bubble gum on one of the many TV ad campaigns that failed to save it, Smash Hits simply went pop. (http://www.guardian.co.uk/media/2006/feb/06/mondaymedia-section.pressandpublishing<accessed 2/7/10>)

Since then, *Smash Hits* has been revived for a couple of special issues, notably after Michael Jackson's death.

Bella and *Best* (H Bauer; G&J of the UK, NatMags: 1985–) spearheaded an attack by German publishers H Bauer and Gruner & Jahr that successfully challenged the cosy dominance of IPC's weeklies *Woman, Woman's Own* and *Woman's Weekly*. This was a de facto, and perhaps inevitable, globalisation of magazine market that has been analysed in *Women's Weekly Market In Great Britain* (Evans, Evans and Ungersma, Cardiff: nd) but it also led to a major shake up of women's weeklies, one result of which was …

Take A Break (H Bauer: 1990–), which has become a consistent leader in its field and is one of the few magazines to have nurtured its own political party – twice: the Mum's Army of 2006 and Voices For Women of 2010 (http://blogs.pressgazette.co.uk/wire/6745).

Heat (Emap, Bauer: 1999–), which started as a general entertainment title but soon became the touchstone of snide celebrity reportage, was another by-product of the shake-up in women's publishing. Although it came after the launches of *Hello* (1988) and *OK!* (1993), that had between them established the genre in the UK, *Heat* took the form to a higher – or lower – level than its precursors.

Customer Magazines

High Life (Highgate Publications; Cedar Communications: 1973–) was founded by Bill Davies, one of the busiest, yet comparatively unsung, journalists of the 20th century. Davies's career encompassed the *Financial Times*, the *Evening Standard*, the *Guardian*, BBC radio (he presented the *World at One* in its early days) and television (the *Money Programme* was his idea) and *Punch*. *High Life* was among the first in-flight magazines and is a very early, and long lived, example of modern Customer publishing. It has been joined by siblings *Business Life* and *High Life Shopping*.

Sky TV Guide/SKY: The Magazine/SkyMag/Sky Magazine (Redwood, John Brown, News Magazines, BSkyB Publications: 1994–) deserves its place here because it is the biggest magazine, by far, in the UK. Its ABC-audited circulation for the period July to December 2009 was 7,423,570. It started as a straightforward television guide for BSkyB subscribers but developed into a full blown magazine as it passed through the skilled hands of first Redwood Publishing and then John Brown Citrus, two of the country's most successful contract magazine publishers. When News Corporation set up News Magazines in 2006, the company bid for and, perhaps unsurprisingly, won the contract to produce *Sky*. Sadly, magazines proved one field that Rupert Murdoch's empire could not successfully conquer and the title has moved in-house to BSkyB.

The M&S Magazine (Redwood: 1987–) was the UK's first retail customer title and it changed both the face of this type of magazine and the way they are published. As Redwood's editorial director Sara Cremer notes:

> Not only was this the first retail customer magazine, but it was a turning point for Redwood in determining the content and positioning of all future customer magazines. The power of the planning department was born as focus groups and research revealed what readers demanded of the magazine: 'More information about M&S products and services please!'

> The magazine, which was to have been called *Seasons*, was promptly renamed *The M&S Magazine* and every page would be a selling page 'only it wouldn't look that way to customers'. From that moment on, relevance became the guiding light for Redwood editors in shaping editorial content. (Personal communication)

B2B Magazines

Management Today (Haymarket et al: 1966–) was a joint venture by Haymarket, the British Institute of Management, the *Financial Times* and the *Economist*. It gave business managers a lively, well informed, interesting and good looking publication of their own. The didactic purpose was to help improve the quality of management in the UK, but it was presented in an extremely palatable way. Lessons learned from this were soon applied to …

Campaign (Haymarket: 1968–) was launched, phoenix like, from the remains of a periodical called *World Press News* that had been bought by Haymarket Publishing, run by Michael Heseltine. Where *WPN* had been dull and worthy, *Campaign* was bright, inquisitive and imbued the advertising industry with a sheen of glamour that has lasted to this day. If nothing else, *Campaign* demonstrated that it was possible, and even desirable, to publish a trade magazine (the sector had not then been dubbed B2B) that borrowed art direction ideas from the consumer press, including stunning photography.

Online Magazines

The online magazine is now commonplace, either as a standalone venture or as a brand extension of a print title. There was a time, however, when launching an online magazine was a leap into the unknown.

NME.com (IPC: 1996–) was highly influential in demonstrating the power of the web to reach a new audience. Launched under the editorship of Brendan Fitzgerald, it was not until Anthony Thornton redesigned the site in 1998 with a focus on news that it began to make waves, winning the PPA Website Of The Year twice and gaining for Thornton the British Society of Magazine Editors Online Editor of the Year award. The ability to present up-to-the-second news was soon allied to the power to purchase gig tickets and albums, creating a strong business model.

Topgear.com (BBC Worldwide) is notable for being one leg of a tri-partite cross-platform strategy intended to give the brand a 360-degree media presence. The other legs are print (the magazine) and television (the programme). Before implementing the plan in 2007, the BBC had to overcome numerous internal barriers to allow all three elements to operate from the same physical space, and it is this integration of all three that warrants *Top Gear*'s appearance here.

Pistonheads.com (Dave Edmonston; Haymarket: 1999–) was set-up by Dave Edmonston as a place where owners of TVR sports cars could discuss panel fit, engine failure and electrical meltdowns. This simple idea captured something essential, the forums expanded to include other marques and topics and by the end of 2006 it was attracting 900,000 unique users and 28 million page impressions every month – a huge 'readership' that rivalled the online versions of well-established print magazines.

In January 2007 Haymarket, publisher of print and online magazines such as *What Car?* and *Autocar*, made Edmonston an offer he could not refuse and incorporated the website into its stable – a brave and radical move considering that the title's main asset was its online community, an entity that could disappear literally at any moment. However, it is also a move that indicates a strong belief in the communitarian aspect of magazine theory and thus the action of a committed *magazine* publisher.

Hybrid/Bookazine/Specials

The bookazine has become something of a staple on the news stand – thicker and less designed than a magazine, thinner and more picture-led than a book and focused on a single topic. The bookazine tradition goes back a long way – for example, roadtests from the American motorcycle magazine *Cycle World* provided specialist publisher Brooklands with the material for many slim volumes: pages from the magazine literally reproduced and bound together behind an index. Next step up is for a large newsagent (such as WH Smith) to commission an author (or, increasingly, publisher) to write 20,000 words on a particular subject (such as tv programme *Heartbeat*) and market the resulting bookazine as an 'exclusive' publication.

Pistonheads: The Best Bits 2009 (Haymarket) went one further in taking a selection of material from the website, including reader contributions such as forum postings, and publishing it as a 200-page paper edition.

This is a phenomenon we will almost certainly see more of; for example, in June 2010 Future Publishing announced that it was launching a 132-page print version of its online technology portal *TechRadar* and more are planned. In the USA, Hearst's CEO Cathie Black explained:

> Another retail strategy we're using to drive growth is the 'bookazine', a magazine generated from branded Hearst content. As part of our overall strategy to offer consumers and advertisers multiple access routes into Hearst-branded content, we are also planning more products that convert digital content to print. (http://news.ipda.org/march-10/march-10/hearst-magazines-president-on-the-power-of-retail.html)

Hearst's British outpost is the National Magazine Company (NatMags), whose titles include *Cosmopolitan, Good Housekeeping* and *Esquire*, so this is another trend that will almost certainly spread across the Atlantic.

Whatever the exact form or format, one thing is for sure – magazines will survive. Compare what *The Spectator* wrote on 2 April 1831 with the situation today and make your own judgement:

> We are afraid the day for Magazines is gone by; it is a form of publication which does not suit the wants of the reading world, in the present state of literature. The Newspapers and the Weekly Reviews, in their improved and extended form, have taken the ground formerly occupied by the Magazines, and with great advantage of more frequent publication ... Magazines formerly occupied the precise position of some of the present Weekly Papers; witness the list of bankrupts, the obituary, the prices of stocks, etc., which formerly adorned them, and which are now omitted simply because they are forestalled by the Newspaper. (Herd, 1952: 204)

BIBLIOGRAPHY

Books & articles

Abrahamson, David (1996a) 'The bright new-media future for magazines', *Magazine Matter*, The Newsletter of the AEJMC Magazine Division, Summer.

Abrahamson, David (1996b) *Magazine-Made America: The Cultural Transformation of the Postwar Periodical.* Cresskill, NJ: Hampton.

Akbar, Arifa (2008) 'Scarlett sees red over fake interview', the *Independent*, 16 December, accessed online at www.independent.co.uk/news/media/press/scarlett-sees-red-over-fake-interview-1128202.html

Aldridge, Meryl (1998) 'The tentative hell-raisers: identity and mythology in contemporary UK press journalism', *Media, Culture & Society*, 20 (1): 109–127.

Allan, Stuart (2004) *News Culture* (2nd Edn). Maidenhead: Open University Press.

Altick, Richard D. (1957) *The English Common Reader: A Social History of the Mass Reading Public 1800–1900.* Chicago: University of Chicago Press.

Altick, Richard D. (1974) *Victorian People and Ideas.* London: JM Dent.

Amos, Owen (2009) 'Reed Business Information journalists in strike ballot', *Press Gazette*, 17 February, accessed online at www.pressgazette.co.uk/story.asp?storycode=43107

Anderson, Benedict (1983) *Imagined Communities: Reflections on the Origin and Spread of Nationalism.* London: Verso.

Anderson, Chris (2009) *Free: The Future of a Radical Price.* London: Random House.

Andrews, Amanda (2006) 'Teenagers turn backs on lifestyle magazines', *The Times*, 12 August, accessed online at business.timesonline.co.uk/tol/business/industry_sectors/media/article606912.ece

Angeletti, Norberto and Oliva, Alberto (2004) *Magazines That Make History: Their Origins, Development, and Influence.* Gainesville/Barcelona: University Press of Florida/Editorial Sol 90.

Ballaster, Ros, Beetham, Margaret, Frazer, Elizabeth and Hebron, Sandra (1991) *Women's Worlds: Ideology, Femininity and the Woman's Magazine.* Basingstoke: Macmillan.

Barrell, Joan and Braithwaite, Brian (1988 [1979]) *The Business of Women's Magazines.* London: Kogan Page.

Barthes, Roland (1974) *S/Z* (translated by Richard Miller). New York: Hill and Wang/The Noonday Press.

BBC online (2006) 'Cameron must offer alternative', 23 January, accessed online at news.bbc.co.uk/1/hi/uk/4637948.stm

Beetham, Margaret (1990) 'Towards a theory of the periodical as a publishing genre', in Laurel Brake, Aled Jones and Lionel Madden (eds), *Investigating Victorian Journalism*. Basingstoke: Macmillan. pp. 19–32.

Beetham, Margaret (1996) *A Magazine of Her Own*. London: Routledge.

Beetham, Margaret and Boardman, Kay (2001) *Victorian Women's Magazines: An Anthology*. Manchester: Manchester University Press.

Benwell, Bethan (ed.) (2003) *Masculinity and Men's Lifestyle Magazines*. Oxford: Blackwell.

Berger, Maurice, Wallis, Brian and Watson, Simon (eds) (1995) *Constructing Masculinity*. New York: Routledge.

Billings, Claire (2008) 'Monkey magazine expands into mobile tv', 13 March, accessed online at *Brand Republic* www.brandrepublic.com/Discipline/Media/News/790633/Monkey-magazine-expands-mobile-TV/

Bird, S. Elizabeth (1992) *For Enquiring Minds: A Cultural Study of Supermarket Tabloids*. Knoxville: University of Tennessee Press.

Bjørnsen, Gunn, Hovden, Jan Fredrik and Ottosen, Rune (2007) 'Journalists in the making: findings from a longitudinal study of Norwegian journalism students', *Journalism Practice*, 1 (3): 383–403.

Black, Jeremy (1992) 'The eighteenth century British press', in Dennis Griffiths (ed.), *The Encyclopedia of the British Press 1422–1992*. London: Macmillan. pp. 13–23.

Bonham-Carter, Victor (1978) *Authors By Profession, Volume 1*. London: Society of Authors.

Boyce, George (1978) 'The Fourth Estate: the reappraisal of a concept', in George Boyce, James Curran and Pauline Wingate (eds), *Newspaper History from the Seventeenth Century to the Present Day*. London: Sage. pp. 19–40.

Boyce, George, Curran, James and Wingate, Pauline (eds) (1978) *Newspaper History from the Seventeenth Century to the Present Day*. London: Sage.

Boyd-Barrett, Oliver (1970) 'Journalism recruitment and training: problems in professionalization', in Jeremy Tunstall (ed.), *Media Sociology: A Reader*. Chicago: University of Illinois Press. pp. 181–201.

Braithwaite, Brian (1995) *Women's Magazines: The First 300 Years*. London: Peter Owen.

Brake, Laurel (1994) *Subjugated Knowledges: Journalism, Gender & Literature in the Nineteenth Century*. Basingstoke: Macmillan.

Brake, Laurel, Jones, Aled and Madden, Lionel (eds) (1990) *Investigating Victorian Journalism*. Basingstoke: Macmillan.

Brants, Kees, Hermes, Joke and van Zoonen, Liesbet (1998) *The Media In Question: Popular Cultures and Public Interests*. London: Sage.

Brog, Annabel (2005) 'Teenage girl still has time for magazines, whateva' she says', *Press Gazette*, 25 August.

Brook, Stephen (2009) 'Sales slump hits homes magazines', the *Guardian*, 12 February, accessed online at www.guardian.co.uk/media/2009/feb/12/magazine-abcs-sales-slump-hits

Brown, Lucy (1992) 'The British Press 1800–1860', in Dennis Griffiths (ed.), *The Encyclopedia of the British Press 1422–1992*. London: Macmillan.

Buckingham, David (1993) *Children Talking Television: The Making of Television Literacy*. London: Falmer.

Burrell, Ian (2008) 'A new woman climbs aboard Redwood stage', the *Independent*, 19 May, accessed online at www.independent.co.uk/news/media/a-new-woman-climbs-aboard-redwood-stage-830553.html

Careers Advice Service (2008) Magazine Journalist Job Profile, accessed online at careersadvice.direct.gov.uk/helpwithyourcareer/jobprofiles/profiles/profile124/

Carr-Saunders, Alexander Maurice and Wilson, Paul Alexander (2001 [1933]) 'Journalists', in Jeremy Tunstall (ed.), *Media Occupations and Professions: A Reader*. Oxford: Oxford University Press. pp. 37–41 (originally published in *The Professions*, Oxford: Clarendon Press).

Cassidy, Anne (2008) 'Asda admits "mistake" in magazine distribution row', *Brand Republic*, 31 July, accessed online www.brandrepublic.com/News/835790/Asda-admits-mistake-magazine-distribution-row/

Chambers, Deborah, Steiner, Linda and Fleming, Carole (2004) *Women And Journalism*. London: Routledge.

Clair, Colin (1965) *A History of Printing in Britain*. London: Cassell.

Clarke, John, Hall, Stuart, Jefferson, Tony and Roberts, Brian (1975) 'Subcultures, cultures and class' in Stuart Hall and Tony Jefferson (eds), *Resistance Through Rituals*. London: Routledge. pp. 9–74.

Click, William J. and Baird, Russell N. (1990) *Magazine Editing and Production*. Dubuque: William C. Brown.

Cole, Peter (2003) 'Escaping from the timewarp', *British Journalism Review*, 14 (1): 54–60.

Conboy, Martin (2004) *Journalism: A Critical History*. London: Sage.

Considerine, Guy (2002) *How Magazine Advertising Works IV*. London: PPA.

Coyle, Martin, Garside, Peter, Kelsall, Malcolm and Peck, John (eds) (1990) *Encylopedia Of Literature and Criticism*. London: Routledge.

Cozens, Claire (2006) 'What women want', the *Guardian*, 23 January accessed online at www.guardian.co.uk/media/2006/jan/23/nationalmagazinecompany.pressandpublishing

Crawley-Boevey, Sarah (2009) 'Marketing Special Report: The marketers' perspective', *Marketing*, 27 January, accessed online at www.marketingmagazine.co.uk/news/877052/Marketing-Special-Report-marketers-perspective/

Crewe, Ben (2003) *Representing Men: Cultural Production and Producers in the Men's Magazine Market*. Oxford: Berg.

Curran, J., Gurevitch, M. and Woollacott, J. (eds) (1977) *Mass Communication and Society*. London: Edward Arnold/Open University.

Curran, James and Seaton, Jean (1997) *Power Without Responsibility: The Press and Broadcasting in Britain* (5th edn). London: Routledge.

Curran, J., Smith, A. and Wingate, P. (eds) (1987) *Impacts and Influences: Essays on Media Power in the Twentieth Century*. London: Methuen.

Currie, Dawn H. (1999) *Girl Talk: Adolescent Magazines and Their Readers*. Toronto: University of Toronto Press.

Cushion, Stephen (2007) 'Rich media, poor journalists', *Journalism Practice*, 1 (1): 120–129.

Davies, Loraine (2010) 'Launch of MagNet', *InPublishing*, InPub Weekly #011 23 July, available online at www.inpublishing.co.uk/kb/articles/launch_of_magnet.aspx

Davies, Nick (2008) *Flat Earth News*. London: Chatto and Windus.

Davis, Antony (1988) *Magazine Journalism Today*. London: Focal.

de Bruin, Marjan (2000) 'Gender, organizational and professional identities in journalism', *Journalism* 1 (2): 217–238.

de Burgh, Hugo (ed.) (2005) *Making Journalists: Diverse Models, Global Issues*. Abingdon: Routledge. pp. 25–43.

De Castella, Tom (2008) 'The seven ages of magazine readers', *Media Week*, 30 September, accessed online at www.mediaweek.co.uk/news/849870/seven-ages-magazine-readers/

Delano, Anthony (2000) 'No sign of a better job: 100 years of British journalism', *Journalism Studies*, 1 (2): 261–272.

Duffin, Amy and Nacer, Rachel (eds) (2010) *FIPP World Magazine Trends 09/10*. London: FIPP.

Duffy, Margaret and Gotcher, J. Michael (1996) 'Crucial advice on how to get the guy: the rhetorical vision of power and seduction in the teen magazine', *YM Journal of Communication Inquiry*, 20: 32–48.

Duke, Lisa (2000) 'Black in a blonde world: race and girls' interpretations of the feminine ideal in teen magazines', *Journalism and Mass Communication Quarterly*, 77 (2): 367–392.

Dyson, Lynda (2007) 'Customer magazines: the rise of "glossies" as brand extensions', in Tim Holmes (ed.), *Mapping the Magazine: Comparative Studies in Magazine Journalism*. London: Routledge. pp. 113–120.

Ernst & Young India (2010) *The Indian Magazine Segment: Navigating New Growth Avenues*. New Delhi: Ernst & Young.

Errigo, Jackie and Franklin, Bob (2004) 'Surviving in the hackademy', *British Journalism Review*, 15 (2): 43–48.

Evans, Ellis D., Rutberg, Judith, Sather, Carmela and Turner, Charli (1991) 'Content analysis of contemporary teen magazines for adolescent females', *Youth and Society*, 23: 99–120.

Evans, Jessica and Hesmondhalgh, David (2005) *Understanding Media, Inside Celebrity*. Maidenhead: Open University Press.

Feng, Yang and Frith, Katherine (2008) 'The growth of international women's magazines in China and the role of transnational advertising', *Journal of Magazine and New Media Research*, 10 (1): 1–14.

Ferguson, Marjorie (1983) *Forever Feminine: Women's Magazines and the Cult of Femininity*. London: Heinemann.

Festinger, Leon (1962) *A Theory of Cognitive Dissonance*. London: Tavistock.

FIPP (2003) bit.ly/FIPP_Lat_Am

FIPP (2010) bit.ly/FIPP_abril

Franklin, Bob (1997) *Newszak and News Media*. London: Arnold.

Franklin, Bob (2008) (ed.) *Pulling Newspapers Apart: Analysing Print Journalism*. London: Routledge.

Frazer, Elizabeth (1987) 'Teenage girls reading *Jackie*', *Media Culture and Society*, 9 (4): 407–425.

Friedan, Betty (1963) *The Feminine Mystique*. New York: Dell.

Frith, Simon and Meech, Peter (2007) 'Becoming a journalist: journalism education and journalism culture', *Journalism*, 8 (2): 137–164.

Gauntlett, David (2008) *Media, Gender and Identity* (2nd edn). London: Routledge.

Gillmor, Dan (2004) *We the Media: Grassroots Journalism by the People, for the People*. Sebastopol: O'Reilly Media.

Glover, Stephen (1999) *Secrets Of The Press: Journalists on Journalism*. London: Penguin.

Goldstein, Tom (1985) *The News at Any Cost: how journalists compromise their ethics to shape the news*. New York: Simon and Schuster.

Gough-Yates, Anna (2003) *Understanding Women's Magazines Publishing, Markets and Readerships*. London: Routledge.

Greenberg, Susan (2007) 'Theory and practice in journalism education', *Journal of Media Practice*, 8 (2/3): 1–9.

Greenslade, Roy (2006) 'What newspapers can learn from magazines', Greenslade blog, the *Guardian*, 22 September, accessed online at www.guardian.co.uk/media/greenslade/2006/sep/22/whatnewspaperscanlearnfrom

Greenslade, Roy (2007) 'Why I'm saying farewell to the NUJ', the *Guardian*, 25 October, accessed online at www.guardian.co.uk/media/greenslade/2007/oct/25/whyimsayingfarewelltothe

Greenwood, Ernest (1966) 'Attributes of a Profession', in Howard M. Vollmer and Donald L. Mills (eds) *Professionalization*. Englewood Cliffs, NJ: Prentice Hall. pp 10–19.

Griffiths, Dennis (ed.) (1992) *The Encyclopedia of the British Press 1422–1992*. London: Macmillan.

Grogan, Sarah (1999) *Body Image: Understanding Body Dissatisfaction in Men, Women and Children*. London: Routledge.

Habermas, Jürgen (1989) *The Structural Transformation of the Public Sphere: An Inquiry into a Category of Bourgeois Society*. Cambridge: Polity.

Hailin, Henry He (2009) *China In Their Hands*, available online at http://bit.ly/FIPP-Hailin

Hall, Stuart and Jefferson, Tony (eds) (1975) *Resistance Through Rituals*. London; Routledge.

Hampton, Mark (2004) *Visions of the Press in Britain, 1850–1950*. Urbana & Chicago: University of Chicago Press.

Hanna, Mark and Sanders, Karen (2007) 'Journalism education in Britain', *Journalism Practice*, 1(3): 404–420.

Hargreaves, Ian (ed.) (2002) *Journalists at Work*. London: Journalism Training Forum.

Harris, Michael and Lee, Alan (eds) (1986) *The Press in English Society from the Seventeenth to Nineteenth Centuries*. London and Toronto: Associated University Presses.

Hartley, John (2000) 'Communicative democracy in a redactional society: the future of journalism studies', *Journalism*, 1 (1): 39–47.

Hebdige, Dick (1979) *Subculture: The Meaning of Style*. London: Methuen.

Henningham, John and Delano, Anthony (1998) 'British journalists', in David Weaver (ed.), *The Global Journalist: News People Around the World*. Cresskill, NJ: Hampton: pp. 143–160.

Hepworth, David (2006) *Media Guardian*, 6 February, p. 3.

Hepworth, David (2007) 'The end of teenage', *And Another Thing* blog, 11 July, accessed at whatsheonaboutnow.blogspot.com/2007/07/end-of-teenage.html?showComment=1184169960000

Hepworth, David (2008) 'OK for some – but celeb weeklies suffer', the *Guardian*, 18 February, accessed online at www.guardian.co.uk/media/2008/feb/18/abcs.pressandpublishing

Herd, Harold (1952), *The March Of Journalism: The Story of the British Press from 1622 to the Present Day*. London: Allen & Unwin.

Hermes, Joke (1995) *Reading Women's Magazines An Analysis of Everyday Media Use*. Cambridge: Polity.

Hicks, Joe and Allen, Grahame (eds) (1999) A *Century of Change: Trends in UK Statistics since 1900*: House of Commons research paper 99/111, 21 December. Westminster: House of Commons.

Holmes, David and Nice, Liz (2009) '"The 'End Generation": Will the internet kill print media?', unpublished paper.

Holmes, Tim (2007) 'Mapping the magazine, an introduction', *Journalism Studies*, 8 (4): 510–521.

Holmes, Tim (ed.) (2008) *Mapping the Magazine: Comparative Studies in Magazine Journalism*. Abingdon: Routledge.

Houghton, Walter E. (ed.) (1966) *The Wellesley Index to Victorian Periodicals, 1824–1900*. Toronto: University of Toronto Press.

Hujanen, Jaana, Lehtniemi, Ninni and Virranta, Riiki (2008) *Mapping Communication and Media Research in the UK*. Jyvaskyla: University of Jyvaskyla.

Jackson, Peter, Stevenson, Nick and Brooks, Kate (2001) *Making Sense of Men's Magazines*. Cambridge: Polity.

Johnson, Sammye (2007) 'Why should they care? The relationship of academic scholarship to the industry', *Journalism Studies*, 8 (4): 522–528.

Johnson, Sammye and Prijatel, Patricia (1999) *The Magazine From Cover To Cover: Inside a Dynamic Industry*. Chicago, IL: NTC.

Journalism Practice, 1 (3): 383–403.

Klancher, John (1990) in Martin Coyle, Peter Garside, Malcolm Kelsall and John Peck (eds), *Encylopedia Of Literature and Criticism*. London: Routledge.

Korinek, Valerie (2000) *Roughing it in the Suburbs: Reading* Chatelaine *Magazine in the Fifties and Sixties*. Toronto: University of Toronto Press.

Langer, John (1998) *Tabloid Television, Popular Journalism and the 'Other News'*. London: Routledge.

Lee, Alan J. (1976) *The Origins of the Popular Press in England*. London: Croom Helm.

Lin, Linda and Reid, Kathleen (2008) 'The relationship between media exposure and anti-fat attitudes: the role of dysfunctional appearance beliefs', *Journal of Body Image,* 6 (1): 52–55.

Livingstone, Sonia (2007) 'The challenge of engaging youth online: contrasting producers' interpretations of websites', *European Journal of Communication,* 22 (2): 165–184.

Matejko, Aleksander (1970) 'Newspaper staff as a social system', in Jeremy Tunstall (ed.), *Media Sociology: A Reader*. Chicago: University of Illinois Press. pp. 168–180.

McCracken, Ellen (1993) *Decoding Women's Magazines From* Mademoiselle *to* Ms. Basingstoke: Macmillan.

McKay, Jenny (2000) *The Magazines Handbook*, London: Routledge.

McLuhan, Eric and Zingrone, Frank (1995) *Essential McLuhan*. London: Routledge.

McLuhan, Marshall (1969) *Counterblast*. London: Rapp & Whiting.

McNair, Brian (2003) *News and Journalism in the UK* (4th edn). London: Routledge.

McNair, Brian (2005) 'What is journalism?', in Hugo de Burgh (ed.), *Making Journalists: Diverse Models, Global Issues*. Abingdon: Routledge. pp. 25–43.

McNally, Paul (2008) 'David Hepworth: 'Magazines should stop doing cheap TV', *Press Gazette*, 22 October, accessed online at www.pressgazette.co.uk/story.asp?section code=6&storycode=42290&c=1

McNally, Paul (2009) 'Natmag plans to make up to 15% of staff redundant', *Press Gazette*, 27 February, accessed online at www.pressgazette.co.uk/story.asp?sectio ncode=1&storycode=43196&c=1

McRobbie, Angela (1978) '*Jackie:* An Ideology of Adolescent Femininity'. Stencilled Occasional Paper, Centre for Contemporary Studies, Birmingham.

McRobbie, Angela (1991) *Feminism and Youth Culture: from 'Jackie' to 'Just Seventeen'*. Basingstoke: Macmillan Education.

McRobbie, Angela (1999) *In the Culture Society: Art, Fashion and Popular Music*. London: Routledge.

Milburn, Alan (ed.) (2009) *Unleashing Aspiration: The Final Report of the Panel on Fair Access to the Professions.* London: Cabinet Office.

Milmo, Dan (2006) 'Smash Hits falls victim to fans' eclectic tastes and internet', the *Guardian*, 2 February, accessed online at: www.guardian.co.uk/business/2006/feb/02/media.pressandpublishing

Moeran, Brian (2006) 'More than just a fashion magazine', *Current Sociology*, 54 (5): 725–744.

Morrish, John (2003) *Magazine Editing, How to Develop and Manage a Successful Publication* (2nd edn) London: Routledge.

Mott, Frank Luther (1930) *A History of American Magazines 1841–1850.* Cambridge, MA: Harvard University Press.

Muddiman, Joseph George (1920) *Tercentenary Handlist of English and Welsh Newspapers, Magazines and Reviews.* London: *The Times.*

Negroponte, Nicholas (1995) *Being Digital.* New York: Knopf.

Nevett, Terence (1994) 'Advertising', in J. Don Vann and Rosemary T. Van Arsdel (eds), *Victorian Periodicals and Victorian Society.* Aldershot: Scholar.

Newall, Sally, Hudson, Hannah and McNally, Paul (2009) 'Young ideas', *Press Gazette*, March, pp: 16–17.

Nice, Liz (2007a) 'Magazine journalism: targeting print publications to reflect a desired audience', in Fran Blumberg (ed.), *When East Meets West: Media Research and Practice in the US and China.* Newcastle: Cambridge Scholars.

Nice, Liz (2007b) 'Tabloidisation and the teen market: are teenage magazines dumber than ever?', *Journalism Studies*, 8 (1): 117–136.

Nordenstreng, Kaarle (1998) 'Professional ethics: between fortress journalism and cosmopolitan democracy', in Kees Brants, Joke Hermes and Liesbet van Zoonen (eds), *The Media In Question: Popular Cultures and Public Interests.* London: Sage. pp. 124–133.

North, John S. (ed.) (1997) *The Waterloo Directory of English Newspapers and Periodicals 1800–1900, Vols 1–10.* Ontario: North Waterloo.

NUJ (2007) *Shaping the Future*, Commission on Multi-media Working, December, accessed online at www.nuj.org.uk/innerPagenuj.html?docid=605

NUJ (n.d.) www.nujtraining.org.uk/page.phtml?id=692&category=Training%20Policy&finds=0&string=&strand=

Oates, Caroline (1999) 'Designing women's magazines'. Paper presented at the 'Design Culture' conference, Sheffield Hallam University and the European Academy of Design, 30 March–1 April (cited in Gough-Yates, 2003: 17–18).

Ofcom (2006) *Communications Market Report*, available online at www.ofcom.org.uk/research

Ohmann, Richard (1996) *Selling Culture: Magazines, Markets and Class at the Turn of the Century.* London: Verso.

Orwell, George (1937) *The Road To Wigan Pier.* London: Left Book Club.

Paine, Fred K. and Paine, Nancy E. (1987) *Magazines: A Bibliography for Their Analysis, with Annotations and Study Guide.* Metuchen and London: Scarecrow.

Panagiotarea, Anna and Dimitrakopoulou, Dimitra (2007) 'Newspapers and young audiences: a relationship of participation or rejection'. Paper to Future of Newspapers conference, Cardiff, September.

Periodical Publishers Association (2000) *Handbook.* London: PPA.

Peterson, Theodore (1964) *Magazines in the Twentieth Century.* Urbana; University of Illinois Press.

Phillips, Angela (2005) 'Who's to make journalists?' in Hugo de Burgh (ed.), *Making Journalists: Diverse Models, Global Issues.* Abingdon: Routledge. pp. 227–244.

Plant, Marjorie (1939) *The English Book Trade*. London: Allen & Unwin.

Poole, William Frederick (1963 [1882]) *Poole's Index to Periodical Literature, Vol 1 Part 1 A-J*. Gloucester, MA: Peter Smith.

Postgate, Raymond (ed.) (1969 [1930]) *The Conversations Of Dr. Johnson*. London: Alison & Busby.

PPA (2009) Periodicals Training Council Work Experience Guidelines, accessed 15 January at www.ppa.co.uk/cgi-bin/wms.pl/916

PPA online (2005) accessed at www.ppa.co.uk/press-and-media/news/2005/june/eu-commissioner-praises-magazine-industry/

PPA online (2008) PPA Marketing, Data and Trends, accessed 12 November at www.ppamarketing.net/cgi-bin/go.pl/data-trends/index.html

PPA online (2009) 'Latest NRS figures reflect ABC trends', accessed 26 February at www.ppamarketing.net/cgi-bin/go.pl/research/article.html?uid=360

Prensky, Mark (2001) 'Digital natives, digital immigrants' *On the Horizon*, 9 (5): accessed October 2001 at www.marcprensky.com/.../Prensky%20-%20Digital%20Natives,%20 Digital%20Immigrants%20-%20Part1.pdf

Press Gazette (2005) 'Authority says teen mags are way to go for sex education', 11 November, p. 11.

Press Gazette (2007) 'Natmags closes Jellyfish', 14 August, accessed online at www.pressgazette.co.uk/story.asp?storyCode=38501&sectioncode=1

Preston, Nikki (2007) 'The demise of teen magazines', Mad.co.uk, 15 August, accessed at www.mad.co.uk/Main/ABCs/Articles/5698478f2257402f934270d94 dc9a4a6/The-demise-of-teen-magazines.html

Preston, Peter (2008) 'The curse of introversion', *Journalism Studies*, 9 (5); 642–649.

Pykett, Lyn (1990) 'Reading the periodical press: text and context', in Brake et al. (eds), *Investigating Victorian Journalism*. Basingstoke: Macmillan. pp. 3–18.

Raeymaeckers, Karin (2002) 'Research note: young people and patterns of time consumption in relation to print media', *European Journal of Communication*, 17: 369–383.

Raeymaeckers, Karin (2004) 'Newspaper Editors in search of young readers: content and layout strategies to win new readers', *Journalism Studies*, 5 (2): 221–232.

Raeymaeckers, Karin, Hauttekeete, Laurence and Hoebeke, Tim (2007) 'Newspapers in education: a qualitative press policy to preserve future readership for newspapers'. Paper to Future of Newspapers conference, Cardiff, September.

Reed, David (1997) *The Popular Magazine in Britain and the United States 1880–1960*. London: The British Library.

Rooney, Dick (2000) 'Thirty years of competition in the British tabloid press: the *Mirror* and the *Sun* 1968–1998', in Colin Sparks and John Tulloch (eds), *Tabloid Tales: Global Debates over Media Standards*. Lanham: Rowman & Littlefield. pp. 91–110.

Rowan, David (2001) 'Magazine covermount wars', *Evening Standard*, 20 June.

Sampson, Anthony (1996) 'The crisis at the heart of our media', *British Journalism Review*, 7 (3): 42–51.

Seal, Rebecca (2007) '*Cosmo* at 35 – still sexy and campaigning. But is it really cutting edge?', the *Observer*, accessed online at www.guardian.co.uk/media/2007/feb/04/ pressandpublishing.genderissues

Self, Abigail and Zealey, Linda (eds) (2007) *Social Trends No. 37*. London and Basingstoke: Office for National Statistics/Palgrave Macmillan.

Servan-Schreiber, Jean-Louis (1987) *The Power To Inform*. New York: McGraw-Hill.

Sheahan, Tim (2009) 'Customer magazine circulation rises while consumer falls', *Print Week*, 12 February, accessed online at www.printweek.com/RSS/News/880795/ Customer-magazine-circulation-rises-consumer-falls/

Shevelow, Kathryn (1989) *Women and Print Culture*. London: Routledge.

Simon, James and Merrill, Bruce D. (1997) 'The next generation of news consumers: children's news media choices in an election campaign', *Political Communication*, 14: 307–321.

Snoddy, Raymond (1992) *The Good, the Bad and the Unacceptable: The Hard News about the British Press*. London: Faber & Faber.

Sparks, Colin and Tulloch, John (eds) (2000) *Tabloid Tales: Global Debates over Media Standards*. Lanham, MD: Rowman & Littlefield.

Splichal, Slavko and Sparks, Colin (1994) *Journalists for the 21st Century: Tendencies of Professionalization Among First-year Students in 22 Countries*. Norwood, NJ: Ablex.

Steinem, Gloria (1994) *Moving Beyond Words*. London: Bloomsbury.

Stephenson, Sian (2007) 'The changing face of women's magazines in Russia', *Journalism Studies*, 8 (4): 613–620.

Stewart, James D., Hammond, Muriel E. and Saenger, Erwin (1955) *British Union-Catalogue of Periodicals*. London: Butterworth.

Sutton Trust (2006) *The Educational Backgrounds of Leading Journalists*, available online at www.suttontrust.com/reports/Journalists-backgrounds-final-report.pdf

Swaine, Matt (2010) *'A former academic's view on life and realities on the other side of the fence'*. Presentation to PTC Academics and Industry Forum, 23 June.

Tagiev, Ruslan (2006) *Russia Makes Way For A Magazine Boom*, available online at http://bit.ly/FIPP-Russ

Temple, Mick (2008) *The British Press*. Maidenhead: Open University Press.

Thompson, E.P. (Edward Palmer) (1968) *The Making Of The English Working Class*. Harmondsworth: Penguin.

Ticknell, Estella, Chambers, Deborah, van Loon, Joost, et al. (2003) 'Begging for it: "new femininities", social agency, and moral discourse in contemporary teenage and men's magazines', *Feminist Media Studies*, 3 (1): 47–63.

Tönnies, Ferdinand (2001) *Gemeinschaft und Gesellschaft* [Community and civil society], edited by Jose Harris and translated by Jose Harris and Margaret Hollis. Cambridge & New York: Cambridge University Press.

Townend, Judith (2008) 'SoE08: New multi-platform journalism forum will "converge" journalism training', *Journalism.co.uk*. 11 November, accessed online at www.journalism.co.uk/2/articles/532786.php

Tulloch, John (2000) 'The eternal recurrence of new journalism', in Colin Sparks and John Tulloch (eds), *Tabloid Tales: Global Debates over Media Standards*. Lanham, MD: Rowman & Littlefield. pp. 131–146.

Tumber, Howard and Prentoulis, Marina (2005), 'Journalism and the making of a profession', in Hugo de Burgh (ed.), *Making Journalists: Diverse Models, Global Issues*. Abingdon: Routledge. pp. 58–74.

Tunstall, Jeremy (ed.) (1970) *Media Sociology: A Reader*. Chicago: University of Illinois Press.

Tunstall, Jeremy (1971) *Journalists at Work: Specialist Correspondents: Their News Organizations, News Sources, and Competitor Colleagues*. London: Constable.

Tunstall, Jeremy (ed.) (2001) *Media Occupations and Professions: A Reader*. Oxford: Oxford University Press.

van Cuilenberg, Jan (1998) 'Diversity revisited: towards a critical rational model of media diversity', in Kees Brants, Joke Hermes and Liesbet van Zoonen (eds), *The Media In Question: Popular Cultures and Public Interests*. London: Sage. pp. 38–49.

van Leeuwen, Theo and Machin, David (2005), 'Language style and lifestyle: the case of a global magazine', *Media, Culture & Society*, 27 (4): 577–600.

van Zoonen, Liesbet (1998a) 'A professional, unreliable, heroic marionette (M/F): structure, agency and subjectivity in contemporary journalisms', *European Journal of Cultural Studies*, 1 (1): 123–142.

van Zoonen, Liesbet (1998b) 'One of the girls? The changing gender of journalism', in Cynthia Carter, Gill Branston and Stuart Allen (eds), *News, Gender And Power*. London: Routledge. pp. 33–46.

Vance, Carole S. (1995) 'Social Construction Theory and sexuality', in Maurice Berger Brian Wallis and Simon Watson (eds), *Constructing Masculinity*. New York: Routledge. pp. 37–56.

Vann, J. Don and van Arsdel, Rosemary T. (1978) *Victorian Periodicals: A Guide to Research*. New York: The Modern Language Association of America.

Vann, J. Don and van Arsdel, Rosemary T. (1994) *Victorian Periodicals and Victorian Society*. Aldershot: Scholar.

Veblen, Thorstein (1994) *The Theory of the Leisure Class*. New York: Dover.

Wade, Matt (2010) 'Mobile phone helps reshape Indian politics and the poor', *Sydney Morning Herald*, 22 May, available online at http://bit.ly/India-mobiles

Watt, Ian (1974 [1957]) *The Rise of the Novel: Studies in Defoe, Richardson and Fielding*. Harmondsworth: Penguin.

Weaver, David H. (2005) 'Who are journalists?', in Hugo de Burgh (ed.), *Making Journalists: Diverse Models, Global Issues*. Abingdon: Routledge. pp. 44–57.

Weiner, Joel H. (1988) 'How new was the New Journalism?', in Joel H. Weiner (ed.), *Papers For The Millions: The New Journalism in Britain, 1850s to 1914*. New York: Greenwood. pp. 47–71.

Wharton, John (1992) *Managing Magazine Publishing*. London: Blueprint.

White, Cynthia (1970) *Women's Magazines 1693–1968*. London: Michael Joseph.

Wilby, Peter (2008) 'A job for the wealthy and connected', the *Guardian*, 7 April, accessed online at www.guardian.co.uk/media/2008/apr/07/pressandpublishing4

Williams, Francis (1957) *Dangerous Estate: The Anatomy of Newspapers*. London: Longmans, Green & Co.

Williams, Kevin (1998) *Get Me A Murder A Day!* London: Hodder.

Winship, Janice (1987) *Inside Women's Magazines*. London: Pandora.

Winston, Brian (1998) *Media Technology and Society: A History: From the Telegraph to the Internet*. London: Routledge.

Wood, James Playsted (1956) *Magazines in the United States* (2nd edn). New York: The Ronald Press Co.

Woodward, Paul (2010) *25 Years In Asia – The Giant Woke*, available online at bit.ly/WoodwardP

Woolf, Michael, North, John S. and Deering, Dorothy (eds) (1977) *The Waterloo Directory of Victorian Periodicals 1824–1900, Phase 1*. Ontario: Wilfrid Laurier University Press.

Wykes, Maggie and Gunter, Barrie (2005) *The Media and Body Image: If Looks Could Kill*. London: Sage.

Xueqing, Jiang (2010) *Magazines Turning New Page In Battle For Readers*, available online at bit.ly/Xueqing

Yuan, Zhiyi (2009) 'The surviving conditions of Chinese alternative magazines'. Unpublished MA thesis, Cardiff University.

Zhang, Bohai (2008) 'The development of Business-to-Business magazines in China', *Pub Res Q*, 24: 54–58.

Interviews and personal communications

Abbott, Robin (2008) Creative Director, Future Publishing, 30 October.

Barrie, Giles (2008) Editor of *Property Week*, 24 October.

Barrie, Giles (2009) Editor of *Property Week*, 26 February, talk to students at the University of Sheffield.

Bown, Jonathan (2008) Assistant Editor of *New*, 31 October.

Brett, Nicholas (2010) Deputy Managing Director, BBC Magazines, personal communication, 13 August.

Coffey, Margaret (2008) Editorial consultant, ETC, 30 October.

Cole, Peter (2009) Director of Journalism, University of Sheffield, personal interview, 12 February.

Conklin, Margi (2006) Editor in Chief of *Page Six* (supplement of the *New York Post*), 17 January.

Conklin, Margi (2009) now Deputy Editor of the *Sunday New York Post* (US), personal interview, 13 February.

Cooper, Will (2008) Deputy News Editor, *New Media Age*, 13 November.

Davies, Loraine (2008) Director, Periodicals Training Council, 30 November.

Douglas, Jim (2008) Editorial Director, Future Publishing, 4 November.

Genower, Peter (2008) Editorial consultant, 28 October.

Gent, Helen (2008) Freelancer, 30 October, 6 November.

Harris, Mike (2008) Editor of *Golf Monthly*, 5 November.

Hart, Sarah (2008) Former Editor of *Mother and Baby* and *Pregnancy and Birth*, 28 October.

Holden, Moira (2008) Freelancer, completed questionnaire.

Illsley, Yvonne (2008) Freelancer, former Features Editor, *Daily Express, Take a Break*, 25 November.

Kyriacou, Eleni (2008) Freelancer, 6 November.

Moore, Martyn, (2008) Editor, *Fleet News* (formerly *Bauer Automotive*), emailed questionnaire, 10 December.

Nicols, Mel (2009) Editorial Director, Haymarket Consumer Media, 20 November.

Nieto, Kristin (2009) Deputy Style Director, *Life and Style* (US), personal interview, 19 February.

O'Riordan, Marie (2008) Editor of *Marie Claire*, 2001–2008, 6 November.

Pyper, Sarah (2009) Former Editor, *Sugar*, Executive Editor, *In Touch*, US weekly, Deputy Editor, *Closer*, 1 March.

Ram, N. (2007) Editor-in-Chief, The Hindu group, Chennai, 25 July.

Rawlings, Michelle (2008) Freelancer, runs Outline Features Agency, 1 November.

Todd, Sarah (2008) Freelancer, former Editor of *Yorkshire Life*, 5 November.

Toner, John (2009) Freelance representative, NUJ, 29 January.

Wright, Sharon (2008) Senior Content Editor, ukfamily.

INDEX